In memory of my late parents, Tommy and Ida Hullah,
who gave life to five daughters and one son while farming
within Nidderdale. West Riding of Yorkshire

## Hole Bottom Farms, Dacre, Nr Harrogate

Author Gwen Hullah's parents, Tommy and Ida Hullah owned and farmed Hole Bottom Farms for many years (and there giving birth to five daughters and one son). They were shorthorn dairy farmers - with sidelines of breeding large whites, sheep and free-range poultry.

Tommy & Ida Hullah's wedding day 1931

# THE FOUR SEASONS

'Revenge dressed in its Sunday best'

### GWEN HULLAH

She And The Cat's Mother

First published as Safe In Killer Hands: The Original Screenplay in 2017
by She And The Cat's Mother

This revised and updated edition first published in 2019 by She And The Cat's Mother

SheAndTheCatsMother.co.uk

Copyright Gwen Hullah 2017
All rights reserved
Author blog site ==>> SilverSplitter.com

The Four Seasons, adapted into 4 episodes (running time approx' 90 minutes per episode)
by Gwen Hullah; script editor Zizzi Bonah; from the novel,
Safe In Killer Hands: Money, Madness, Murder, by Gwen Hullah

Extract lyrics from song 'Come Closer' written by Ida Barker
Copyright 2009 Beatroute Records International
www.IdaBarker.live

All characters in this publication are fictitious and any resemblance to real persons, living or dead, is purely coincidental

This book is sold subject to the condition that it shall not, by way of trade or otherwise, be lent, re-sold, hired out or otherwise circulated without the publisher's prior consent in any form of binding or cover other than that in which it is published and without a similar condition including this condition being imposed on the subsequent purchaser.

A CIP catalogue record for this book is available from the British Library

ISBN: 9781916047402

For a PDF of this screenplay, please contact the publisher

Cover and interior design by She And The Cat's Mother
Printed and bound by Lightning Source

## Mum, Daughter & Moggy the cat

**In 2016 Mother and Daughter** - Gwen Hullah and Ida Barker, set up in partnership a **book publishing** business, aptly called **She And The Cat's Mother**

**All in house**, complete format: writing, editing, proof reading, formatting paperbacks and ebooks, to raising profile on social media - the only tasking they have not done is the printing. The acid test is getting their books into the highway of readers' minds. They are authorpreneurs!!

# CONTENTS

Letter-of-praise from Dame Julie Walters    9

Episode 1 - Winter    11

Episode 2 - Spring    143

Episode 3 - Summer    277

Episode 4 - Autumn    421

Glossary
Screenplay terms and Yorkshire words    575

List of characters    579

About the author    581

Letter-of-acknowledgement
from HRH the Duchess of Cornwall    582

Other books    583

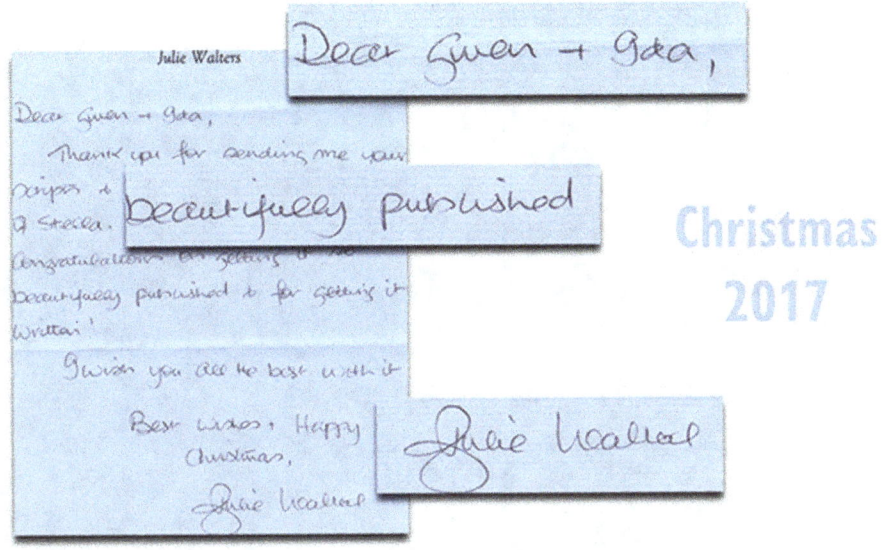

A letter-of-praise from *Dame Julie Walters*
to book publishers, She And The Cat's Mother, for paperback,
SAFE IN KILLER HANDS: THE ORIGINAL SCREENPLAY

'beautifully published' - *Dame Julie Walters*

Episode 1

# Winter

## EPISODE 1
## WINTER

**SCENE 1**
**EXT. YORKSHIRE – WINTER RURAL LANDSCAPE – 3:15 PM**

*The year is 1947. We see vast acreage of desolate winter-white moorland, then sight lower-land where blackfaced sheep shelter behind stone walls, their fleeces congealed with icy-snow – stillness broken occasionally by their haunting bleating.*

**SCENE 2**
**EXT. STOCKDALE FARMS – 3:16 PM**

*Two adjoining stone farmhouses with attached outer buildings silhouetted against snow laden sky. Dim lights seen from three windows. We are drawn down to a snow-banked beck aligned with gaunt trees; to stepping stones; flagged water-splash; towards icicle waterfall. We view dark depth to copious flow beyond.*

**SCENE 3**
**INT. STOCKDALE FARMS – STELLA'S LIVING ROOM – 3:17 PM**

*Furnished with over-large furniture. A full sized black leaded fireplace, surrounded by horse brasses and rosettes.*

*We see STELLA ASQUITH, aged 46, handsome, proud woman with naturally wavy ginger-red hair which frames vivacious features. She is sat rigid at bureau, pen in hand. Suddenly rises. Goes over to window and stares outwards.*

## SCENE 4
## EXT. STOCKDALE FARMS - MOORLAND - DAY (FLASHBACK)

We see SAM ASQUITH, aged 72, tall formidable man, alienated, staggering blindly through violent snow blizzard wholly exhausted - falling - rising to finally fall into contracted position, frozen through death's open door.

## SCENE 5
## EXT. STOCKDALE FARMS - MOORLAND - DAY (FLASHBACK)

Three days after fatal blizzard.

We see and hear JAKE SWALES, aged 65, farm-man, stoic, vigorous with psycho-tendency - shabbily dressed, overcoat has no belt, hanging loose revealing worn trousers strung chest high by faded braces exposing long-legged boots, and ABE ASQUITH, aged 64, less-fortunate-begrudging cousin of SAM, a large man, deadpan expression, rarely smiles.

Shovels in hands, hacking, digging, scraping - SAM'S body being prised from ice-bound grave.

## SCENE 6
## INT. STOCKDALE FARMS - STELLA'S LIVING ROOM - 3:18 PM

STELLA turns away from window. Her face creased in sorrow. Returns to desk and dates letter page, 24TH JANUARY 1947.

## SCENE 7
## EXT. COUNTRY ROADS - TWO WEEKS LATER - 2 PM

We see snowplough reopening snow-bound country roads. Blizzards filling in the cuttings almost as fast as man and machine can dig. They decide to call it a day.

**SCENE 8**

**EXT. STOCKDALE FARMS - MAIN GATE ENTRANCE - 3 PM**

*GRACE ASQUITH, aged 26, a smallish woman, neither frail nor chunky, phenomenally strong willed, known for speaking her own mind, yet has sensitivity she rarely puts into words.*

*We see GRACE zigzagging a route in deep uncut slip-road. She heads for main gate entrance. Rubs coat sleeve over gate sign: STOCKDALE FARMS, hitches rucksack to other shoulder, turns up overcoat collar, shivers, climbs up and over gate wedged by snowdrift and heads home along the mile-long cart-road.*

**SCENE 9**

**INT. STOCKDALE FARMS - STELLA'S KITCHEN - 4 PM**

*Large kitchen. Flag-stoned floor. No electricity or gas supplies and no hot water flows.*

*STELLA is ladling hot water from back boiler into a bucket. We hear the lifting of the iron door sneck, then the dull drop, we see the draft of snowflakes as GRACE pushes door open to vacillate inside. She bangs it shut, leaving herself on the inside.*

                    STELLA
                  *(pleasantly)*
        I knew you'd come ... given time ...
        but not to put too fine a point on it
        our Grace, you'd rather be late than
        wrong.

*STELLA drops the boiler lid down and places wet jug on the hot surface where it sizzles away - unnoticed to them.*

GRACE *removes rucksack, then headscarf. She runs her fingers through her damp hair.*

          GRACE
    It's hard to be punctual in the snow, Mother.

*There's no overbearing welcome between them, only a toughness and philosophical attitude. Love is known, no need to be said.*

STELLA *carries bucket of hot water to the sink and pours half into sink bowl.*

          STELLA
    I've missed you over the last two years, more than I can ever say ...
        *(she dashes soap flakes into bowl and stirs vigorously)*
    Easy enough when I carry a private conversation in my head ...
        *(she smiles)*
    At least I can say, thank God you've arrived home safely which is more than I can say about your father ...
        *(smile wavers)*
    We could tell by his footprints in the snow that he'd been crossing and re-crossing the frozen-over beck trying to locate the fort shelter ...
        *(her voice quails)*
    Cousin Abe said Sam had most likely become disoriented by the snow blizzard ...

GRACE

*(takes overcoat off and drapes it over wooden clothes horse)*
Uncle Abe and Aunt Winny, as Grandma Blanche said last week ...

*(scornfully)*
have the belief that Father, the elder Cousin, would bequest them an adjoining farm, knowing you and Father have no son to pass it onto just to keep the Asquith name alive in the farming community!

STELLA

*(washing crockery)*
I believe you're right Grace, and I may be wrong, but I'm certain that Abe took perverse pleasure in breaking your father's limbs so he and Jake could lay him flat on the field gate, and the rope ...

*(her voice breaks)*
the cart rope was not equal to the purpose of securing Sam to the gate spars ...

*(voice rises)*
then to crown it all, he had the asperity to say ...

*(she swallows her pain)*
"By Gawd! He looks more human dead than ever he did alive!"

GRACE

And Jake ...?

*(sits down at table)*
Did he rise to the insinuation?

STELLA

Too shocked. Never known him so quiet. Hardly spoke a word. His answer was to barge over to Bonny then back her within inches of the gate ...

(pause)

Abe took the chain traces from the horse's harness and hitched them onto the gate hinges ...

(begins to wipe plates dry)

I led Bonny while the men hauled on side-ropes to prevent the gate striking the back of Bonny's limbs by sliding forward on the icy ground ...

We hear crockery clatter as STELLA stacks them onto cupboard shelves ...

STELLA

As for Jake, well, he was quite unchaste, more so than when his wife died of shingles.

(pause)

He did say after working and living alongside the Asquiths for near on fifty years, he'd never once thought it would come to this.

GRACE

(suddenly vacates chair, words bitter to taste)

Money talks! Money can whitewash! That's what Father use to say, but death was one deal he couldn't buy his way out of, as Grandma Blanche said, "Hell won't want him because he'd take control"!

*GRACE abruptly leaves the room.*

*STELLA stretches her arms out to her and gathers emptiness. We see grief expressed unguarded.*

## SCENE 10
**EXT. STOCKDALE FARMS - TOP COW-HOUSE - 6 PM**

*Tilly lamps glowing from inside a cow-house window. We glimpse JAKE shabbily dressed wearing hobnailed boots walking towards the building. He is carrying a milk bucket on crook of his arm and a storm lamp in one hand and a three legged stool in the other hand. He enters the building.*

## SCENE 11
**INT. STOCKDALE FARMS - TOP COW-HOUSE - 6:01 PM**

*We see SOPHIE ASQUITH, aged 22, gentle by nature, a wholesome girl but splendidly indiscreet, and STELLA already hand-milking TWO OF TWELVE DAIRY COWS chained by the neck within individual wooden stalls.*

*JAKE strides across the manure channel behind cattle, plonks his stool down by RHODA'S hindquarters, sits down, rams bucket between his legs to rest rim on his heels. Shoves his flat capped head onto RHODA'S flank while endeavouring to pull and squeeze on two opposite teats.*

*We hear occasional lowly "mooing" and the steady rhythm of the ejecting milk as it penetrates into the depths of the already drawn down milk within their three buckets.*

**SCENE 12**

**INT. STOCKDALE FARMS - STELLA'S LIVING ROOM - 7:30 PM**

*STELLA is placing logs on fire as GRACE enters, washed and re-dressed in khaki dungarees and multifarious fair-isle jumper.*

>               STELLA
>           *(turns round and half-smiles
>           sadly)*
>       Your name never passed your father's
>       lips again, and dear Sophie, every now
>       and then, she'd wear that jumper
>       Grandma Blanche knitted for you years
>       ago, as an indication of keeping you
>       close to her. She really has missed
>       her older sister more than words could
>       ever say ...
>
>               GRACE
>       Yes, my leaving was with the distinct
>       feeling of separateness ...
>               *(pause)*
>       Do you think Father suffered a great
>       deal between the difference of life
>       and death?

*She crosses the room to turn the wireless knob to the HOME SERVICE.*

>               GRACE
>       And do we know when we do something
>       for the last time?

*STELLA turns back to fire and rakes poker through bottom grate.*

                    STELLA
    Hard to say, lass. He was very much
    dead when we found him ... and when I
    took my last look at your father
    before Cousin Abe screwed down the lid
    of his coffin, I saw that his face was
    covered by his overcoat ... and when I
    lifted it from his face, his eyes were
    open. He was looking straight back at
    me ...
            *(her voice catches her throat)*
    And I wanted to keep him here where he
    belonged, instead I said to Abe that
    Sam should be wearing it, because he
    would feel the cold. Abe pulled me
    aside and said ...
            *(her voice falters)*
    "He doesn't belong to you anymore".

*STELLA brushes away excess ash from hot fire-bars, then turns to look at GRACE.*

                    STELLA
    But I will say this, you're a sure
    reminder to me ...
            *(pause)*
    A smaller image of course - that Sam
    Asquith is not completely dead.

*We hear muted voices coming from wireless.*

*They go unheard to STELLA and GRACE.*

                    GRACE
    The more I think about it, the more I
    believe death is the absent one who

sees to it that family business will remain unfinished.

>                    STELLA
>               *(drops another log on the fire)*
>          And goodbyes remain unspoken forever
>          and a day. Your father was no good at
>          writing letters because he was already
>          very skilful at hiding his feelings
>          and dealings ...
>                    *(her eyes reflect anger and*
>                    *heartache)*
>          If only Sam had shown more of his
>          heart ...

>                    GRACE
>               *(bitterly)*
>          Instead of showing a lack of interest
>          that was calculated to dishearten all
>          but the fanatical.

GRACE folds her arms tightly across her breasts and sits down on sofa. Her eyes meet her mother's in a polished stare, faces claiming a portion of quiet desperation that is not altogether quiet, displayed in a succession of disturbances of faint moans, tormented grunts and unguarded coughing.

From across the room, like an uninvited guest, the HOME SERVICE NEWS ANNOUNCER gives out a warning ...

>                    HOME SERVICE (WIRELESS)
>          Look out for helicopters dropping food
>          and animal provisions over the cut-off
>          areas ...
>                    *(voice more authoritative)*
>          German Prisoners of War have arrived

>                    on camp sites in the North of England
>                    and these men are being placed at the
>                    disposal of the Highway Surveyors to
>                    aid snow clearances ...

GRACE springs swiftly from the sofa. Switches off wireless. One suffering expression superimposed on another. Her mouth hardily moves at all.

>                              GRACE
>                    I remember the day I left home,
>                    remember how slowly I reacted when
>                    Father said Hertz had hung himself
>                    from a beam in the bottom barn, and I
>                    don't think that I was convinced at
>                    the time – but I was ready to believe
>                    anything when the alternative was so
>                    unbelievable ...
>                              (turns distressed face to the
>                              wall)
>                    And ... and ... feeling within myself
>                    a sense of loss so ... so deep that it
>                    shook my soul.

STELLA comes to stand close to GRACE'S rigid back and slowly wraps her arms around her.

FLASH – We see a young Prisoner Of War hanging from a beam in the barn. Castrated. Accentuated by the beams of sunlight filtering from the narrow slat glassless windows to depict SAM and JAKE, slowly they turn to stare coldly at STELLA standing transfixed within the doorway ...

FADE TO DARKNESS.

**SCENE 13**

INT. STOCKDALE FARMS - STELLA'S KITCHEN - 9:20 AM

*JAKE wrenches farmhouse kitchen door open. His flat capped head juts round the edge of door frame, letting a brisk draught sweep into kitchen.*

*STELLA is stood at sink washing breakfast crockery.*

> JAKE
> Ah thought ah heard thee clatterin' about in bottom o' sink ...

*His eyes sagaciously take in the full draining board and STELLA busy scouring iron pans.*

> JAKE
> When tha's a minute t' spare ...

*He pauses to place his big boned shoulder to the open door and stop it buffing against his body.*

> JAKE
> Will tha come an tek a look at owld Bonny?

> STELLA
> (wiping hands and wrists dry)
> I'll come right away, Jake.

> JAKE
> Aye, t' owld horse doesn't seem able t' shake it off. Reckon outin' t' church other week must have taken its toll on her ...
> (he pauses to straighten up)

>                    Tha'll not be ower long then!

*And with that said, he bangs door shut.*

## SCENE 14
**EXT. STOCKDALE FARMS – FARMYARD – 9:30 AM**

*Everything iced over, STELLA heads for stables, we hear crunching underfoot as she walks on frosted snow. She enters stables.*

## SCENE 15
**INT. STOCKDALE FARMS – STABLES – 9:31 AM**

*JAKE already busy shovelling away heaps of steaming horse manure into wooden wheelbarrow.*

*FOUR SHIRE HORSES stand tied by halters to the sides of their partitioned stalls. Their barfins and bridles are arranged along each division, while the rest of the harnesses hang clean and orderly behind them on the far wall.*

*He places shovel down inside of barrow, takes a curry comb and dandy brush from windowsill and begins to brush the lost bloom of the black mare, BONNY.*

>                    JAKE
>               *(said without hardly a pause of breath)*
>          T' think we use t' have six pairs o' horses setting off wi' their harnesses janglin' and their steel shoes ringin' out as they struck yard flagstones an' ploughmen sittin' sideways on t' horses' backs an' all afore four o'clock in a mornin' an' then we'd

work reight through till nearly dark.

*He nods his head in a flagellant way and steps back from BONNY to study her.*

*STELLA moves closer to BONNY and begins to stroke her along the tell-tale signs of aging. STELLA'S fingers pass over sunken eyes with their benign expression ... in response, the workhorse thrusts her neck forward.*

          STELLA

Funny what you can see coming without really knowing it ... It's not her fault that she's grown old and now ready to be turned out to grass.

          JAKE

Ah can see t' way Bonny reacted t' thy handlin' her, missus. Proud arch o' her neck, it's no longer theer. An' ah spotted in that moment her condition had undergone a difference. Ah permanent difference.

          STELLA
        *(with constrain)*

Could it possibly be only colic, Jake? I don't think I'm ready for another tragedy.

*We see BONNY awkwardly strain and before the mare can right herself, she coughs – a violent convulsive cough which leads to a deep inhalation of breath.*

          JAKE

She's brokken winded. Did t' see the

double lift t' her belly as she
breathed out? Aye, poor owld horse,
she's needin' some extra effort t'
force air out ...

                STELLA
        *(wearing a rictus smile)*
Over many gruelling years, I've come
to the belief that hope is the second
cousin of the unhappy, and now I can
vouch to that. Optimism ought to be
criminalised.

                JAKE
Best we can do reight now is t' mek a
cough drench an' if she's none t'
clever in ah couple o' days maybe we
should consider callin' vet.

*He walks away and begins to rummage amongst SAM'S assortment of drench bottles, dented measuring spoons and dry corks stacked on the inner windowsill – unwillingly, STELLA'S eyes follow his movements.*

                STELLA
Dear God, it's so painful seeing the
pallid futility of those overshared
objects left ownerless and now, in as
much reduced to junk. Sam's meanness
always needed a little tempering ...
        *(courageously)*
Everyone knew he was a man cast in a
mould of iron ...

                JAKE
Aye, an' everyone knew he'd skin ah

flea for its hide ...
>   *(his mouth slides sideways)*

As for mesen, ah'm steeled by duty an' faith in t' order o' things ...
>   *(allows himself a twisted smile)*

As tha knows missus ah've worked from boy t' man for Asquith family an' did what had t' be done.
>   *(squeaks a cork back into a bottle neck)*

An' I've heard confessions that even close friends would hesitate t' share wi' each other.

They stand perfectly still staring at each other. Sizing each other up.

                    JAKE
Ah swore t' a lifelong silence t' keep safe secrets shackled inside my soul. Price ...
>   *(his lips curl into a thin smile)*

A home at Stockdale till ah die!

                    STELLA
You're a cornerstone to Stockdale Farms, Jake. That should not be questioned by anyone ...

                    JAKE
>   *(abruptly)*

Does ta feel wind o' change?

STELLA
*(with decision)*
If you mean, without saying so, does Cousin Abe and son see themselves as benefactors of Stockdale Farms ... or Farm, which would offer them scope to oust the Asquith women, leaving us high and dry ...

JAKE
Aye, ah do! An' what about mesen? I'll not be shoved back inta workhouse!

STELLA
*(adamant)*
Don't fret yourself, Jake. You're as safe as houses here, and I'll not hear another word of doubt coming from you or anyone else. Anyway ...
*(smiles)*
What would we, the Asquith women do without you? As I said earlier, and I'll say it again, you are now our cornerstone of Stockdale ...

JAKE
*(returns her smile, just)*
For what it's worth, ah'll put thee inta picture.
*(he's back to his sinewy self)*
Aye, ah still feel saddled wi' shame havin' been ah workhouse inmate. Ah pauper's bairn. Father among others, buggered off an' made some sort o' livin' searchin' sewers for what they could find ...

                    STELLA
Your mother and any other siblings
...?

                    JAKE
          *(returns bottle to windowsill
          with a clatter)*
It were ah savage life, full t' brim
wi' poor folk all classed as bottom o'
society. Folk who had no hope in hell
o' bein' rescued except applyin' or
pleadin' for entry inta paupers'
workhouses.

*JAKE selects a dandy brush, begins to groom a SHIRE HORSE.*

                    JAKE
It's ah gurt grey stone buildin' still
operatin' on edge o' yon moorland.
          *(points westward)*
It were over-crowded wi' under-
employed owld men an' worn-out women
an' sickly bairns. The place stunk o'
piss, shit an' diseases.
          *(his nostrils fluctuate)*
Matchmakin'!

*JAKE swings round to face STELLA with fierce eyes.*

                    STELLA
Matchmaking?

                    JAKE
Aye. Matchmakin'. That spelt out jaw
disease.
          *(pause)*

                    Owld John Asquith's wife explained
                    years later that it were caused by
                    slow combustion comin' from compounded
                    phosphorus.
                              *(his eyes widen)*
                    We'd nivver heard them words mentioned
                    ... nah ... not once. Inmates use t'
                    call it the Lord's Last Supper because
                    poor buggers jaws were slowly eaten
                    away ... putrid.

                              STELLA
                         *(with unnecessary delicacy)*
                    You sound as though you're meeting
                    ghosts on the landing, Jake.

                              JAKE
                    That's as may be.
                         *(bitterly)*
                    Mesen an' other young lads were given
                    two choices. Either t' go round
                    collectin' dog shit t' sell t'
                    tanneries, or chimney sweepin' room
                    wheer trainin' were bloody brutal.

**SCENE 16**
**INT. WORKHOUSE – CHIMNEY SWEEPING ROOM – DAY (JAKE'S MEMORY)**

*We see a dank, dark room with a black leaded fireplace. A fire is burning red-hot in the grate. A row of YOUNG EMACIATE BOYS stand in a row, wearing loin-cloths.*

*MASTER 1 stands over the BOYS with a blooded cane.*

*MASTER 2 takes each BOY in turn and begins rubbing strong brine onto elbows and knees.*

*TWO ASSISTANTS drag a whimpering BOY and stronghold him in front of the hot fire. BOY yells; struggles; lashed with the cane.*

*This procedure is repeated and repeated, getting bloodier and bloodier until the BOYS' kneecaps look as though they've been pulled off.*

**SCENE 17**
**INT. STOCKDALE FARMS - STABLES - 9:36 AM**

*JAKE savagely cuts a plug of tobacco and wedges it against his gum.*

                    JAKE
           *(features awry, voice guttural)*
Aye. Tha cruel bastards called it ...
           *(harshly emphasises letter "H")*
<u>H</u>ardenin' o' the flesh!

                    STELLA
           *(looks exquisitely troubled)*
Thank you, Jake for sharing and shedding light on your disturbing past with me, I'll not steal it away ...
           *(pause)*
Life has taught me to leave looking in from the outside unsaid.

                    JAKE
John an' Sam Asquith said more than once Stockdale would allus keep a roof ower my head until day ah was carried out feet first! So theer!

*STELLA acknowledges his strange sinuous gestures with only her eyelids.*

>STELLA
>
>I cannot for the life of me imagine Sam even transiently thinking anything other than that. After all, I worked and toiled alongside him, day in day out for the last twenty-eight years. I mean twenty-eight years of marriage does shape minds, and I know he would have told me ...
>
>JAKE
>
>*(he clicks his tongue in agitation)*
>
>Ah'd bet on thee life, missus if tha'd died before him, if asked instead o' saying ah loved her an' I'll miss her, the boss would have said, she was a grand worker. Worth every damn penny!

*STELLA'S expression fixes, stares straight ahead and tightens her coat belt so tightly that he holds his breath, but never takes his eyes off her.*

>STELLA
>
>That's that, then!

*She stumps across flagged stone floor to suddenly spin round making cobwebs flutter in her draft.*

>STELLA
>
>I read somewhere in the Farmers' Weekly that approximately two hundred and seven fatalities happen each year in the countryside ...

*JAKE nods his head violently willing her to go on. She does not disappoint him.*

                    STELLA
          Which brings my thoughts strictly back
          to Abe and his son.

                    JAKE
              *(as though he's found her*
              *hiding in some darken place)*
          Aaaaah!

*With the agility of a man twenty years younger he side-steps her to open stable door wide, then standing to attention, he touches his flat cap in a salvable way.*

                    JAKE
          Tha can rely on mesen from start t'
          finish, boss!

*His conviction and loyal words take her to the door and out of the stables.*

## SCENE 18
**INT. STOCKDALE FARMS - STABLES - 10:45 AM**

*SOPHIE'S sat at ease on a three legged milk stool, shaking the measure of the horse's draft while JAKE is straightening the horse cloth draped over BONNY'S back.*

*STELLA and GRACE enter.*

*JAKE and GRACE attend to BONNY by way of running a rope under her nose-band and throwing it over a beam in the stable roof.*

                    STELLA
          Have you re-checked the two cows-in-
          calf, Sophie? They're due to calve in
          the next day or two.

                    SOPHIE
          Yes. Although roan Sylvia seems more
          than restless and she's not eaten her
          fodder by half.

*STELLA nods her understanding. JAKE and GRACE are now ready to pull BONNY'S head upwards.*

                    JAKE
          Reight! That's far enough.

*He swings back on rope. STELLA takes bottle from SOPHIE and gives it an extra good shake, hands it back to her, then relieves GRACE of her grip on the rope. STELLA then stands behind JAKE as SOPHIE pushes rickety stool towards GRACE and hands her the drench bottle. GRACE mounts the stool.*

                    JAKE
                 (to GRACE)
          Ista ready, lass?

*He squints up from the other side of BONNY while re-adjusting tension on rope. In response BONNY gives out a gurgling cough and starts to plunge about in the restricting stall. Steel clad hooves clattering on stone floor.*

                    STELLA
                 (shouting; penetrating JAKE'S
                  ears)
          <u>Get on with it, our Grace! Don't take
          all day ...</u>

                    JAKE
              (bawling to BONNY)
    Git up straight theer, yer gurt wick
    bugger!

He jabs his elbow into BONNY'S ribs, then slackens rope slightly. GRACE prises the bottle neck half passed BONNY'S clenched teeth. We see the medicine begin to flow from centre of BONNY'S mouth.

                    JAKE
    It's comin' out o' this end o' horse's
    mouth. What's tha playin' about at?

He juts his head round BONNY'S upturned neck.

                    GRACE
    Come on, Sophie. Don't stand there
    like a spare part, rub under Bonny's
    throat and encourage her to swallow or
    we'll be getting nowhere fast.

Hair flying SOPHIE springs into action as the horse tries to back its hind quarters behind next partition while STELLA and JAKE lean against her.

                    STELLA
              (shouting to SOPHIE)
    Tap her smartly under the chin,
    surprise her before she surprises us!

BONNY grates her teeth against glass bottle - medication flows from her mouth.

GRACE wrenches it away from clamping teeth.

                    GRACE
         Steady. Steady, old lass ... Steady.

*GRACE alights firm footed from cockling stool (one leg of three loose) while JAKE gives some play on the rope and gradually BONNY'S head is lowered.*

                    JAKE
              (empathy strong in harsh voice)
         Ah'll see if ah can tempt her with ah
         warm, light gruel.

*He removes horse blanket, then grooms her sweating coat.*

                    STELLA
         If Bonny's condition worsens in the
         next day or two, we'll have to call in
         the veterinary.

                    GRACE
              (abruptly)
         If we can't get out due to the
         prevailing weather, then it's unlikely
         that he'll be able to arrive here.

*A silence. A sharp to the taste silence.*

                    STELLA
              (her eyes become larger and her
              mouth smaller)
         Thank you, Grace. I can always rely on
         your proficiency skills to be
         annoyingly accurate.
              (pause)
         A rather vexing habit you picked up
         from your father. Saying the right

thing at the wrong time.

STELLA looks over her shoulder at SOPHIE wriggling the loose leg into place.

                      STELLA
Not like your young sister who simply enjoys just being Sophie! Well, I refuse to make changes for the sheer pleasure of refusing to change. Yes ...
        (her eyes aim to scold them)
For Bonny's sake we will dig ourselves out, if we have to and that's final.
        (checks wrist watch)
It's nearly eleven o'clock, which one of you lassies would care to come with me to check the cart-road and side-roads to see if the snowplough has cleared them, or at least tried?

STELLA marches out.

## SCENE 19

**EXT. STOCKDALE FARMS - FARMYARD - 10:48 AM**

GRACE and SOPHIE follow STELLA out of the stables, JAKE, reaching out closes the door.

                      JAKE
We're runnin' a bit late, boss. Ah'll be on me way t' check ewes-in-lamb and see t' jobs in high-barn.

He whistles and BRIDIE the black and white border collie comes to heel from nowhere.

                    JAKE
          Shouldn't be ower long, boss. But weel
          need another farm-man after thaw sets
          in.

*He whistles again and man and dog fall into step and head for moorland.*

                    GRACE
          I'll stay home and cut the hay from
          the baulks for later foddering, then
          feed the calves and ...

*The rest of GRACE'S words are lost as she heads up the yard.*

                    STELLA
          Come along our Sophie before we lose
          the rest of the morning ...

*She charges the yard gate, only to stagger to an undignified stance.*

                    STELLA
          Well! Well! Would you credit it, can
          you see what I can see?

*SOPHIE gives her a conciliatory smile, she is thinking of her latest romance with imperfect thoughts, then comes to a juddering stop on the icy flagstones.*

                    SOPHIE
               (shrieks)
          <u>Harry!!</u>

                    STELLA
               (prods SOPHIE)
          Where has he sprung from? And on a day
          like today! It beggars belief.

*STELLA spreads her arms wide in noxious gestures towards the
snowdrifts, vast beside the stone walls. The ice-bound becks
on either side of the farms, the stark leafless trees,
silver-grey with frost raising their boughs high to the laden
grey sky. All held in a vice-grip of winter.*

                    STELLA
               (she stares at SOPHIE)
          Well, look girl! Never mind him! Look
          at the weather ... it's the worst
          winter in living memory, and yet ...
          in the midst of it all, there is
          Harry! He must think he's in stocks of
          clover.

                    SOPHIE
               (calling)
          Harry. Oh, Harry!

*HARRY BLETCHFORD, aged 25, a fair-haired resilient young
clerk from J. W. HINCHCLIFFE AND CO SOLICITORS crosses the
footbridge - slipping and sliding. He straightens his glasses
while waving.*

                    STELLA
               (postulating)
          Harry! Well ... we can't get our milk
          out and collected ... and we've not
          set eyes upon the postman since last
          week ... and no provisions have been
          delivered since a week on Tuesday and

>             furthermore ... we can't dig our way
>             out to get to the nearest public
>             telephone kiosk!
>                     *(a dangerous infliction in her*
>                     *voice)*
>             Yet Harry simply gets through ... He
>             deserves to be hugged to death.

*HARRY, taking his last accomplishing steps, cogently folds his arms over the top spar of the gate. He gives two, three prefatory coughs between catching his breath back, while managing to look subsidised by SOPHIE'S welcome. And as he hangs there, eventually, his eyes meet STELLA'S.*

*His eyes behind rimless spectacles give him a rather miscreant look of authority, or could he be seeing money?*

*STELLA guards her eyes against him reading too much into her bias thoughts. She changes expressions like four seasons in a day.*

>                     STELLA
>                     *(she elongates the word*
>                     *"trailing")*
>             May I ask, Harry, what brings you
>             <u>trailing ...</u> into the Yorkshire Dales
>             on a day such as today?

*He doesn't appear to have heard one word. He has the appearance of a young man parched in a desert sighting an oasis, SOPHIE'S wholesome smiling face.*

>                     HARRY
>                     *(his answer sounds distant)*
>             You know, Mrs Asquith, we seldom
>             attribute common sense to others

accept to those who agree with us ...

*STELLA stares back at him, mentally reducing him to a midget, who has been kicked out of a nudist colony for sticking his nose into other folk's business.*

*SOPHIE comes to the rescue.*

                    SOPHIE

How did you get here, Harry? Surely not all the way from Holbridge on foot? And what are the roads like ... out there? Are they still unpassable by transport? And what about ...

*He raises his frozen hand in the pleasant easy way of his.*

                    HARRY
          *(his voice lingers over her name)*

One question at a time, Sophie ... Quite simple really. Mr Hinchcliffe arranged for me to be an assisting passenger with Doctor Liddle's practice, which allowed me to be dropped off at the same time as the medical supplies allocated to Kayshaw village, courtesy of an army helicopter ...

                    STELLA
          *(snarls)*
Helicopter!

*She shoots a pair of disbelieving eyes towards the over-cast sky.*

STELLA

(worth saying twice)

Helicopter!

SOPHIE

Helicopter. Did you say, helicopter, Harry?

*SOPHIE'S eyes shimmer upon him favourably. A patient look spreads over his cold, white complexion.*

HARRY

The side-roads are still cut-off in many areas, although the snowplough and grit lorries are making in-roads ...

STELLA

Did you see anything of a milk lorry in the vicinity? Did you spot any milk churns on anyone's milk stands?

*HARRY looks at STELLA politely. STELLA stares back at him abrasively.*

STELLA

Did you see anyone? You must have seen somebody! Somewhere! In some place or another ...

HARRY

(unhurried)

Not so much that you would notice. The Air Ministry forecasted earlier today, Mrs Asquith, there would be two nights' frost in the region of more than minus twenty degrees centigrade, and ...

              STELLA
             (incensed)
You've come all this way to tell us that! How dare you take us for some sort of country bumpkins, who merely exist on fresh air and a good view.

*She yanks gate open. It swings back closing with a sharp contemptuous click, leaving them all standing on the same side of the gate. STELLA marches headlong for the forecourt with SOPHIE in tow. HARRY stands his ground.*

## SCENE 20
**INT. DRILL HALL - SEPTEMBER - NIGHT (HARRY'S MEMORY)**

*SOPHIE and HARRY dancing the HOKEY-COKEY, singing with DANCERS: "Put your left leg in, your left leg out, in, out, in, out and shake it all about. You do the hokey-cokey and you turn around. That's what's all about. Ohhh, lay ..."*

*SOPHIE smiles right into his heart ... HARRY is instantly in love!*

## SCENE 21
**EXT. STOCKDALE FARMS - TOWARDS FARMHOUSES - 10:52 AM**

*Happily HARRY removes an envelope from his inside pocket as he catches up to STELLA and SOPHIE.*

              HARRY
As you know, Mrs Asquith, the mail and goods train have not been fully operational due to the hazardous

weather conditions on the rail tracks, and ...

              STELLA
            (blazing)
Is this all necessary? Explanations take a deal of time, and time means working-time here at Stockdale, young man. Minutes ago, we were going to inspect the outgoing roads, but then, you're a city guy ... what would you know about the ways of countryfolk?

*She strides away angrily.*

*SOPHIE hangs back for HARRY, then re-catching STELLA up.*

              HARRY
Mr Hinchcliffe asked me to hand deliver this important letter to you, Mrs Asquith.

*STELLA suddenly comes to a halt.*

              STELLA
Letter! What sort of a letter?

*HARRY hands over the enveloped letter.*

              HARRY
Mr Hinchcliffe did stress that it was a very urgent matter. A matter with pressing importunity. Therefore an immediate reply will be necessary, despite the weather.

                    STELLA
          This is neither the time or place for
          paperwork.
                    (coldly)
          And you don't have to be a sadist to
          work that out. Harry Bletchford!

## SCENE 22
## INT. STOCKDALE FARMS - STELLA'S KITCHEN - 3 PM

*SOPHIE and HARRY are seated at kitchen table, knives and forks at the ready. They're laughing and talking about cinema venue. STELLA enters, takes top-coat and wellingtons off.*

                    SOPHIE
          Come on, Harry ... think.

                    HARRY
          I know James Mason was cast as ...

                    SOPHIE
          And Margaret Lockwood, leading lady
          ...

*HARRY looks keen, bland, knowledgeable.*

                    HARRY
          From the novel ... I know ... don't
          rush me ...

                    SOPHIE
          The title. Think of it ...
                    (she begins to tickle him)
          Sir ... Sitwell.

*And they burst into laughter all over again.*

*GRACE enters from living room, bearing large tray whereupon plates full of hot sliced farm bacon, scrambled eggs and fried crisp bread all ready to be served.*

                GRACE
We eat very simple at home. I hope you don't mind, Harry. It's bacon and eggs, home produced, not rationed in the countryside. We grow, kill and eat as we please.

                SOPHIE
    *(without heat, turns to STELLA)*
Harry could not possibly make it back to Holbridge before dark. After all, Father ...
    *(she smiles bravely)*
We've all been through a lot lately.

*STELLA'S eyelids quiver. She forces a smile; opens her eyes wide, folds her lips around her impetuosity.*

                STELLA
Well, now. If you're prepared to addle your keep, young man, I dare say we could put you up until tomorrow but we don't carry passengers here at Stockdale.

                HARRY
    *(taken aback)*
If you're sure it's no disposition.

                SOPHIE
    *(eager)*
Will you accept, Harry? Say you will.

> Hospitality is a tradition in the
> Dales. We'd be offended if you refuse
> ...

SOPHIE'S *words seem to caress him.*

> HARRY
> Yes ... yes ... if everyone is
> absolutely sure that I'll not be an
> encumbrance.

> STELLA
> *(pauses rather unkindly long)*
> That's settled then. Until tomorrow.

*STELLA turns to the sink and washes her hands.*

*GRACE dishes out food.*

*SOPHIE and HARRY begin to tattle the food with sheer exuberance.*

> STELLA
> *(to distance herself, she turns*
> *to GRACE and dries her hands)*
> I'll be in the living room if anyone
> needs me ...
> *(lowers voice while passing*
> *GRACE)*
> I can't help but notice your sister's
> blatant behaviour. If she was so upset
> about her father, then she wouldn't be
> able to eat so much.

*STELLA vacates the kitchen, one hand covers her mouth to stifle a sob, the other hand takes the envelope out of the pocket of her breeches.*

**SCENE 23**
**INT. STOCKDALE FARMS - STELLA'S LIVING ROOM - 3:02 PM**

*We hear muffled sounds from the kitchen of SOPHIE and HARRY talking, laughing, talking.*

*We see STELLA lighting two free standing paraffin oil lamps with splinter. They stand with large ornaments and STELLA and SAM'S wedding photograph has prominent position, reflecting her gazing out beyond the solicitations of the photographer as though saying: I came by accident, but I stayed on purpose.*

*She turns away then looks searchingly at the envelope, turns it over.*

*GRACE enters room, carrying two cups of tea on a tray.*

              GRACE
I'll keep you company for five minutes, while those two young persons settle down.

              STELLA
             *(looking up)*
What puzzles me is, what can be so urgent that it can't wait until the thaw comes? I mean, it can't be monetary problems ...

              GRACE
           *(putting saucered cups onto side-table)*
Father was too tight-fisted for that.

He never spend a half-penny where a
farthing would go.

*GRACE sinks onto easy chair.*

*STELLA suddenly fluctuates onto sofa, clutching her throat.*

     STELLA
You don't think we could have buried
your father in the wrong grave?
Someone did say, I can't remember who
... that there had been another burial
scheduled, the same day.

## SCENE 24
**EXT. STOCKDALE FARMS – FARMYARD (STELLA'S MEMORY)**

*The morning of SAM'S burial. We see and hear ominous clattering of chains, steel wheels grinding on icy covered yard flagstones. MEN'S harsh voices echoing in the freezing cold weather, ABE tightening screws on the coffin with a decisive hand which matches his voice ...*

     ABE
Shake a bridle ower ah Yorkshire man's
grave an' he'll rise up and steel thee
horse.

*MOURNERS smile knowingly, then the coffin is secured to the bottom of the hay-cart with cart ropes and BONNY; we see her curry combed, dandy brushed and ribboned, harness brasses polished, gleaming, reflecting the images of STELLA and SOPHIE.*

*BONNY'S standing patiently between the shafts as ABE and his son MIKE settle onto the front cart-rails, reins in hands, clipped hearth rug thrown over their riding breeches and polished boots and leggings.*

*We see JAKE on foot, grasping the leading rein. BONNY pulling and straining within the cart-shafts, driven out of the farmyard towards Kayshaw village – followed by the MOURNERS on foot – all carrying shovels and spades.*

**SCENE 25**
**INT. STOCKDALE FARMS – STELLA'S LIVING ROOM – 3:03 PM**

*STELLA and GRACE exchange bleak looks without self-consciousness.*

> STELLA
> (crying out)
> What a day! What an unforgiving day!
> We, Sophie and myself ... and a few neighbouring farmers turned out, thank God ... followed behind the cart on foot putting shoulders to wheels, hands to shovels, digging out and through snowdrifts all the way to Kayshaw village church. And dear Almighty ... by the time the funeral service ended, a blizzard had been and gone, refilling the grave and leaving no trace or sign behind ...

*She begins to weep silently.*

*GRACE rises, goes to sideboard, opens bottom doors, takes out brandy bottle and pours a measure into STELLA'S teacup, stirs tea, hands it over to STELLA, then sits down next to her.*

GRACE
So, you think, perhaps, Father's buried in some other's family grave?

*She glances at the envelope still clutched in STELLA'S hand.*

GRACE
If you're right it would require an explanation, at least a gratuity ...

STELLA
*(wiping her eyes)*
The vicar kindly invited Sophie and myself into the vestry, and stoked the coke stove before offering us a cup of consecrated wine. There was no tears ...
*(blows her nose noisily)*
We had no tears left. As for the caretaker, well ... he'd hardly introduced himself before the vicar anxious not to be first as we were as anxious not to be last, came back to say ... we could now proceed to assemble around the newly found graveside. And to increase our misery ...
*(her voice quails)*
the vicar ... well ... he's never had a strong voice at the best of times and as we few stood shivering in the driving snow ...
*(pauses to gulp tea noisily)*
Believe me, our Grace. His voice faded in and out to such an extent that I could not even begin to pretend to

myself that I'd understood a word he had said ... and as for lip-reading ...

*STELLA gives an apologetic shrug and puts the envelope back into her pocket before washing down her pain with the medicinal tea ... coughs ungraciously.*

           STELLA

Can't let Harry see that I've been blubbering ...
    *(mouth buckles)*
After all, Sam always said that I was always my own woman, yet I was never bored by the old shapes of everyday farming life, and ...

           GRACE
    *(rises swiftly from sofa)*
Grandma Blanche said Father was a sanguinary man, and having you as his loyal wife papered over his bloody conscience ... of right or wrong.

*STELLA rises from sofa, she's regained her equilibrium, just.*

           STELLA

I am a woman of few illusions, Grace as well you know. And ...
    *(squares shoulders)*
foremost in my mind right now is holding a tight reign onto running the business here at Stockdale Farms. And furthermore, I'll definitely be going through to Holbridge, sometime next week snow or no snow.

GRACE

*(scoops crockery up)*

I hope you read that letter before you go, remember, Mother. Father and J. W. Hinchcliffe were as thick as thieves. There's bound to be a clause ...

STELLA

*(narrows her eyes)*

Their coherent manner, your father explained away as man's talk. And now you come to mention it, our Grace, I remember John Hinchcliffe saying after Sam's funeral service, "No appointment necessary. Sam's business arrangements have been cut and dried. Just a matter of signing on the dotted line." And I also remember, later, our eyes met only fleetingly, but nothing was communicated back to me. However at the time it did cross my mind, perhaps I'd lost the connection in my grief ...

GRACE

*(turns sharply to STELLA)*

The thought has just struck me again, Father may well have bequeathed the adjoining farm to Abe or his son Mike to ensure that the Asquith name is carried on to future male Asquiths!

STELLA

You're not the first one to think that ... as Jake said earlier today, he'll not be ousted out of his home, and by

hell, neither will we ...
>           (mutinous)
> If that's a fact! Then, kid gloves are off! I know what Jake Swales is made of. He's a sadistic man. He'll settle anyone's ash. That I'm absolutely sure of.

## SCENE 26
**INT. STOCKDALE FARMS - STELLA'S KITCHEN - 3:05 PM**

*STELLA and GRACE return to kitchen.*

>           STELLA
>     *(with bare minimum of good manners)*
> Hospitality is no stranger in my home, Harry. What I have yet to understand ...

*She pops boiled bacon between two home-baked slices of bread.*

>           STELLA
> Is the surprise from visiting guests when they find they are almost immediately pressed into work. Farm-work!

*HARRY coughs and clears his throat.*

>           HARRY
>     *(his voice a trifle high)*
> What had you in mind for me to do, Mrs Asquith?

STELLA

(challenge in voice)

How do you feel about lending a hand to assist Jake when he re-drenches the black mare, Bonny? She's rather under the weather these days.

*Hurriedly, he swallows glass of milk to the last drop, while looking, in turn, at the women. Suddenly he rises from the meal table.*

HARRY

That will be a pleasure. The way I see things, I'm not going to learn much by watching everyone doing different things ...

(with approval if not quite enthusiasm)

After all, it can't be more difficult than working with Mr Hinchcliffe ...

(laughs pleasantly)

How could it be worse?

GRACE

(reaches for her overcoat)

Farm-work isn't a job for anyone with a glass back, Harry.

(buttons up coat)

And I reckon drenching Bonny will be more physical than licking stamps for envelopes at J. W. Hinchcliffe's office.

**SCENE 27**

**EXT. STOCKDALE FARMS - APPROACHING STABLES - 5 PM**

*We see STELLA slip-sliding over snow-tracks towards stables, carrying storm lamp.*

**SCENE 28**

**INT. STOCKDALE FARMS - STABLES - 5:02 PM**

*STELLA hangs flickering lamp on nail jutting out of wall.*

> STELLA
> 
> If anyone had to ask me how am I bearing up to my life today, I would have to say that I'm lucky to have kept so sane.

*JAKE is dandy-brushing a young GELDING. Its coat shining like wet coal.*

> JAKE
> 
> Bullshite! Pure bullshite!

> STELLA
> 
> *(she smiles bravely)*
> 
> Grace unwittingly reminded me that the bane of my marriage was that I have no son, and as for Harry ... he's not what Sam or I had in mind for our Sophie ... he's poor! A mere clerk! He smells money here at Stockdale, that's what Sam said - often.

> JAKE
> 
> *(morosely)*
> 
> Weel, if it's any comfort t' thee

lass, it just nivver happened between mesen and me late wife. Just nivver happened! An' by Gawd, we did try some fuckin' antics, enough t' blunt onnybody's appetite.

          STELLA
        *(taking off headscarf)*
So that was that! How's the obstinate young man framing?

          JAKE
Tha means city gent.

*A mixture of amusement and asperity cross his leathery features.*

          JAKE
Aye ... well ... tha knows. We did have a spot o' bother t' begin wi' ...

          STELLA
        *(pugnacity aroused)*
What do you mean ... spot of bother?

          JAKE
        *(droll)*
Pig bother. Aye ... as soon as he shot bolts on pig-house door, store-pigs, all thirteen o' them gruntin' an' squealin' charged out in a solid block. Sent him skittlin' inter air wi' buckets o' feed stuff then as soon as pigs felt shock o' freezin' ice under theer trotters an' afore he'd time t' pick hissen up they did an

>           amazin' quick turn an' bolted back
>           squealin' an' clamberin' all ovver him
>           again t' get back inter pig hole.
>                   *(his eyes water with silent*
>                       *mirth)*
>           By Gawd, boss. He don't half stink!


>                       SOPHIE
>                   *(pokes head over the opened top*
>                       *door of stable)*
>           Do you still need Harry to give a
>           helping hand with Bonny's drench?


>                       STELLA
>                   *(forcefully)*
>           I have definite reservations about
>           Harry's capabilities ...

HARRY enters. His appearance, his stylish clothes, even in the dull glow can be seen splattered with waste matter, hair dishevelled and caked with gruel. Even his glasses have traces of residue upon the lenses, but he maintains his dignity.

STELLA wordlessly hands HARRY a rope.

>                       HARRY
>                   *(politely, not moving a muscle*
>                       *in his face)*
>           Thank you, Mrs Asquith.
>                   *(turns to JAKE)*
>           I understand that I'm going to assist
>           you, Jake.

JAKE jerks his head towards BONNY. He's determined to cut the city clerk down to size.

                    JAKE
          An' tha would know summat about t'
          job, eh? Weel, get crackin' lad let's
          see what tha's made of.
                    (harshly)
          Start framin' an' shove this rope
          under Bonny's nose band!

*Stiffly side-stepping alongside BONNY, HARRY gingerly pokes the rope to where JAKE'S jabbing fingers indicate.*

                    JAKE
          Bugger me! 'Ere ... 'Ere, give it t'
          fuckin' me.

*JAKE snatches rope away, and tosses rope with expertise over beam then begins to haul restless BONNY'S head upwards.*

*HARRY'S eyes behind his smudged lenses look wide open as they follow the tilting head.*

*STELLA pushes stool forward while thrusting the drench bottle into HARRY'S uncertain hand. She inclines her head and eyes in the direction regarding HARRY'S next move, before disappearing to other side of BONNY.*

*We see HARRY climbing onto loose legged stool to stand precariously beneath BONNY'S neck. We hear ruckling sounds coming from her upturned throat, see quivering nostrils. See large yellow clamped teeth, the whites of BONNY'S eyes and her ears laying flat to her greying head.*

*HARRY begins to shake. He breaks out into a sweat. He looks petrified.*

                    JAKE
               (rasps)
          Sharpen up t' job, lad. Tha's not
          bloody shifted. We've not got all day!

HARRY takes several deep breaths ... raises shaking hands
towards BONNY'S upturned restless head. We hear glass clink
against her teeth.

In SLOW MOTION, BONNY'S saliva trickles down the front of
HARRY'S soiled shirt, she rears, bringing a fore-foot
clomping down on HARRY'S head to catch his shoulder.

In REAL-TIME, HARRY is sent spinning back against far wall,
to rebound and slither down amongst falling harness ...
choking and gasping, he flounders to land awkwardly on the
stone floor.

                    JAKE
               (squints across at HARRY)
          Weel! That's a rum un. Ah don't know
          what the hell t' say, except ... hard
          work nivver killed onny-one.

                    STELLA
               (with perfectly natural
               impatience)
          I have an intolerance to sloppy
          workmanship. We've started this job
          and we'll damn well finish it. This is
          not the time for mediation!

HARRY flounders to his knees, rakes fingers through hair,
glasses askew.

> JAKE
> (yelling into HARRY'S distorted face)
> <u>Tha should be grateful t' owld horse in't young anymore. When she was young she'd ah kicked a flea's eye reight out!</u>

HARRY blinks mutely back at him, legs jerking convulsively as he tries again to rise.

SOPHIE'S searching for missing stool leg, finds it, pushes it back into evacuated hole, just in time to slot stool beneath HARRY as he begins to slide off the wall.

> SOPHIE
> Take it easy, Harry.
> (she strokes his back sympathetically)
> Just let yourself settle down naturally.

HARRY opens his mouth wide and let's out a silent scream.

JAKE is standing over him stiff with experience from A to Z.

> JAKE
> Ah've summat t' tell thee lad, ah've been amongst beasts all me workin' life an' ah'm goin' t' tell thee summat! We don't like smart arsed novices practicin' on our good livestock. Tha knows nowt about damn business onny road. So bugger off!

JAKE turns to STELLA with the air of a man who has made

everything plain and within that glance we can see
acknowledgement of their working respect for each other.

                    JAKE
    Ah'll be off then.

He barges out of the stable. We hear him whistling for
BRIDIE.

HARRY clears his throat, making noises to formulate a
sentence that bears no resemblance to any known words,
followed by a long suffering silence.

                    STELLA
        (begins to talk as though no
        one is present)
    It's wonderful to have a few moments
    of peace and quiet ... and ...
    gentility ... and ...

Before her words elapse she's retrieved the unbroken
dandelion and burdock bottle from the hayrack and sheered
away into the night.

## SCENE 29
**INT. STOCKDALE FARMS - STELLA'S KITCHEN - 8 PM**

We see SOPHIE and HARRY enter. Pork is sizzling away in the
Aga oven, and GRACE is spooning vegetables into serving
dishes while STELLA is stacking cleaned pans beneath kitchen
sink.

                    STELLA
        (laconically)
    Poor Sam. It's rather debilitating
    when I think how he loved home

cooking, especially the winter evening meal.

*STELLA heels cupboard door shut and wipes around the sink with dishcloth.*

               GRACE
           *(pops lids over hot food)*
Do you feel the need for a doctor's attention, Harry? I dare say after our meal-time we could ask Jake to harness one of the horses ...

               HARRY
Pardon!

*HARRY slumps flinching onto a chair, turning a pair of streaming eyes in the direction of the voice, spectacles lop-sided. He begins to wring his hands together over his manured smeared clothes, while muttering words that sound suspiciously like rebukes.*

               STELLA
           *(sharply)*
Don't prevaricate, young man. Speak up.

               HARRY
I am not prevaricating.
           *(struggles to sound friendly)*
If a man cannot waste time thinking about his physical or moral condition ... then I'm convinced he'd nearly always discover that he was un-well ... and –

                    SOPHIE
          Harry said that he wondered if, in
          time, he would find that he just
          wasn't here and there would be someone
          else in his skin, in his head, some
          strange person he wouldn't even know
          ...

SOPHIE presses a glass with brandy and warm water into
HARRY'S moving hands.

                    STELLA
               (aware of SOPHIE'S promiscuous
               nature)
          Women get pleasure out of simple
          things such as conversations with
          bairns in arms and ...

                    HARRY
               (desperately)
          Men in love ...

HARRY judders forward to grab SOPHIE'S hand and pulls her
onto his shaking knees. He props his head on her shoulder and
closes his eyes.

STELLA and GRACE exchange uneasy glances; STELLA moves closer
to GRACE.

                    STELLA
               (ungracious undertones)
          An hour earlier, Grace, I might have
          said the accident was wasted on Harry,
          but now I feel certain it could only
          be described as something that serves
          him right.

                    GRACE
           (inclines head in agreement)
        I'm about to dish out everyone, so
        don't take too long deciding when to
        come to the table.

*GRACE picks up loaded tray and heads for living room.*

*SOPHIE springs to her feet, mouth wet with appetite.*

                    SOPHIE
        I'm coming. I didn't realise until I
        smelt the delicious aroma of roasted
        pork and vegs just how ravenously
        hungry I am ...

*She disappears after GRACE into next room. STELLA starts to follow. HARRY stares into the empty space, he looks lost, becomes fidgety.*

                    STELLA
        I'll bring you some of my husband's
        spare clothes so you can get cleaned
        up ... change in your own time, Harry.
        There's plenty of hot water ...

*She points towards back boiler, then crosses to earthenware sink and proceeds to do a little mock demonstration to the mechanical working of the cold water pump.*

*HARRY curdles on the chair.*

                    STELLA
              (getting the edge back in her
              voice)
        No electricity, gas or hot water

66

>               supplies are laid here at Stockdale,
>               but we don't complain ... we maintain
>               a certain decorous restrain, after
>               all, country life is a way of life.

*She turns away and heads for the living room, turns round.*

>                         STELLA
>               It will only take me five minutes to
>               sort out a change of clothes ...

*We see HARRY slumping further down on the chair.*

>                         STELLA
>               And in your own time, Harry, come
>               through and have a bite to eat.

*She leaves the kitchen.*

## SCENE 30
**INT. STOCKDALE FARMS - STELLA'S LIVING ROOM - 9 PM**

*We see STELLA, GRACE and SOPHIE sat in the comfortable living room.*

*GRACE is pouring tea into their cups from a Fabergé teapot. The envelope is propped against the sherry decanter on the Edwardian sideboard.*

>                         STELLA
>                      (demurring)
>               Sometimes I ask myself which is the
>               worst, saying too much or seeing too
>               much and saying nothing?

*They silently stare attentively at the unopened envelope.*

*We see the fire, hear it crackling as flames lick around blazing logs. We see sawn-off logs stacked on the hearth enclosed by a brass fender, and a full coal bucket at the fireside.*

*GRACE leaves the arm-chair, goes to sideboard, opens bottom door and takes out bottle of whisky, turns, their cups are now in alignment.*

                SOPHIE
              *(non-drinker)*
I have no aptitude for drink but tonight, just a drop ...

                STELLA
Don't pour mine out, our Grace as if you're handing out small change!

                GRACE
          *(exercising caution pours)*
We must guard against over stimulating ourselves, Mother.

                STELLA
       *(using a parental expression)*
I'm a devout Christian, but tonight I need a good stiff whisky to get myself off the ground what with one thing and another, Grace, I feel hard pressed to answer that rebuke.

*We see them resettling closer to the fireside, sipping their medicinal tea.*

                GRACE
I'll make up the guest room before

long and put a couple of hot water bottles in the bed just to air the bedding.

STELLA nods, not really listening, her thoughts distant, expression lamentable.

> STELLA
>
> My mind can do nothing right now, but announce its distress to itself ... what has induced John Hinchcliffe, in this diabolical weather, to send Asquith business with a young clerk ... a foolhardy young man with more luck than Sam, your father? What is it that cannot be kept? What is so pressing? Why this immediate and dangerous action?

> SOPHIE
>
> *(her good nature matches her voice)*
>
> Have you made up your mind, Mummy when you're going to open the letter? It's getting late ...

> STELLA
>
> *(gulps down tea, then rebukes gently)*
>
> Sophie, my dear ... your sense of time is no sense at all. Besides ...

STELLA turns her face towards kitchen where HARRY still abides.

STELLA

This is our business. The Asquith's business, in fact I've a good mind to take the family concern out of Hinchcliffe's hands; he's a man's man.

GRACE

*(her voice carries possibilities)*

But for now, will Harry be in a fit state to be left on his own? What if he should slip into unconsciousness during the night?

SOPHIE

*(reproachfully)*

You're surely not suggesting we wet-nurse Harry ... you know I always need eight hours of sleep –

GRACE

*(bluntly)*

He's your friend. Not ours! Letter or no letter.

STELLA

If that letter is carrying bad news, which I fear it could well be, I will not be sleeping tonight so that settles the matter!

*STELLA jumps to her feet and charges the two steps down into the kitchen.*

## SCENE 31

INT. STOCKDALE FARMS - STELLA'S KITCHEN - 9:02 PM

*HARRY is standing by the welsh dresser, solicitously attired in SAM'S three-sizes-too-large clothes - yet somehow they suit him.*

*FLASH - we see SAM superimposed on HARRY.*

*STELLA pulls up short, this unexpected shock she had not bargained for. Resourcefully, pulls herself together.*

      STELLA
   (*keeping to safe ground*)
Food. Do you feel you could hold down something light? Scrambled eggs, all free-range, no powdered stuff here ... The war!
   (*enunciated*)
The war rationing with all its governmental restrictions never really touched the countryfolk. Did you know that, Harry?
   (*she's back in her stride*)
Oh, yes. Our menfolk were exempt from wartime services ... we ... the farmers were and still are the mainstream providers to our wonderful country needs, simply because all the ships were assigned to warfare instead of the usual cargo of fats, oranges and bananas from overseas.
   (*she makes it sound like
   intercourse*)
You see, Harry, just a question of demand and delivery ... but we don't

talk about ...

          HARRY
      *(a tone of benign injustice)*
Black marketing.

          STELLA
And we don't talk about that either, self-reliance and initiative that's what we countryfolk call it, young man.

*She takes a step back from him and sweeps her eyes over him.*

          STELLA
You've lost a bit of ground, Harry. For a start, I'll make you a pot of hot milk with a spoonful of Cousin Abe's pure honey gathered from the heathered moorland ...

          HARRY
      *(his voice reserved, too quiet)*
Your very kind, Mrs Asquith.

          STELLA
      *(truthfully)*
Not at all.

*She leads the way into the living room.*

## SCENE 32
**INT. STOCKDALE FARMS - STELLA'S LIVING ROOM - 9:03 PM**

HARRY hovers astride the steps. SOPHIE springs forward, links arms, guides him to easy chair. He slips slowly down into it like a well fitting shoe with SAM'S clothes, folding about his lean frame to rest where they touch.

GRACE and STELLA lower their sagacious eyes, GRACE to her teacup, STELLA to attend to the fire.

**SCENE 33**

**INT. STOCKDALE FARMS - STELLA'S KITCHEN - 9:04 PM**

We see the inside of the kitchen door opening, then see JAKE leaning half way inside doorway, an empty bucket in one hand and a flickering storm lamp in the other hand.

> JAKE
> (shouting)
> 'Ellow! 'Ellow! Onnybody about?

**SCENE 34**

**INT. STOCKDALE FARMS - STELLA'S LIVING ROOM - 9:04 PM**

STELLA drops poker into the companion set as though red-hot and descends the steps in one swoop.

**SCENE 35**

**INT. STOCKDALE FARMS - STELLA'S KITCHEN - 9:05 PM**

JAKE loiters in kitchen doorway.

> JAKE
> (bawling)
> It's Sylvia! Tha knows! That theer roan beast ... last near far wall, home cow-house. Weel, she's started calvin' an' I'll need ah hand!

                    STELLA
          Just step inside and close the door,
          Jake it's draughty.

*She begins to pull on knee stockings and wellington boots while he starts to fill bucket with back-boiler water. JAKE squints down into the blackness of the boiler in wonderment.*

                    JAKE
          An' who the hell's had all t' hot
          water?

*GRACE enters kitchen and helps STELLA into top-coat as JAKE clatters and scrapes with water jug in and out of boiler.*

                    GRACE
          I'll start siding away the meal
          things, Mother, then clean down
          Harry's clothes ready for tomorrow's
          leave.
                    *(turns top-coat collar up)*
          If you're not back by then, I'll come
          to the calving.

*STELLA and GRACE'S eyes meet and hold in an unspoken understanding and love.*

*STELLA ties headscarf under her chin while casting an enduring glance at HARRY'S plastered clothes draped over chair back.*

                    STELLA
          I maybe wrong, lass. But I would mark
          down that young man as a lateral
          thinker.
                    *(nods thoughtfully)*

There's more to him than meets the
eye. He needs careful watching.

>                    GRACE
>          (ponderously, inspects his
>          daubed clothes)
> Put it this way, Mother. Whichever
> direction he's coming from, if he
> doesn't learn the nature of farming
> quickly then he'll soon feel
> segregated and I can vouch that time
> promises, but it doesn't always fulfil
> ...
>          (pause)
> Time can create cruel coincidences and
> they do take some riding.

>                    STELLA
>          (grips GRACE'S arms)
> Don't be too precious with your
> thoughts, our Grace. I'll not steal
> them away.

JAKE jerks his way passed them with bucket of water.

>                    JAKE
> Ista ready, boss?

STELLA lifts tilly lamp from hook in ceiling beam.

>                    STELLA
> Don't forget, Grace to check the
> wireless for any further weather
> warnings.

STELLA braces herself and follows JAKE out. We hear the drop *of the iron door sneck.*

## SCENE 36
**INT. STOCKDALE FARMS - COW-HOUSE ADJOINING A BARN - 9:12 PM**

*We see a row of SIX SHORTHORN COWS-IN-CALF, all chained by their necks to their individual side-poles, each separated by individual wooden partitions.*

>                    JAKE
>           Hope t' hell it's goin' t' be straight
>           forward calvin' or we'll have a devil
>           of a job gettin' vet out t'night!

*He removes his coat and jacket. Hangs them on nail in wall. He rolls up his shirt sleeves, lathers his hands and arms vigorously with carbolic soap, then rinses them from bucket of water.*

*STELLA hands him hessian sack to dry off. They then wrap sacks round their waists, secure with a large nail.*

*STELLA holds lamp aloft while he makes brief, experienced examination of SYLVIA.*

>                    JAKE
>           Reakon we'll give her a few minutes t'
>           see if she can manage on her own.
>           Nature's a wonderful thing tha knows.

*He reaches up and takes two milking stools and a calving rope from ledge. They sit down. He rolls a mean cigarette, lights it, inhales deeply. Gradually wisps of smoke come from his mouth as he speaks.*

                    JAKE
                (drolly)
            An' how's city gent's head then?

*STELLA settles on stool, props her back against wall, stretches legs out before her, then removes headscarf and runs fingers through her hair.*

                    STELLA
            Like Big Ben. Cracked, but still
            telling the time.

*They sit without further exchange of words, overseeing the CATTLE chewing contently on their cuds while laid forelegs bent and back legs tucked in, resting peacefully.*

*SYLVIA is the only cow standing, the CALF'S fore-feet already showing. We hear painful bawling.*

                    JAKE
            Always a good sign t' see head restin'
            on its forelegs.
                (drags on cigarette)
            Aye ... all goin' weel she shouldn't
            be ower long.

*STELLA rises to shake bracken out behind straining SYLVIA ready for the CALF'S landing.*

                    STELLA
                (empathy strong)
            Cush, cush. Cush ... cush.

*We hear the neck chains clattering as the slack of the steel links contact the stone feeding trough as SYLVIA jerks her head up and down with another loud bellow of pain ...*

*TWO OTHER COWS begin to make "mooing" sounds. Chains gently clanging in response to labouring bawling.*

> JAKE
> *(repeats)*
> Always good sign t' see young un's head restin' on its forelegs.

*He rises, stubs out cigarette under his boot heel, makes a noose and slips it behind CALF'S head and beneath its forelegs, adjusting rope accordingly.*

*They wait until SYLVIA strains again before pulling on rope, in time, in rhythm with her thrusting and bearing ...*

*CALF comes away gradually to slither down onto dry bracken.*

> STELLA
> Looks like we've got a good one.
> *(she smiles)*
> Oh, Sam would be so pleased.

*JAKE removes rope, cleans mucus from CALF'S nostrils and mouth. CALF looks dazed. Then slowly its legs begin to spiral as STELLA rubs down and removes slippery, bloody substance with a meal sack. The stimulation awakens the CALF. JAKE lifts its tail.*

> JAKE
> A heifer.

> STELLA
> *(her delight is immense)*
> Oh, Jake. She's a real champion. Just look at the dark roan markings. Heifers are always good news ... they

enhance the herd given time.

    *(emotional)*

If only Sam could have been here to see her ...

She begins to weep without utterance of sound.

    JAKE
    *(soulful as he contemplates the*
    *toil of her misery)*

Aye ... Weel, lass ... that's as may be ...

He lifts his flat cap and scratches his head; lank hair falls on his forehead. His face lengthens and a corner of his mouth droops.

    JAKE
    *(speaks slowly)*

Tha knows ... nobody can turn clock back an' if we could we'd not only have t' turn our lives back around again but we'd have t' turn ivvery others' lives back that had come in touch wi' ours at that time, an' some folks wouldn't want that! Far rather leave it as the good Lord intended!

He swivels his worn cap back onto his head.

STELLA rises from her knees unable to share her inner feelings the calving has triggered in her.

    STELLA

I'll go and make Sylvia a warm bucket of gruel.

>                    *(she staggers to cow-house*
>                    *door)*
> I'll not be over long.

>                    JAKE
>                    *(brusquely)*
> Ah see it like this. We're all born
> between piss an' shit, an' when we all
> peg out we're all bloody equal!

## SCENE 37
**INT. STOCKDALE FARMS - STELLA'S LIVING ROOM - 10:30 PM**

*The wireless is switched on. We hear the muted broadcasting voices in background.*

>                    GRACE
> Take your time, Harry while I place a
> light in the guest's bedroom.

*She grips a candle-stick holder with a candle inserted. Its translucent tongue of flame licks the air as she sweeps by him.*

*HARRY rises stiffly from chair. He can barely bend to place mug on side table.*

*Concern spreads over SOPHIE'S young face, and plainly not over STELLA'S set expression.*

>                    SOPHIE
> I'll show you the way, Harry. You look
> as though you can scarcely move. Come
> on ...
>                    *(she links her arm through his)*
> I know you'll be soon back to your old

self by tomorrow, I just know you will
...

      STELLA
    (*separates each word carefully*)
But we can never go back. Nobody can.
It's the two second rule.

*STELLA watches them as they leave the room, turns back to place coal on fire.*

*We hear footsteps and young tones of voices as GRACE and SOPHIE descend the stairs and re-enter room.*

      GRACE
    (*she closes living room door*)
I don't think he's got anything left
to offer anyone ...

      SOPHIE
And I'm just sort of tired out. I
think I'll lie down awhile ...
    (*sprawls attractively onto the
    sofa in advanced lethargy*)
I feel all in ... Mummy ...
    (*groans*)
Quite out of sorts.

      GRACE
    (*her smile aims to scold
    SOPHIE*)
I prefer my feet on the ground, action
to a bed of roses, instead of getting
the lion's share of sympathy from the
family.

                        STELLA
            Don't be so stiff and judgemental, our
            Grace. You know, dear Sophie doesn't
            have your stamina ...

*STELLA is at SOPHIE'S side in a flash. She feels her brow, examines her eyes, looks at her tongue and presses her neck.*

                        STELLA
            How do you feel, love?

                        SOPHIE
            Mmmmmm ...

                        STELLA
            That's no answer at all.

*She re-checks for signs of sickness.*

                        SOPHIE
            Sort of under the weather ... sort of
            sickening ... it's been such a long
            day, even with Harry in it ...
                    (mouth droops)
            Just feeling off colour. I'll be okay
            after a bit.

                        STELLA
                    (places a throw-over cover
                    around SOPHIE)
            Get some sleep and try to get a sense
            of time together! Grace and I will be
            on call throughout the night. Now, get
            some rest. There's a good lass.

*SOPHIE needs no second telling. She closes her eyes*

*thankfully against the rigours of the day.*

**SCENE 38**

**INT. STOCKDALE FARMS - STELLA'S GUEST ROOM - 10:50 PM**

*We see HARRY off his head, turns painfully over in bed and enters a room without walls.*

**SCENE 39**

**INT. STOCKDALE FARMS - STELLA'S LIVING ROOM - 10:51 PM**

*STELLA rearranges the loose cushions on her easy chair and leans back as though to restore herself.*

> STELLA
> There's nothing I would like better right now than to have a small aperitif and ten minutes of peace and quiet before I open that darn letter.

*GRACE switches off wireless, then heads for the sideboard. Opens bottom cupboard door. We see a wide variety of home brewed wines of many colours in labelled bottles.*

> GRACE
> Elderberry! I think elderberry will go down a real treat.

*GRACE twists and turns the cork causing an outburst of gaseous force.*

*STELLA blinks herself alert, then gracefully accepts a full glass of the wine. She holds it up to the firelight.*

> STELLA
> Looks good enough to be champagne.

*STELLA smells it, then takes a sip and another at leisure, she half laughs.*

              STELLA

The bubbles are fairly bursting on my tongue ... Wonderful experience!
      *(sips more and more)*
Absolutely divine. You really are a dab-hand at this wine making business ... the distillery ... very make-shift by anyone's standards, but very adequate for ...

*STELLA takes a larger sip, then a good swallow and puts hand to throat.*

              STELLA
     *(she closes her eyes)*
The bottom barn ...

              GRACE
One of the best I've made so far.

*GRACE rolls wine around her mouth with a faraway look on her face.*

              GRACE
Made this and others the year before I left home. It was a very good year for harvesting ... a fruitful year.

              STELLA
     *(she reopens her eyes and turns towards her)*
Do you want to talk through those two, long years when ...

                    GRACE

          Not just yet, Mam. They're still too
          raw ... alienation and loss, rubs the
          soul raw.


                    STELLA
                (studies GRACE)
          We all tend to shy away from painful
          matters one road or another, but there
          does come a time for reckoning, we all
          know that given time ... of course.

STELLA replenishes their glasses, then extends herself before the blazing fire.

                    STELLA
          When you're ready, love ... When
          you're ready ...

**SCENE 40**

**EXT. STOCKDALE FARMS – MOORLAND – DAY (STELLA IMAGINES)**

We see a blurred sighting of SAM, isolated, striving blindly through snow blizzard, which fades as STELLA speaks.

                    STELLA (V/O)
          If I had to be honest, our Grace. I
          could say there are times when I can't
          hold a clear image of your father's
          face, nor hear his voice in my head
          ... yet ...
                (gulps wine)
          Yet I am poignantly conscious of him
          throughout each day and night ...

**SCENE 41**

INT. STOCKDALE FARMS - STELLA'S LIVING ROOM - 10:53 PM

*STELLA suddenly rises to seize the unopened envelope.*

                STELLA
    I've just noticed ...
        *(she turns envelope over)*
    I've been addressed as, Mrs Stella
    Asquith. Not Mrs Samuel Asquith.

*STELLA'S mouth tightens and her eyes grow wilder as she pushes her thumb slowly beneath the sealed envelope. She takes a quick glance at SOPHIE sleeping peacefully.*

                STELLA
    It just goes to show that it doesn't
    take long for some folk to alter
    things ...

                GRACE
    I'll go and make a quick check on
    Harry.

*GRACE vacates chair discreetly and picks up a lighted paraffin lamp.*

                GRACE
    If you ask me it's not so much Bonny's
    fault as Harry's misfortune.

*GRACE leaves the room, STELLA appears not to have heard.*

*STELLA slips the headed writing paper from its envelope. It's folded in three. She straightens it out but it doesn't lay flat. Words, handwritten. Sentences short, ending with flourishing signature. She folds the letter back into its groves in a state of shock and replaces it back into its envelope.*

*Half a minute later, she retrieves it. This time attending to each single word.*

*GRACE re-enters room.*

*We see STELLA sitting bolt upright, like a Prussian General, staring unseen into the fireback. GRACE quickly replenishes their drinks.*

>            GRACE
>         *(abruptly)*
>    Take this, Mother! You look half dead
>    and in need of a little tempering ...
>         *(pause, searching STELLA'S*
>         *face)*
>    I hope I haven't spoken unkindly, but
>    I expected more of a show from you,
>    and as for Father, as far as I'm
>    concerned, he performed his last
>    noteworthy act by dying.
>
>            STELLA
>         *(as though speaking to herself)*
>    Just then, you sounded like an
>    Asquith. A ruthless Asquith.

*STELLA takes full glass and raises it mechanically to her lips and empties the glass of its contents.*

>            GRACE
>         *(looking angry)*
>    Father surely hasn't left the

adjoining farm to Abe has he?

*GRACE pours them both a large drink, then sits down heavily. At length STELLA moves shooting glances like bayonets to the right and to the left of herself. Her face as white as driven snow.*

           STELLA
      *(through clenched teeth)*
This is the most violating letter I have ever read! I don't think this is the sort of ambience to which I should be subjected to!
      *(her lips begin to curl)*
What sort of game was he playing? And without so much as an inkling to me all though our twenty-eight years of marriage ...
      *(shakes letter injuriously)*
And all those years I foolishly believed I was without any encumbrances!
      *(voice rising to a crescendo)*
<u>Now I find I have gained an encumbrance!</u>

           GRACE
Encumbrance?

           STELLA
A supernumerary encumbrance!

*STELLA stares at the letter in the cadmium yellow lamplights.*

           STELLA
After nearly thirty years of working

> hard alongside your father ... all
> that loyalty and dedication I gave him
> and Stockdale Farms ... and now ... to
> be handed this ... this ...

*She holds letter up as though she's holding a reptile, then leaps to her feet with frightening agility.*

>                    STELLA
> You know what I think, our Grace. It's
> the living who are the victims of the
> dead!

>                    GRACE
> I need another drink. You're sounding
> ominous, and quite unlike you ... I
> hardly recognise you.

>                    STELLA
>              *(smiles deferentially)*
> We've been through a great deal lately
> ... so debasing ... so severely
> lowering ...
>          *(struggles to keep voice level)*
> But this. It's a shocker! A real
> shocker by anyone's standards.

*STELLA sits close to the fire, both doing the slow burn.*

>                    STELLA
> You know, Grace I was barely twenty
> when I married your father and he was
> over twenty years older than me ...
>          *(re-fills glasses)*
> and wealthy ...

GRACE

What were you seeking? A father figure or purely a husband with money? I don't hear you mention love.

STELLA

Your father was more use to being loved than giving love so I settled for security. I wanted security with a good social and material return within marriage ...
    *(pause)*
Believe me, those insurances were uppermost in my mind even at that early age. I knew what I wanted and I went out to get it, as Grandma Blanche always said, "a complimentary arrangement" if ever she saw one.

*The homemade beverages begin to relax them. STELLA slackens off.*

STELLA

This turnip wine is truly unbelievable ... it quite awakens my taste buds ...
    *(eyelids droop)*
the exquisite bouquet ... is incredulous ...

GRACE

The letter, Mother ...

STELLA

Shall we try the dandelion ...

*GRACE reaches out and pats her mother's arm kindly.*

GRACE

By the time we've finished sampling these delicious wines, Mother you'll be incapable of seeing anyone's point of view but your own and -

STELLA

(insidiously)

The bugger! To think he managed to take his secret right through to his grave without so much as a nod or a wink to anyone in the family. He was too damn mean to even share it.

GRACE

Father was always economical with words and the telling of his deeds ...

STELLA

(voice beginning to slur)

Not all his deeds, my dear ... underneath his diplomatic veneer, if anyone crossed him, he was a sanguinary man ...

SOPHIE

(waking up suddenly)

Is that a compliment?

STELLA *turns her head proudly to face* GRACE *and* SOPHIE.

STELLA

If there's one thing I can say ... quite ...

(marginally fluffs words)

categorical ... cally ... You've both

been able to depend on my honesty and
sincerity. Someone you can talk to
openly and whoo ... whooommm ... you
can be candid wiv ...

*STELLA'S delivery is inarticulate as she droops her gaze and begins to flatten out the folded letter.*

               STELLA
I shall now endeavour to po ... ceed.

*STELLA struggles to keep her voice from broadening out into mispronounced words.*

               STELLA
    *(face uninviting)*
The plain truth is ... Mr J. W.
Hinchcliffe, our family solicitor has
forwarded ... via Harry ... this ...
this ...
    *(falters tongue twisting*
    *erroneously)*
prelimmee ...
    *(takes another stab at it)*
pre ... limm ... mmmy ...
    *(splutters like a firework*
    *ready to go off)*
It's an impeee ... im ... pi ... us
... impious osten ... ta ... shus ...
letter and it doesn't even read well,
the shithouse!

*They stare at STELLA as though they don't recognise their mother.*

STELLA

*(voice belligerent)*

Hinchcliffe states ...

*(suddenly her irregular words become regular, just)*

And I quote ... "Due to the worse winter on record and the Dales total isolation, to save an impassable journey by you, into Holbridge, the gratuity is straight forward. Your deceased husband, Samuel John Asquith of Stockdale Farms, Kayshaw, near Holbridge, West Riding of Yorkshire, died 21st January 1947. He bequeathed in his will that the adjoining farm (known as Stockdale Farm) to his son, Francis Spencer-Asquith, born out of wedlock on the 17th March 1904, to a then, Miss Evelyn Ridgeholm of Woodclose, near Holbridge, (also deceased). A written acknowledgement would be advisable so that we can proceed to a satisfactory transaction of the legacy by early spring 1947." Unquote.

*An irksome atmosphere prevails in the room.*

STELLA

In a nutshell! A bastard son! An illegitimate son and we are the last to know!

SOPHIE

*(whispers)*

Did you say ...? Did you just say ...?

A son?

                    GRACE
An illegitimate son?

STELLA *jerks to her feet.*

                    STELLA
            *(yelling into their faces)*
Yes. A bastard son. Do you want me to
spell it out to you both? Right! Shall
I start with bast? Would you both like
me to give you the definition of the
bast as in packsaddle ...?
            *(pounds letter mercilessly)*
Here I'm referring to the old locution
... and just when I need it ... I've
lost it ...

                    SOPHIE
            *(bewildered)*
Where has he cropped up from?

STELLA *gestures very disreputably at the solicitor's letter.*

                    STELLA
Canada!

                    SOPHIE and GRACE
            *(with astonishment)*
Canada!

                    STELLA
Yes. Canada. A maverick. A packsaddle.
            *(sits down suddenly)*
I wonder if Cousin Abe knows?

SOPHIE

*(counting on her fingers)*

1904 ... that makes him 43 years old. How come we've never heard or seen head or tail of him ...?

*(bitterly)*

And how are we suppose to handle a complete stranger bequeathed into our family business and -

GRACE

*(sharply)*

He, this so-called son of father's cannot walk straight into our lives and our livelihood from somewhere else, and by the sound of the letter - bringing nothing, absolutely nothing with him, apart from himself ...

SOPHIE

*(speaks with a kind of gasp)*

And he's too old to be mothered, and what if he's married? Will he have bairns? And if he has, then they're likely to be teenagers - with a forty something mother.

GRACE

If we're not very careful, Mother, our lives will be taken over by a complete stranger - and what could or would we do with a stranger or a stranger's family in our home, or Jake's home?

STELLA
*(holds up a hand to indicate silence)*
Questions! All questions. Plans will have to be made ...
*(she smiles peculiarly)*
Fortified with Jake's loyal and sadistic nature, after all, he was your father's side-kick, and besides, Jake and I did touch down yesterday on the possibility of Cousin Abe or his son, Mike being possible benefactors to our homes here at Stockdale Farms ... but ...
*(snarls)*
Never once did I envisage this catastrophe ... this ...

*STELLA stares at the letter, screws it savagely into a crumpled ball and throws it virulently into the fire-flames.*

GRACE
*(with sufficiency)*
We can not allow this man to take half-share of everything. It's not as if he's earned it. We, the Asquith women helped Father to accumulate his wealth by toiling like men here at Stockdale ...
*(voice hardens)*
Day in, day out, week in, week out, season in, season out, and now this Francis Spencer-Asquith, an unknown to us ...
*(her voice falters)*
Out-of-wedlock Asquith ... and besides

all that, there's not room for another Mrs Asquith here, I mean, our mother is the patriarch of the Asquith family, even Aunt Winny and Uncle Abe begrudgingly concede to that ...

          STELLA
    *(eyes are fierce)*
I do not need a solicitor or a psychologist to tell me that Sam Asquith, your father, would have known if there were additional family members and John Hinchcliffe would have doubly checked and seen to that, and knowing your father's calculative nature, he would have made provisions for them, if they exist. After all, Grace, your father crossed you out of his mind and his earlier will. He said that you had brought disgrace and betrayal to his whole family by fraternising with that German Prisoner Of War, our wartime enemy.

          GRACE
    *(face twists painfully and*
    *voice quails)*
Hertz and I fell in love, unconditionally, even though neither one of us could barely speak the other's language ... we connected ... and now ...
    *(swallows with difficultly)*
all those special memories belong only to me.

> SOPHIE
> *(softly)*
> Love doesn't have to be spoken, it's just known.

> STELLA
> *(too angry to be agreeable)*
> There's an invisible line that divides love from hate, my mind felt bruised when Doctor Liddle told me, confidentially, that your father had ordered him to terminate ...

*STELLA bites her bottom lip too late on the guarded secret.*

*A silence falls.*

*STELLA closes her eyes upon them and appears to give herself over to intense thoughts.*

> GRACE
> *(speaks with restrain)*
> To end the sweet core of life ...
> *(pause)*
> Father deserved to die hard.

*SOPHIE looks hot and bothered. She stumbles ungainly to the sideboard, opens a bottle of wine and pours herself a full glass.*

> SOPHIE
> *(between gulps)*
> I'm beginning to feel a trifle pooched due to family confessions.
> *(sits down and nurses the half empty glass of wine)*

I'm not used to it. I'm more use to being loved.

                GRACE
           (voice harsh)
How right Grandma Blanche was when she said, Father was a murderous man. And on top of that, a bloody hypocrite himself, having sired a bastard son. A son never once spoken of in our whole lives.

*STELLA and GRACE exchange hollow glances.*

                SOPHIE
           (whispers wide-eyed)
A half-brother ... he's our half-brother.

*STELLA and GRACE appear not to have heard her claim.*

                STELLA
We don't want to lose face by suffering social death by not embracing this kept-in-the-dark inheritor. We can't allow him to rattle about in the community like a lost part. We must invite him into our homestead graciously – then once we've gained his trust, we will have our plans ready ... Riddance plans.

            GRACE and SOPHIE
Plans!

*STELLA'S face reveals a curious set of the mouth.*

                    STELLA
          Jake and I have already set the seeds.
          Farming accidents do happen.
                    (pause)
          Whether they're instigated or purely
          accidental, these things happen.

*Conspiratorial glances pass between them which become united
in consolidation. STELLA replenishes glasses, they raise
them, then clink them together, and systematically drink
deeply, then STELLA smiles very slightly at each daughter in
turn.*

                    STELLA
          It's in the nature of farming.

## SCENE 42
**EXT. STOCKDALE FARMS - FARMYARD - 9 AM**

*GRACE is hoisting ash bucket and dashing out coal cinders
liberally over the icy flagstones.*

*JAKE leads broken winded BONNY, out of the stables. STELLA is
standing by, overseeing.*

                    STELLA
          What we want is a change for the
          better or is that asking too much?

*BONNY clops by on the parameter of the ashes.*

                    JAKE
                (bawling over his shoulder)
          Any horse looks fast moving agenst
          trees ...

*He brings BONNY to a stilted stop. He hands the halter-lead to GRACE. BONNY gives a sharp cough with a detectable stiffening of the muscles, then cocks her tail and gingerly lowers it.*

>STELLA
>*(anxiously)*
>Could be a touch of colic?
>>*(her eyes seek JAKE'S)*
>Or should I stop kotowing?

>JAKE
>Aye. Theer's summat else, but ah don't know if tha's ready for it.

*He examines BONNY with experienced hand and eyes. He shakes his head, face dead-pan and turns away.*

>STELLA
>Take Bonny back into the stable, Grace out of this freezing weather, then try her with some warm gruel.
>>*(she swings round to JAKE)*
>I take it that she's still consuming food?

>JAKE
>Weel ...

*He regards his boss stoically, a cigarette butt hanging from his lower lip.*

>JAKE
>She's been none t' clever wi' it last few days or so ...

STELLA

That does it! Jake! We're going to get the Rover out and make a telephone call to the veterinary for an urgent farm visit, and while we're about it, we'll be going through to Holbridge!
    *(tone absolutely final)*
To call on J. W. Hinchcliffe! The damn rotter. I'll not have him writing me off ... yet!

JAKE

Fuck me! Holbridge! Did t' say Holbridge?

STELLA

We'll need chains fixed to all four car wheels, and I'll get our Sophie to assist you ...
    *(hollowing to the right and to*
    *the left of herself)*
Sophieeee ... Sopheeeee ...

*JAKE juts out his chin and butts his head about in the air.*

JAKE

Tha'll nivver in a month o' Sundays git car up or down roadways nivver mind inta bloody Holbridge, all them gurt hills for a damned start!

*STELLA turns a full circle upon him and we can see she is smiling at him, but the smile doesn't reach her eyes.*

STELLA

We're going! And that is the end of

the matter!

>JAKE
>*(a ring of defiance in his rasping voice)*

We're goin'! Who's we're?

>STELLA

You and me, Jake. Just you and me!

>JAKE

Me! That means ... me? Ah've nivver set foot - let alone sat down in thee cars throughout thirty years I've known thee ... an' now, all o' a sudden tha springs this hoi polloi job ont' mesen wi'out warnin'.

>STELLA
>*(eyes waiting to lock into his eyes)*

It's a matter of some incoherent rigmarole in my late husband's will ...

She looks as though she's swallowed a jug of raw lemon juice.

>STELLA

A mere conjecture!

JAKE struggles to read her meaning. His mouth gaps open.

>STELLA

Which would make all the difference to my status, and it could include you having to relinquish the roof over your head!

                    JAKE

What the hangman!

*Two startled round eyes in his rubicund face expand. He cups his large hand behind his ear as though he hasn't heard.*

                    JAKE

What did t' say? Ah didn't catch what tha said.

                    STELLA
                    (brutally)

You heard me! I shall go and get a cat lick then get changed, and you will have all the amenities in place within the hour, if you know which side your bread's buttered on!

## SCENE 43
## I/E. ROVER CAR - STOCKDALE FARMS - FORECOURT - 10 AM

*Rover stood with engine running. Chains secured around wheels with binder twine and expertise.*

*We see STELLA slithering towards parked vehicle. She is dressed serviceable but expensively; green cord riding breeches, flat heeled long-legged leather boots, wool jumper and Harris tweed jacket. Overcoat, barely black, Astrakhan swagger coat. Upon her head an Astrakhan Russian styled hat which comes to rest upon her eyebrows and earlobes.*

*STELLA looks impressive, powerful and quite grand.*

*SOPHIE is busy arranging sheep skins over front seats, edges herself out of car.*

              SOPHIE

Extra comfort, Mam, and I've put a few extra blankets on the back seat, just in case ...

              STELLA
        *(nods her thanks)*

Has Jake put any extra weights in the car boot to hold the back-end down?

*STELLA skids along the frozen snow to check – we see two hessian sacks trussed-up contents already turning them black.*

              STELLA
        *(shouting)*

<u>Coal!</u>
        *(slams boot door shut)*

Let's hope to God, we don't catch fire.
        *(turns to SOPHIE)*

Where's Jake?

*STELLA seats herself onto the driving seat while GRACE shunts a couple of shovels and a spade onto the floor of Rover behind her seat.*

              STELLA

We should be back before dark. The postman said only this morning that the grit lorries had been out earlier and they had made in-roads into the side-roads ...
        *(she looks them in the eyes)*

Anyway, today is as good as any to get

> out and necessitate and that for now
> is enough nourishment ... And where's
> Jake?

We hear the Rover engine accelerating loudly.

> STELLA
> Surely he knows time is precious, and
> precious is the essence of our time.

Cursing under his breath, JAKE lowers himself awkwardly onto the passenger seat, while GRACE, SOPHIE and BRIDIE pile onto the back seat.

> STELLA
> (laughs)
> Just for the joyride to the end of the
> cart-road. Hold onto your hats girls.
> It's going to be a bumptious ride.

STELLA turns her attention to the clutch and the gear stick. The car shoots forward. The back swings round. The chains chisels and chomps into the frozen snow as they clunk towards the water-splash.

JAKE bathed in female atmosphere, feels his senses dulled amongst dainty fare.

> JAKE
> (bawling)
> <u>Tha's not on a bloody race track an'
> ah'll tell thee for nowt, ah don't
> want t' end up between two brass
> handles like boss did!</u>

He immediately folds his arms, his face, his whole body into *a hard ball of entire occupation of bloody mindedness.*

*STELLA barely stops the car to drop the girls off.*

                STELLA
            *(in expansive mood)*
      Expect us when you see us, my dears.
      And keep the home fires burning.

*SOPHIE manages to touch the back bumper with a finger as STELLA rams her foot level to the boards, swings the motor out of the entrance gate and up the road towards Kayshaw village.*

### SCENE 44
### I/E. ROVER CAR - APPROACHING KAYSHAW HILL TOP - 10:20 AM

*STELLA determinedly grips the steering wheel. JAKE is back to jutting his head and thrusting his chin forward as he peers through car window at the approaching hill top.*

                JAKE
      Don't thee forget t' drive inta a
      skid, not bloody well out o' it. That
      way tha might save us a lot o' bother!

                STELLA
      I dare say you're wondering why I
      bought you with me instead of one of
      my daughters.

                JAKE
      Aye, an' wonderin' nobut lasts for a
      few days an' then pup's eyes are
      oppened. Thee just concentrate on thee
      drivin'.

STELLA snorts and stomps on the accelerator.

                    STELLA
That's a poor attitude to take, Jake. It shows a paucity of imagination on your part. So just sit back and enjoy the view.

He rives back onto the seat. They round a bend a trifle too wide ... Silence falls between them as they head for Kayshaw downhill.

We see a red cattle wagon trundling along. We hear its engine grinding away in bottom gear while travelling in the centre of the roadway.

                    STELLA
       (shouting antagonistically and
       waving to WAGON DRIVER)
<u>You've no business to be here. Move over you great road-hog! You're not fit to be let loose.</u>

She breaks. The car slews. The wheels keep skidding, chains spit out bullets of solid ice combined with grit which ricochets back onto the car windows and bodywork.

                    JAKE
       (bawling)
<u>Put them theer bastard wipers on, afore ah shit mesen!</u>

We get a fleeting glimpse of a large startled face behind the steering wheel of the red wagon as STELLA fights to deviate from the line of proper course – a head-on collision.

*And within seconds they realise there is only one way to go ... down!*

                  JAKE
          *(closes harassed eyes)*
     Ah can see mesen being laid next t'
     Sam Asquith down in Kayshaw cemetery
     ... all brokken up like boss were ...
     an' wallflowers! Aye ... wallflowers
     always me favourite flowers ...

                  STELLA
         *(through clenched teeth)*
     I do not for one premonitory moment,
     Jake imagine myself laying on top of
     Sam Asquith ... not today or any day
     ... let alone in Kayshaw's graveyard.

*We see them shunting down the icy steep hill with increasing speed. Passing a row of terrace houses, family grocers, ale house with its chimney puffing smoke out into the frosty air.*

*The Rover sheers at the bottom of the hill and by its own directing means, ploughs through a monstrous heap of snow gatherings which disintegrate in the air with impact, icy congealed edges scrape over and down the bodywork of the Rover, and splinter through the impaired window screen.*

*We see STELLA squinting, still gripping onto the steering wheel like grim death until by chance, she crashes into a stationary delivery van, consequently rebounding off to slam into the village telephone kiosk. The impact spins the car, juddering round precariously before keeling over on the snow covered village green.*

*JAKE, bent lopsided below apron of dashboard, his teeth still* barred against death. Slowly juts his head above the board.

STELLA, slightly leaning towards JAKE, still gripping steering wheel, feet wedged abstrusely between peddles. She looks as though she's anally sucked up everything beneath her and in return everything holds STELLA upright in the power of retention.

They watch abstractedly. A front car wheel with its disarranged chains spinning round until mind over matter and gravity prevail.

Both shunt themselves out of the damaged vehicle, aware SEVERAL VILLAGERS eyeing them from behind moving lace curtained windows.

STELLA retrieves her handbag while adjusting her Astrakhan hat, then JAKE silently inspects dents, scratched bodywork, one headlight smashed, other hanging, mudguard missing and boot lid misplaced by protruding sacks of coal.

JAKE turns to STELLA, then kicks dishevelled chains.

          JAKE
     Sam Asquith would turn in his grave if
     he saw this ...

          STELLA
     And if I had to see him, I'd wring his
     balls!

She inhales a few deep breaths and slowly exhales, to becoming obscurely composed.

          STELLA
     Come along, Jake. Let's see what the

blacksmith can do for us and don't you bugger things up for us by cursing, because he's a Methodist lay preacher and he won't tolerate any filthy language.

*They head towards the forge.*

*We see JAKE shove the door open, the BLACKSMITH is shoeing a CLYDESDALE HORSE. Furnace burning red-hot.*

## SCENE 45
**INT. BLACKSMITH'S FORGE - KAYSHAW - 10:30 AM**

*BLACKSMITH is hammering the white hot metal into shape on the anvil.*

          JAKE
      *(expansively)*
Ah recognise yon geldin' ... that theer horse is one o' Jeff Harrison's.

         BLACKSMITH
Aye! Does t' want t' make somethin' of it?

          JAKE
      *(trying to smile and not*
      *succeeding)*
All reight ... all reight ...

         STELLA
      *(steps forward, open to*
      *conversation)*
I'm Mrs Sam Asquith ...

*She pumps BLACKSMITH'S free hand heartily but with a certain philosophical sternness.*

                STELLA
We need a horse when you've finished your excellent work, as a means of assistance to place my motor car back on the road ...

*She looks at the BLACKSMITH as though it is a real treat to see a real human being.*

                BLACKSMITH
        *(he looks back at her as though*
        *he's known her all his life)*
Tha what! What did t' say tha wanted?

                STELLA
I have an appointment at eleven o'clock this morning with J. W. Hinchcliffe ... solicitor, in Holbridge ...
        *(she swallows the lie and*
        *pauses)*
What with poor Sam dying like that... and I've still to call the veterinary ... left the children ...

*She pauses too long.*

                JAKE
        *(ardent zeal)*
By heck! Ah've seen some bloody changes in me time ...

*JAKE lifts his cap and scratches his head then swivels it*

*back on his head, catching STELLA'S eye.*

                JAKE

Take t' day for a <u>bloooomin'</u> start!

               STELLA

        *(grandly)*

I'm not taking, Jake. I'm merely appropriating.

        *(turns to BLACKSMITH*

        *flirtatiously)*

Would you kindly let us borrow Mr Jeffery Harrison's Clydesdale horse simply to pull my motor car upright ... Mr ... Mr ...

*His name completely escapes her memory. Diplomatically, she places a fluttering hand to the side of her hat band as though developing some sign of migraine or pertaining to menstrual tension.*

            BLACKSMITH

        *(impressively a tower of*

        *strength)*

Say no more, Mrs Asquith. Don't thee fret thesen. When ah've finished shoein' t' hoss, we'll be reight with thee, lass. And in meanwhile, tha can use me household telephone. The missus should be at home.

*STELLA graciously tries not to overdo things and disappears thankfully out of the forge.*

## SCENE 46

I/E. ROVER CAR - KAYSHAW VILLAGE GREEN - 11:30 AM

STELLA climbs back onto driving seat of Rover, settles down. She's ready.

JAKE cranks away with starting handle. The robust engine bursts into life. He withdraws handle. Stomps around battered car, throws it into car and lurches himself onto back seat.

We see roads narrowed by banking of snowplough's sidings, several delivery vehicles chug passed them on the gravelled roads.

                STELLA
            (conversational)
      How exhilarating, Jake to see that
      we're all taking advantage of the last
      forty-eight hours forecast of no
      further snowfalls ...

                JAKE
      Just thee keep an eye on road!

                STELLA
           (slows down speed, looks
           straight ahead)
      Now, is as good a time as any time to
      get to the heart of the matter. Did
      you know Sam has a son, Jake?

A long silence prevails.

A Fordson tractor with a trailer load of hay grinds passed them, she glances over her shoulder to see the trailer disappear round distant bend, and also sees JAKE'S face with *morbid interest.*

*His face is dark with bitter resentment. A face resisting change.*

                JAKE

No! Nobody breathed ah word t' me about a bloody son! Ista sure tha's not drempt it?

                STELLA
    *(speaks quietly but with pent up emotion)*

It's no dream. It's a registered fact. Does the name Evelyn Ridgeholm mean anything to you?

                JAKE

A son! What son ...? An wheer does that leave me? No! Nobody mentioned ah son t' me ... because ...
    *(begins to rive about on back seat)*
An' ah'll tell thee why! A son spells out changes, an' ah'd be shoved back t' workhouse that's wheer ah came from. Lived hand t' mouth. Knocked from pillow t' post ... nivver been able t' shake it off ... if it hadn't been for John Asquith spottin' me standin' under clock-tower in Mottley market town on Martinmas hirin' day November time fifty years ago ... given me a good home ...
    *(his voice almost breaks)*
This is me home Stockdale. They said

ah'd always have a home here ... till day ah died.

     STELLA
    (reproachfully)
One only has to pause a moment and a woman will find that a man will be talking about something else ... Did you hear me, Jake? Evelyn Ridgeholm. Have you heard of her?

     JAKE
    (snarls, he's back to his old
    self)
Eve Ridgeholm! She use t' be old John's housekeeper after his missus pegged out ... nobut at Stockdale for couple o' years then she upt' an' buggered off all o' a sudden ... here ... wheer's this all leadin' ta?

     STELLA
I'll tell you where it's all leading to ... what was she like? Any woman would want to know ... it's only natural.

     JAKE
    (voice harsh)
A gurt monumentous sort o' woman ... her gait was real heavy an' awkward ... trailed about like a bloody Neanderthal man!

*She flinches as though struck. She cascades through gears, not once but twice.*

                    STELLA
          Well, by all accounts she's the mother
          of Sam's son ... an illegitimate son!

*He rives himself to the edge of the seat. He breaths heavily
down her Astrakhan collar.*

                    JAKE
          By hell! They kept that bugger dark,
          talk about been given fuckin' mushroom
          treatment ...

                    STELLA
               (aggrieved, swings round as
               though seated on a swivel
               chair)
          And what's fuckin' mushrooms got to do
          with anything?

                    JAKE
               (shouting unbridled anger)
          <u>Weel! Kept in bloody dark an' fed on
          bullshit! An' more t' point what's tha
          goin' t' do about it?</u>

*They drive down into Holbridge in stony silence. Not even
seeing or feeling the exhilarating view of the Dales.
Everything stretching before them has a pale yellowish tinge
from the faint winter sunshine. Slowly she drives into the
ancient town of Holbridge to park in HINCHCLIFFE'S carpark.*

*JAKE coldly, begrudgingly waiting for her response, his eyes
dark, impervious to the rays of light.*

*STELLA takes car out of gear and pulls brake on. Her eyes as
dark as his.*

STELLA

Champion! Splendid! We've arrived in one piece.

(pause)

Don't you really mean, Jake, what are <u>we</u> going to do about it? After all, Sam has willed the adjoining farm and half of his enterprises to his son ... by the name of Francis Spencer-Asquith.

JAKE

We? Thee an' me!

STELLA

Yes! We! You and me.

JAKE

What about thee daughters ...

STELLA

Subordinating daughters.

*He rests his forearms along the back of the front seat, interlocks his fingers, rests stubble chin upon them and almost in a dilatory fashion he turns his capped head and looks her straight in the eyes. Their eyes lock. They gradually smile at each other, granted the smile does not reach their eyes.*

JAKE

Tha knows how old John died?

STELLA

More or less. Gored by a shorthorn bull ...

JAKE

An' tha cottoned onta job accomplished on that young German Prisoner O' War ...?

STELLA

Sam barely mentioned, but ...

JAKE

Weel ...

*He leans over passenger seat and peers attentively through cracked window screen.*

JAKE

(voice droll)

Weel, these things happen ... farm accidents happen so t' speak ... misfortunes, carelessness. Call it what tha likes ... these things happen ... it's in nature o' farmin'.

STELLA

That's settled then, Jake!
  *(gets out of car, rummages in handbag, finds shopping list)*
Tell them to forward the bills as usual, but now to Mrs Stella Asquith.
  *(hands him the list and car keys)*
See you in half an hour, Jake.

*And off she stomps towards J. W. HINCHCLIFFE AND CO SOLICITORS entrance and without any intervention, recedes from his view.*

**SCENE 47**

INT. HINCHCLIFFE'S OFFICE - HOLBRIDGE - 12:36 PM

*HINCHCLIFFE is of medium height, legs of a shorter man. His crowning glory - thick, straight silver hair and bank holiday blue eyes. We see him bending over his large oak desk, stubbing out a half-smoked cigar into an over-flowing ash tray as STELLA sweeps in unannounced.*

> HINCHCLIFFE
> *(startled)*
> Good heavens, Mrs Asquith. Where have you sprung from?

*His eyes move rapidly around his office as though she's popped out from behind the oak wall panels. He finds his way back behind the authoritative desk. He indicates she should sit down. STELLA sits down slowly, her back as straight as a ramrod.*

> HINCHCLIFFE
> *(pleasantly)*
> The weather ...

> STELLA
> *(snaps)*
> Don't straddle with me, John Hinchcliffe! The operative word is bequeathed! I've not come all this way to talk about the blasted weather!

> HINCHCLIFFE
> *(instantly brusque)*
> Indeed! We will get down to the business in hand, Mrs Asquith ...

*He consults his wrist watch slowly, deliberately giving the broad hint that she is sitting in unscheduled time, and time is short even in this weather. He punches a bell on his desk - almost at once his SECRETARY cocks her head around the door edge.*

                  HINCHCLIFFE
    Samuel John Asquith's documents. Thank you.

*The door closes. HINCHCLIFFE makes a palaver relighting the half cigar while STELLA holds her tongue and nurses her inner rage.*

*The door reopens. We catch a glimpse of a green sleeve slipping a buff bulky folder onto the corner of his desk. The door closes with a little efficacious click.*

*Then only the rustle of pages turning, the ticking of the wall clock and the pull of the gas fire can be heard in the room. Then their back to business.*

                  HINCHCLIFFE
        *(holds out legal form for her to take)*
    Would you please sign this document between the two little crosses ...

                  STELLA
        *(looks mystified and refuses to take it)*
    Sign ... What? Quackery!
        *(eccentrically, like a wounded duck)*
    Quack, quack.

                    HINCHCLIFFE
            *(he doesn't appreciate her word*
            *foreplay, and it shows)*
    I take it that you have read the
    letter I sent through for you which
    deserved to be read properly ...

*Her fickle eyes become larger and her wide mouth becomes smaller.*

                    STELLA
    I read it, but it made no sense. No
    sense at all. Perhaps you would be
    good enough to explain the
    circumstances to me ... We've been
    through such a lot lately.

                    HINCHCLIFFE
            *(uses his cigar as a pointer)*
    Simple! Sam Asquith, your late husband
    had an illegitimate son to a Miss
    Evelyn Ridgeholm of Holbridge. She's
    dead. He's alive. Samuel John Asquith,
    his father, left the legacy of the
    adjoining ...

                    STELLA
            *(demands rapidly, shooting to*
            *her feet and straddling her*
            *legs wide)*
    Adjoining farm! Which one of the farms
    are you, or was Sam for that matter
    referring to?

                    HINCHCLIFFE
    Well ... Well ...

> *(he puffs hard on his phallus shaped cigar)*

The adjoining farm, presumably the one Jake Swales inhabits ...

              STELLA
> *(with benign menace)*

Presumably! Mr Hinchcliffe, you call yourself a legal man, yet here you are astonishing me with such a negative corollary. Surely, the act of presuming that which is presumed, is pure supposition. A hypothesis! It would not stand up in court for five minutes.

*STELLA stares defiantly back at the shrewd face, trying to remember, what if anything, she knows about the law.*

             HINCHCLIFFE

In that case I can look forward to a protracting case with substantial legal fees, Mrs Stella Asquith!

              STELLA
> *(speaks bluntly)*

By all means, and send this Francis personage to Stockdale Farms. We need a new labourer. He will be paid the usual going rate. Good day!

*She marches out of the room.*

## SCENE 48

I/E. ROVER CAR - HINCHCLIFFE'S CARPARK - 12:50 PM

*We see JAKE rubbing his coat cuff over the cracked car window screen. STELLA climbs onto the back seat.*

> STELLA
>
> Let's get cracking, Jake. We've a couple of calls to make yet. First call, Doctor Liddle's surgery, then the Wheat Sheaf ... just two or three queries to iron out.

*With settled purpose he arranges himself behind the steering wheel. He drives cautiously out from the carpark and onto the street.*

## SCENE 49

EXT. ROVER CAR - BOTTOM OF MAIN ST - HOLBRIDGE - 12:55 PM

*JAKE drops STELLA off.*

## SCENE 50

I/E. ROVER CAR - BOTTOM OF MAIN ST - HOLBRIDGE - 1:05 PM

*We see STELLA getting into car.*

> STELLA
>
> Doctor Liddle is always so obliging ... perhaps a little too familiar, in a good way, though.
>     *(leans forward)*
> Just remember to stop at the Wheat Sheaf ... shouldn't be too long, they'll not be over busy in this weather.

## SCENE 51

**I/E. ROVER CAR - WHEAT SHEAF INN - HOLBRIDGE - 1:35 PM**

*As good as her word, STELLA clambers into the motor car. Her face set.*

                STELLA
You know, Jake. Some folk I find think they're too big to do the small things when really they're too small for the big things; and at close quarters, neither are easy company.

## SCENE 52

**EXT. STOCKDALE FARMS - FARMYARD - 3:05 PM**

*STELLA and JAKE arrive safely back at Stockdale to see MR DAVIS - the veterinary - about to leave.*

*SOPHIE and BRIDIE come to meet STELLA and JAKE as they step out of the Rover.*

                SOPHIE
      *(her young face serious, her*
      *eyes sending warning signals)*
I don't want to spring it on you, Mam, but the vet has already examined Bonny and ...

                JAKE
Aye ... it's just ah matter o' time before ...

*He takes the rest of his words with him as he charges towards the stables.*

                    STELLA

Go put the kettle on, that's a good
lass and arrange a bite to eat ...
it's been quite an inelegant morning,
on the other hand, Doctor Liddle told
me, confidentially, a few home truths
...
          *(pause)*
And where's our Grace?

                    SOPHIE

Feeding poultry and collecting the
eggs. Should be back home anytime to
start feeding the calves and -

                    STELLA
          *(glances at her watch)*
Make haste, Sophie. It will be fairly
dark in an hour's time.

*STELLA heads for stables. MR DAVIS meets her halfway. A man
not to hold his punches.*

                    MR DAVIS
          *(abruptly)*
A case of tetanus, Mrs Asquith.

                    STELLA
          *(stands her ground)*
Lockjaw! Oh, dear God! What a crying
shame.

                    MR DAVIS
          *(fixes her with stern eyes)*
Your daughter confirmed to me that the
Shire had lost a shoe about three

weeks ago, resulting in a foot injury.

                STELLA
            (gravely)
The blacksmith at Kayshaw re-shoed her on the same day as the family funeral ... Cousin Abe will vouch to that.

                MR DAVIS
          (shows her no favours)
A pity she didn't have an anti-tetanus injection at the same time! The Shire horse is in very poor shape.

                STELLA
       (chooses her reply carefully)
In case you are not aware, Mr Davis. We had a state here at Stockdale Farms in which there was a total and permanent cessation ...

She lurches towards stable door with MR DAVIS in tow.

## SCENE 53
**INT. STOCKDALE FARMS - STABLES - 3:08 PM**

We see JAKE, yard brush in hand already bristling down the stalls.

MR DAVIS strides over the neat furrow of dung behind the TETHERED HORSES, and stands alongside BONNY. He taps her under the jaw, in the eye socket, then casts an experienced, fanatical eye over her.

                MR DAVIS
She's broken-winded and her jaws are

>           locked together ... her age is against
>           her ... combine these vital bodily
>           functions and you have here, two real
>           choices, Mrs Asquith.

*JAKE looks barbed. STELLA looks choked. MR DAVIS has the look on his face of: Keep a man waiting long enough and he'll start counting your faults.*

>                    MR DAVIS
>           There's a fifteen to twenty percent
>           recovery rate here, or I can get my
>           humane killer from the car right now.

## SCENE 54
**EXT. STOCKDALE FARMS - MOORLAND - 11:30 AM**

*Raining. The thaw is setting in.*

*STELLA and JAKE, attired in overcoats with hessian sacks draped around their shoulders, secured with a fencing nail prodded into twisted lugholes. They are searching the moorland with BRIDIE; and find BLACKFACED IN-LAMB-EWES dead - upstanding under the banks of the swollen beck.*

*We see muddy waters unmercifully churning against and around the half-submerged bodies, their skins split open along their backs where the fleece has parted under the weight of the frozen ice accumulated on their unsheered fleeces.*

>                    JAKE
>              (gestures with his head)
>           Theer they are ... looks like they
>           were tekin' shelter under banks o'
>           beck an' then weight o' snow on bank
>           edges broke away an' bore 'em down

inta freezin' water.
>   *(bottom lip droops wayward)*

Cudn't escape poor buggers.

>               STELLA
>   *(she takes halted strides
>   towards the dead IN-LAMB-EWES)*
>
> I'll be so thankful to see the back-
> end of this destructive winter ...

*She raises distressed face to the stormy, elevating clouds riding low across the darkened sky.*

>               STELLA
>
> Dear God, there must be something we
> can do. Anything!

>               JAKE
>
> If it's onny comfort t' thee, lass.
> They'll eventually get washed down t'
> home bridge. I'll not risk thine nor
> my life for knacker meat!

*He rams a thumb and forefinger into his mouth and whistles to BRIDIE, stalking along the ridge above the swirling waters. Soulfully they turn their backs on the grim tragedy, and discover their walking on snow with rain water beneath. STELLA labours against the withdrawal suction of each wellington boot stride, looses balance, twists her ankle.*

>               JAKE
>
> If tha's not damn careful, boss ...
> tha'll be endin' up handin' yon
> bastard Stockdale on ah fuckin' silver
> plate.

He turns his grimacing face aside from driving rain, then works everything back in place before looking at STELLA with a re-arranged look as though bearing her good tidings.

STELLA laughs, just. Then regulates the wet hessian sack draped around her shoulders. She re-prods the fencing nail into fresh lugholes. She shivers, hunches her shoulders and glances at his austere face.

                STELLA
           (speaks passionately)
      About Bonny ...

## SCENE 55
**EXT. STOCKDALE FARMS - FARMYARD - 3 PM**

STELLA and JAKE return to Stockdale from moorland in silence, which turns to surprise at sighting Cousin ABE'S Austin 12 car parked within yard - and even more surprise at seeing his head and broad shoulders jut over the open half-door of the loose-box where BONNY is bedded down.

                ABE
           (shouting)
      <u>Aaaah! Good afternoon t' yah both!</u>

JAKE spits contemptuously into the slushy snow as he yanks bottom yard gate open.

                JAKE
           (to STELLA)
      He only reakons t' call once ah year
      an' already he's been here three times
      since boss died an' we've not even
      seen backend o' bloody winter yet!
      He's after summat, mark my words.

>                    Nivver had same drive as boss had.
>                    Aye, ah bit t' laid back for old Sam
>                    ... an' mesen.

*With a look to quell the dislike on JAKE'S face, STELLA inclines her head knowingly.*

>                            STELLA
>                          (to JAKE)
>                    Well, you know Abe. He'll never
>                    change. He's either a bruiser or a
>                    skin-deep charmer. Today, of all days,
>                    I'll play it by ear.

*She advances on ABE as eloquently as she can muster with her turned over heel and saturated clothes which hamper her style.*

>                            STELLA
>                         (calling out)
>                    <u>I was just saying to Jake, I thought
>                    that looked like your vehicle -</u>

>                            ABE
>                          (bawling)
>                    <u>Hasta called vetnerie yet?</u>

*ABE strides out of the building and shoots bolt across with brute force, which sends BONNY into a violent spasm. We see her stagger stiffly inside the stone building, eyes ablaze, saliva frothing and escaping between clamped teeth.*

*JAKE shoves ABE roughly aside with such a careless grace as he enters building.*

>                    JAKE
>          (speaks firmly, caringly to
>          BONNY)
>     Steady ... Steady on theer, lass.
>     Steady.

STELLA and ABE leave JAKE talking softly to stricken BONNY as they head for the farmhouse.

>                    JAKE (O/S)
>     Don't thee go rivin' about in theer,
>     owld gal ... Steady on ... Nah then,
>     nah then ... Steady on ...

>                    STELLA
>          (she speaks more to herself
>          than ABE)
>     Bonny will have to be destroyed when
>     the vet calls again ... won't she?

>                    ABE
>          (nods assent)
>     Just a matter o' time afore she's
>     down. You don't hear of many tetanus
>     cases pulling through, not at her age.

## SCENE 56

**INT. STOCKDALE FARMS - STELLA'S KITCHEN - 3:07 PM**

STELLA pulls out a chair from beneath table for ABE, then places glasses and bottles of brown ale near his elbow.

>                    STELLA
>          (smiles pleasantly)
>     I'll not keep you long, Abe. Just
>     change out of these wet clothes.

**SCENE 57**

**INT. STOCKDALE FARMS - STELLA'S KITCHEN - 3:20 PM**

*STELLA enters, dried off and assailable with her head high.*

*ABE eyes her sagely over the rim of his glass of beer. He sees a handsome woman rather than pretty, and as buoyant as ever. A woman in her prime. He puts his toe in the water first.*

                    ABE
     An' how's t' managin' farms, lass?
     Quite a handful ah should imagine ...

*STELLA eyes his dead-pan expression. A face set in purpose.*

*Compulsively she speaks while nodding her head; enough to compel any auctioneer to drop the gavel.*

                    STELLA
     Champion!

*As if to then find herself the purchaser of a first class, dark roan shorthorn bull.*

                    STELLA
     Champion!

*A lull falls. He tilts and refills his glass.*

                    ABE
       (he struggles to keep jealousy
       and envy out of his voice)
     Ah can see that you've rallied round
     remarkably well from Cousin Sam's
     unexpected death ... Ah rum way t' go.

*He fixes the wealthy widow with a hypnotic stare.*

                ABE
          *(voice deliberately slow and droll)*
Aye ... frozen up, shovelled up, boxed up ... and t' cap it all, a cock-up in cemetery.

*STELLA pours herself a drink and slowly quenches her thirst. She then sighs deeply and nods gravely.*

                STELLA
Sam certainly gave us all a severe shock. A real perturbation of the body, mind and soul ...
          *(wipes froth from her upper lip with corner of table cloth)*
As you so rightly say, Abe. A double barrelled shock whichever way one looks at it. Just shocking.

                ABE
          *(narrows his watchful eyes and guzzles down his beer)*
Jeff Harrison ...
          *(pause)*
told me t' other day, his hoss snigged thee Rover off Kayshaw Green ...
          *(replaces empty glass on table with a smack)*
Heard tha'd made a right old hash of it. By all accounts repairs an' bodywork will cost thee more than loose change.

> STELLA
>
> *(sternly)*
>
> In my family, Abe, we never discuss money. It's a chastening thought though, but in the meanwhile, remind me Abe, what do we owe you to warrant this unexpected visit?
>
> *(pause)*
>
> As you know we're shorthanded now ... and time is precious.

*He beams, swinging round on the chair with surprising nimbleness for one of such bulk.*

> ABE
>
> Tha knows our Michael, second eldest, bit of a lad ...
>
> *(lowers tone confidentially)*
>
> Weel, he get's married next month ...

*His hand slips casually into his inside pocket and re-appears with a fist full of dog-eared bills and receipts. He diligently opens ... refolds them ... hayseeds and chaff flutter from their folds ... until three fluted edged wedding invitation cards can be seen. He props them whimsically between the empty ale bottles.*

> ABE
>
> Theer ... lass ... we were wondering ... like ... if tha'd consider us taking adjacent farm off thee hands ... like?

> STELLA
>
> *(doesn't bat an eyelid; eyes wide in mock astonishment)*

In what way? Whatever do you mean,
Abe? And what have you in mind?

              ABE
    *(warming to his own proposal)*
Simple. Either our Michael moves in as
a tenant and works for you, or I'll
offer thee market price ... after all,
your two girls will be getting wed and
going their own different ways afore
long. This way, we'd have a chance of
passing on the name to yet another
committed generation of Asquiths.

*He gives the relation by marriage only, a broad wink and a knowing smile. These gestures are not returned.*

            STELLA
Committed! What kind of word is that?
You could say he was committed to an
institution for the mentally insane
... or he was committed to prison
because he committed manslaughter.
    *(draws a deep breath then*
     *exhales noisily)*
Not, I feel, a crucial word in any
partnership as serious as family
heritable property, beside ...
    *(gives him a reproachful look)*
What about Jake? That has been his
home for fifty years, he's part of
Stockdale ...
    *(voice rises slightly)*
Jake Swales is a cornerstone of
Stockdale Farms.

                    ABE

    Pension bugger off an' have done with
    him! Family blood should come first!


                    STELLA
                (with decision)
    Jake stays. It's awfully kind of you
    to take the trouble to bother yourself
    about our welfare, Abe. But we're
    hardy, resilient women here. Indeed,
    we're all well accustomed and
    conditioned to hard graft, and I thank
    Sam Asquith for that!

*She vacates her chair and pushes it firmly beneath the table.*

*In a nonchalant manner, ABE places his hand again into an inner pocket to expel a worn wallet. He flicks through contents. And when he answers, his tone suggests: We don't want you to think you're home and dry m'lady.*

                    ABE
    Aaaah! Got thee!

*Rising from the chair, he plucks a held-in-reserve playing card and props it delicately with the rest of the wedding invitations.*

                    ABE
                (spoken heartily to be almost
                brutal)
    Canada! The prodigal son! Fetch him
    along as well. After all, he's more
    one of us than tha'll ever be!

*137*

STELLA

(officiously)

Thank you, Abe, for that bleak reminder. I am very much aware that I'm related to the Asquith family by marriage only - an outsider - and it seems to me that all you Asquith men think about is handing down your wealth to your sons, and even a bastard son, while completely disregarding your daughters' entitlements, because unlike sons, daughters, when they marry, take their father's wealth with them and amalgamate it into another man's estate, which not one of you Asquiths could or would be able to stomach ...

ABE

(struggles to stay amicable)

Ah can see you've grasped t' handle o' our logistics, Stella. Aye, it's a man's world, always has been, an' always will be. And as for Jake Swales, tha should return him back t' where eh came from - workhouse! It's still operatin' on t' edge o' moorland ...

STELLA

(adamant)

Less of that kind of talk, Abe. Jake stays right here, and I will abide by the understanding between John and Sam Asquith and him - the set-down price for Jake's silence pertaining to their treacherous and murderous wheelings and dealings, and in return for his loyalty, they promised him there would be a roof above his head, here, at Stockdale Farms until the day he died.

          ABE
    *(harshly)*
That were their promise, not your promise, so don't go bitin' off more than you can chew ... We Asquith men aren't to be played with.
    *(a faint smile breaks on his
    thin lips)*
An' while I'm here, if ah don't say it some bugger else will ... did t' know how old Sam's offspring came about?

          STELLA
    *(grasps back of her chair)*
I think you ought to go, Abe.

          ABE
    *(sits down)*
Aye! Ah one-off. Ah one-off by all accounts.
    *(looks thoughtful)*
Aye, it must have been like givin' ah strawberry t' ah pig.

*Before STELLA can collect her hostile thoughts in some sort of sequence, the kitchen door is flung open and GRACE, dear reliable GRACE leans inside breathless with urgency.*

          GRACE
It's Bonny! She's fallen and laying

>           rigid on the loose-box floor, and she
>           can't get upright. She's completely
>           distressed ...

And with that GRACE slams the door shut.

>                    STELLA
>                  (shouting)
>           <u>I'm coming! Wait for me! I'm coming!</u>

STELLA grabs a coat then thrusts her feet back into damp wellingtons, while flashing a glance at ABE, then she opens the door.

>                    STELLA
>           Don't just sit there looking gormless,
>           Abe ... do something and as sharp as
>           you can.

ABE rises clumsily.

>                    STELLA
>             (she pushes him towards the
>             door)
>           Go and ring through for the vet and
>           remember, Abe ... not the knackerman
>           first. His bullets are more repulsive
>           than Davis'.

STELLA seizes a headscarf, folds it into a triangle and places it on her head and ties the two corners under her chin.

>                    STELLA
>                  (voice quails)
>           You know as well as I do the slaughter

>                    man's testimony will always leave
>                    behind the drag marks from where he's
>                    winched the dead animal from and into
>                    his wagon ...
>
>                              ABE
>                         *(austerely)*
>                    Not all will be lost. Tha'll be paid a
>                    fiver from knackerman an' as for Bonny
>                    ... she'll end up as cat an' dog meat.

*He allows himself to be manoeuvred through the open doorway.*

**SCENE 58**
**EXT. STOCKDALE FARMS - FARMYARD - 4:30 PM**

*We see KNACKERMAN'S wagon and veterinary MR DAVIS' vehicle parked.*

*MR DAVIS gun in hand. JAKE carrying rope. STELLA a stride behind them with BRIDIE as they head for the loose-box.*

*JAKE slides bolts back into brackets and opens loose-box door.*

**SCENE 59**
**INT. STOCKDALE FARMS - LOOSE-BOX - 4:31 PM**

*We see BONNY emaciated, labouring for breath. She struggles to rise. Barely able to rise.*

*JAKE and MR DAVIS enter.*

### SCENE 60
### EXT. STOCKDALE FARMS - LOOSE-BOX - 4:32 PM

*JAKE exits loose-box and hands BONNY'S leading halter to STELLA, he re-enters loose-box.*

*We hear GUN SHOT!*

*SILENCE.*

### SCENE 61
### INT. STOCKDALE FARMS - LOOSE-BOX - 4:34 PM

*We see BONNY laid stone dead.*

*We see a CLOSE UP of BONNY'S eye - a polished open eye reflecting the image of JAKE.*

*FADE OUT.*

*END CREDITS ROLLS TO SONG BY IDA BARKER, "I FORGOT TO FORGET".*

*END OF EPISODE 1.*

Episode 2

# Spring

:
## EPISODE 2
## SPRING
:

### SCENE 1
### EXT. STOCKDALE FARMS - SPRING RURAL LANDSCAPE - 10 AM

*We see wide blue skies - springtime sunshine - a cluster of larks clambering and trilling happily with the angular April breeze. We hear distant, insistent bleating of spring LAMBS and the answering bass tones of the LAMBED EWES.*

*We see STELLA carrying a bucketful of hen-jock and SOPHIE with a bucketful of mash as they leisurely make their way up the hillside towards a cart-road, in accordance with stone walls where snow still lays in long, white ridges behind the wall-backs.*

*STELLA and SOPHIE approach cart-road leading to hen-houses.*

          STELLA
     (melodramatic)
If I could make a day last forever, it would be a day such as today ...
     (suddenly her mood changes as
     she swings bucket to her other
     hand)
But there would be no place for Cousin Abe or that benefactor son of your father's to walk all over it!

          SOPHIE
     (puts down her bucket and faces
     STELLA with winsome smile)
Will it be all right for Harry to stay

here over the weekend? He is kind of getting the hang of our farming methods.

        STELLA
    *(sternly)*
Harry! He surely must have other things to do at weekends, besides causing friction here at Stockdale ...

        SOPHIE
Harry really is all right once you get to know him, Mam. And he does live a long way from his home.

        STELLA
Sophie, my dear, are you truly aware that this young man is unhealthily besotted by you? And I can't help thinking he's so damn seriously minded.
    *(pause)*
And if you're not careful, he could quite easily dampen your aspirations.

        SOPHIE
    *(smiles, gaze is distant)*
I have no conventions that I'm aware of ...

SOPHIE *hooks her arm through the handle of the bucket then swivels it upon her hip.*

        STELLA
    *(narrows her eyes)*
Just remember, my girl. We have no

room here at Stockdale for idle suppers or benefactors –

          SOPHIE

Such as Francis Spencer-Asquith? So far he's only a name on paper to us.

          STELLA
      *(anger surfaces)*

And that's where he'd stay if I had my way. In the meantime Doctor Liddle is keeping his nose to the ground for us. He's always been like a father to me.

          SOPHIE
      *(slightly disconcerted)*

All this faffing about, Mam. Isn't it about time this Francis showed his face, I mean, it's nearly three months since we first heard about him and all we know, according to Uncle Abe, is that he's here – somewhere in the vicinity by way of wedding invitations.

          STELLA
      *(tone is acid)*

Abe always plays his cards close to his chest. Hardly spoke a word last time he called. He just sat and stared at me. Anyone would have thought that I was one of your father's prized cows!

*STELLA and SOPHIE now reach the cart-road along the hill-top. The hen-houses are a stone throw away.*

Dumping the full buckets to the ground, they rattle the handles against the containers.

>               SOPHIE
>         (calling out encouragingly to
>         HENS)
>     Chuck-chuck ... Chuck-chuck ...
>         (shakes out the mash grain feed
>         into outside feeding troughs)
>     Chuck-chuck ... Chuck-chuck.

We see scattered peacefully, ROAD-ISLAND-REDS foraging daintily amongst rough pasture land.

>               STELLA
>         (two octaves higher)
>     Chuck-chuck ... Chuck-chuck ...

The ROAD-ISLAND-REDS' heads shoot up collectively. They break into a cumbersome run, plumage of coppery-reddish with tones of blue and green flashing like aluminium in the morning sunlight.

STELLA and SOPHIE call, recall, again and again.

>               STELLA
>     Come on, our Sophie. We'd better shake
>     our feathers and get moving.
>         (checks her wrist-watch)
>     It's gone ten o'clock and Jake will
>     already be re-checking the ewes for
>     signs of late lambing.

STELLA and SOPHIE stride towards the meadows, surrounding a large field barn.

## SCENE 2

## INT. STOCKDALE FARMS - FIELD BARN - 10:08 AM

*We see JAKE examining a BLACKFACED EWE-IN-LAMB. He's knelt on one knee with his behind resting on his boot heel. One hand is inserted into the EWE'S birth channel.*

*STELLA and SOPHIE enter.*

> JAKE
> (without looking up)
> Reckon twin lambs are already dead, an' by stink o' them they've been still-born for more than ah day or two.

*JAKE removes his hand, wipes it on handful of hay. Takes out packet of Woodbines, selects one, scrapes a loose match against boot cap and lights cigarette, inhaling deeply. Moves it to corner of his mouth. The smoke trickles up one nostril.*

> JAKE
> Reight. Let's get on wi' job. Hold onta ewe's horns, boss. An' keep her steady, an' Sophie take a leg so ah can see what ah'm doin'.

*STELLA and SOPHIE crouch to level themselves with the lambing EWE - the animal bleats as JAKE re-inserts his hand and wrist.*

> JAKE
> Twin lambs all reight. Legs tangled t'gether.
> (pause)
> Not much room t' move about in.

*We hear the EWE making guttural sounds.*

                JAKE
Just ah question o' singlin' each limb apart from its twin's.
    *(pause)*
Afore attemptin' t' deliver an' at same time, ah don't want t' take too long ...
    *(face creases in concentration)*
Cos she's beginnin' t' go dry, an' ah could tear her insides.
    *(spits out cigarette stub)*
Or tear lambs apart an' bring on blood poisonin'.

                STELLA
My hands are smaller than yours, Jake, shall I ...

                JAKE
Just thee stay put. Ah've started job an' ah'll bloody well finish it.

*We hear painful bleating sounds coming from the EWE as JAKE delivers FIRST DEAD LAMB – followed by SECOND DEAD LAMB – to lay each out on the barn causeway. The EWE shows no sign of getting to her feet, her breathing is irregular.*

                JAKE
Ah'll clean one o' them up an' then skin it.
    *(he looks at the FIRST DEAD LAMB)*
If we're sharp it will definitely postpone its mother's death.

## SCENE 3
**EXT. STOCKDALE FARMS - MEADOWS - 10:23 AM**

*We see STELLA, SOPHIE and BRIDIE hurrying down meadows to where BLACKFACED SHEEP are grazing - YOUNG LAMBS; some suckling their mothers, others frolicsome in the mild warmth of sunshine.*

*STELLA whistles commands to BRIDIE who skilfully separates a EWE with TWIN LAMBS from flock. STELLA hooks handle of walking stick round the neck of FIRST TWIN - the EWE circles, baying - the FIRST TWIN bleats.*

*SOPHIE scoops the FIRST LAMB up into her arms. The remaining SECOND TWIN frolics to its mother's side and begins to suckle her. The EWE smells it, ruckles - she recognises her own. Her eyes pin-point the FIRST TWIN.*

>         SOPHIE
>     *(lamentably)*
> Do you think she knows that she's only
> the one lamb now?

>         STELLA
> Mothers always know, but she'll settle
> for one - eventually.
>     *(whistles BRIDIE to heel)*
> This is a practised method which goes
> back to kingdom come.

## SCENE 4
**INT. STOCKDALE FARMS - FIELD BARN - 10:30 AM**

*STELLA, SOPHIE and BRIDIE enter. SOPHIE is holding the alive FIRST TWIN. JAKE has finished skinning FIRST DEAD LAMB. He's ready.*

                    JAKE
                (to SOPHIE)
            Just hold tha lamb still while ah fit
            this jacket onta it.

We see JAKE place the moist lamb skin over the alive FIRST
TWIN'S back so that it also drapes over fore and back limbs,
to tie it with just enough play so the skin will not fall off
but dry on.

                    STELLA
                (with parental approval)
            She'll be one in a thousand if she
            doesn't take to this little bobby-
            bazzler.

JAKE brings the distressed EWE to her feet. She staggers
weakly. SOPHIE introduces the LAMB to her. The ewe shows
little interest, then slowly shows interest.

                    JAKE
                (to SOPHIE)
            That's reight, lass. Let her get scent
            o' her own lamb first afore we coax it
            t' her teat, otherwise she'll reject
            it.

We see the EWE sensitively breathing the smell of her own
LAMB'S skin – then very slowly she begins to lick it, then
again and again.

                    STELLA
            It's a known fact that sheep give up
            on life if they lose their new-borns.
                (smiles)
            This is a beatific solution to a

crisis.

                    JAKE
               (nods)
          Yah can't beat some ancestral methods.
               (to SOPHIE)
          Thee grandfather taught me no end o'
          skills. He called this here ...
               (points to alive LAMB)
          Skinnin' ah lamb ta save a life!

## SCENE 5
## EXT. STOCKDALE FARMS - FIELD BARN - 10:40 AM

*STELLA and JAKE are standing outside the barn. STELLA is holding empty feeding buckets, JAKE is cutting plug from tobacco stick.*

                    STELLA
          We'd better make haste, Jake. We've
          another potential farm-worker coming
          sometime before dinner, and what with
          the muck-leading and the muck-
          spreading still to attend to ...

                    JAKE
          Hope t' hell this one's goin' t' fare
          better than last one.

                    STELLA
               (nods in agreement)
          A real time waster that one. He set us
          back - way back behind schedule.
               (frowns)
          Lose an hour in a morning and you'll
          find yourself chasing it for the rest

of the day.

                    JAKE
                 (brusquely)
He'd no farmin' experience, even ah
blind man could ah seen that! He'd no
bloody gumption from start t' finish!

                    STELLA
On first sight I quite liked him. I
felt sure he was a decent man, but -

                    JAKE
But me arse!

*STELLA raises appraising eyes to the larks soaring high in the clear blue sky.*

                    STELLA
I'm sure those larks are flirting with
providence.
                 (pause)
I'll just have a quick word with
Sophie, we need her to oversee the ewe
and lamb for the next hour or so.

**SCENE 6**
**INT. STOCKDALE FARMS - FIELD BARN - 10:42 AM**

*We see SOPHIE coaxing the LAMB to the EWE'S teat, it latches on, the EWE takes in its scent - SOPHIE remains cohesive. STELLA enters barn.*

                    STELLA
                 (smiles at SOPHIE)
By the time the skin begins to fall

off in a few days time its foster mother will have accepted it as her own – rarely fails.

          SOPHIE
        *(her smile comes willingly)*
And what about acceptance to Harry, Mummy?

          STELLA
        *(her tone wantonly generous)*
Oh what the hell. Life's too short. All right, Sophie love, you can invite Harry back for the weekend, and if he's not already made other plans, he's welcome to spend his spring holiday here too, either way, we'll lick him into shape soon enough.

**SCENE 7**

**EXT. STOCKDALE FARMS – FIELD BARN – 10:43 AM**

STELLA joins JAKE and together with BRIDIE they make headway home.

          JAKE
        *(abruptly)*
Doesta think yon bastard son of Sam Asquith's will speak in brokken English?

          STELLA
        *(her eyes suddenly flash daggers)*
If he doesn't now, the bugger will before we've finished with him!

                    JAKE

            *(considers her reply with*
            *liking)*
An' what wi' double summertime
operatin' from 13th April we'll have
ample daylight t' work him t' death if
all else fails.
            *(jarring laugh)*
Ah'd ah thought wild horses couldn't
have kept him from Stockdale
considerin' size o' windfall!

                    STELLA

            *(dredges up a thin smile)*
He'll show up as surely as the poppies
crop up in the cornfields, and we'll
be ready for him. We have plans.
            *(stares at JAKE)*
Remember!

                    JAKE

Aye! Tried an' trusted plans. Plans
enough t' settle his ashes once an'
for all!

*STELLA and JAKE stride purposely back towards cart-road, to barely reach the bottom of the hillside. We see GRACE running to meet them.*

                    GRACE

            *(shouting)*
<u>That blasted temporary postman must
have left the first gate open while I
was letting out the dairy cows from
the back cow-house ...</u>
            *(gasps for breath)*

They've roamed over the beck and along the lane -

                    STELLA
Now then, our Grace. Hold onto your tongue. You know as well as I do, livestock that's been chained up in their stalls for six months of the year, do have this dire need, come springtime, to get to the lush green grass and to feel the sun on their backs ...

                    GRACE
          *(not easily pacified)*
Townies! Why are they postmen? They simply have no concept towards the country-way of life.

                    STELLA
          *(takes a prodigious intake of*
          *breath, expels with imprudence)*
Mmmm ... I would liken the lack of understanding to the countryfolk's way of life, as poetry read out badly, so badly phrased that it comes between the meaning and -

                    JAKE
          *(overbearingly)*
Wheer's farm dog raked off ta?

*JAKE whistles shrilly, time and time again. GRACE looks on tight lipped. STELLA looks ready to be quarrelsome. BRIDIE, appears in sight barking.*

                    JAKE
              *(gesturing heavy handed towards*
              *main cart-road)*
        Git away theer! Bridie! Off tha goes.
        Away wi' yah.

*BRIDIE obeys. Pursuing the last of the shorthorn DAIRY COWS frolicking one after another up the cart-road.*

                    JAKE
        No good us all chasin' after them
        beasts. Ah'll finish off muckin' out
        the cow-houses, then hold on just in
        case that new chap turns up trumps.

*Without a backward glance JAKE stumps towards cow-houses.*

## SCENE 8

**EXT. STOCKDALE FARMS - ALONG CART-ROAD - 10:47 AM**

*We see STELLA and GRACE soldiering up cart-road to see the first gate has been left wide open.*

                    STELLA
              *(panting but optimistic)*
        Look on the bright side, Grace, just
        look what a view we're getting.

*Instead of answering, GRACE whistles to BRIDIE. They head for the far end of the field where the DAIRY COWS are now grazing on the lush grass.*

                    STELLA and GRACE
              *(both calling out*
              *encouragingly)*
        Cush-cush ... Cush-cush ...

GRACE whistles commands – BRIDIE works close to the ground, clipping with her teeth at the DAIRY COWS' resisting hocks – gradually they are manoeuvred up the field towards open gateway.

RHODA, the leader – a large red shorthorn cow with curved horns, bars the entrance – then she moves to the gate-post and leisurely begins to rub her neck up and down the stone column.

STELLA and GRACE impatiently pace behind the gathering, waving their walking sticks and shouting encouragements, while BRIDIE is toing and froing behind the cattle.

RHODA suddenly wheels a half-circle then makes a cumbersome dash back down the field, which sets off the other DAIRY COWS.

>STELLA
>(frustrated)
>Would you credit it?

>GRACE
>No!

>STELLA
>It's pure spring madness.

STELLA and GRACE trudge back down the field with excitable BRIDIE to eventually herd the DAIRY COWS back towards the gateway – until MARIGOLD gripes a COW savagely in the groin with her sharp horns.

Bawling, the injured COW breaks away from the gathering herd to run back down the field, which in-turn causes a re-start of joyous gallivanting ...

STELLA
(exasperated)
By Jove, our Grace I'm beginning to think one needs the patience of a saint to endure such set-backs.
(pants)
We're already short on time ...

GRACE
(voice modulated)
I've put sentimentality aside long since, Mother - old sayings carry consequences that can modify anyone's personality.

STELLA smiles, slightly, shrugs her shoulders and leaves it at that.

They manage a third attempt to herd the DAIRY COWS to the gateway - except for JUNIPER, she will not follow through.

STELLA
(coaxingly, stretches out to scratch the root of JUNIPER'S tail)
Just go through the gateway, moo moooo. For your muth-er moo moooo cow ... That's a good old moo moooooo ...

STELLA catches GRACE'S tolerant expression.

STELLA
(her mouth droops uninvitingly)
I feel like I'm descending to the lowering level of cow-talk.
(pause)

> Your father would have called it
> "animalism by intelligentsia".

*We see STELLA glowing with splendid enmity. GRACE hesitating between gauging JUNIPER'S reactions and STELLA'S mixture of malice – so much so, not noticing the rugged heads of the other DAIRY COWS begin to reappear in the gateway, to spontaneously lumber through, kicking their hind legs up, udders and tails swinging preponderantly as they gad joyously back down the field.*

> GRACE
> *(scowling)*
> What a sight for sore eyes.

> STELLA
> There's no denying, they do have a certain ferine energy when they're let loose from chains. This wild behaviour is the onset of springtime, rather like the springtide, it's the syndrome of nature.

*GRACE catches sight of the Rover being driven down the cart-road.*

> GRACE
> *(shouts over her shoulder)*
> <u>The Rover!</u>

> STELLA
> Rover?

> GRACE
> Manpower! Just when we need it most
> ...

STELLA
(renewed vigour)
Manpower!

We see STELLA running towards the approaching motor car. The car purrs to a slow stop. We see TWO MALE FIGURES sitting on the front seats. STELLA acknowledges them with a graceful gesture of her head, before skirting round the Rover in no time at all.

FLASH - of severely damaged Rover - and now restored, repaired and resprayed.

STELLA
Wonderful. Immaculate restoration Mr Holmes ...

STELLA beams upon the repaired vehicle and the garage owner - MR HOLMES at the wheel. She looks the soul of geniality as she grasps the driver's door and swings it wide open.

STELLA
(eyes bright with purpose)
Come now gentlemen, you could not have timed your arrival better if you had tried ... We're persevering with the drawbacks of ferine beasts who simply refuse to go through an open gateway.
(making it sound like reciprocation)
It's spring fever and who can blame them on such a glorious morning.

We see STELLA, MR HOLMES and his PASSENGER drabbling down the field where further signs of unrest is evident.

*The PASSENGER stares around the pasture field with keen surmise. He has an attractively ugly face, framed by thick straight dark hair, broad shoulders accentuating the well-cut tweed suit, with a diagonal ribbed tie and highly polished brogues.*

                    PASSENGER
                *(pleasantly)*
        I'm not suggesting you should adopt a different strategy by any means, but -

                    STELLA
                *(her lips curl with excited repellence)*
        You mean to say ... we are actually doing it all wrong?

*Her dishevelled hair falls in unruly waves around her rosy face.*

                    STELLA
        I cannot for the life of me, even imagine there is another way of getting wandering cows through an open gateway, apart from leaving them until milking time, in which case they would head home instinctively -

                    GRACE
        And that will not be for at least five hours.

                    STELLA
                *(staring defiantly at PASSENGER)*
        You're surely not going to suggest we

>                    move the gate-hole.
>                         *(pause)*
>                    Mr ... Mr ...

*STELLA and GRACE stare boldly at the PASSENGER for the first time, they take in his appearance sagely; furthermore they note – women-like – he carries himself with an upfront and out-front swagger.*

>                         PASSENGER
>                    *(tone sounds arbitrary)*
>                    No! I was going to propose a more
>                    short term solution ...

*We see in that instance a fawn, short haired DOG with a bow shaped back, sharp featured head; chasing excitedly about the field on thin spindly legs.*

>                         STELLA
>                    *(judiciously)*
>                    And what pray is that? Creature?

>                         PASSENGER
>                    *(emits enthusiasm)*
>                    A whippet!

>                         STELLA and GRACE
>                    A whippet!

*They stare with growing repugnancy as the highly strung WHIPPET darts in and around the thorough bred DAIRY COWS, yapping over zealously in a high pitched manner.*

>                         STELLA
>                    To whom does this uncontrollable dog
>                    appertain to?

MR HOLMES takes a step backwards and looks the other way. He begins to shuffle through his pockets – for the Rover's repair bill – obviously not his dog. The PASSENGER'S smile seems destined to be eternal – his dog!

> STELLA
> *(with vexation)*
> I'll have you made aware that most of our dairy cows are in the early to middling stages of being in-calf, and if a dog – any dog found unauthorised running loose amongst them will not be tolerated.
> *(she whumphs backwards and points her stick at WHIPPET)*
> It will be shot stone dead!

STELLA charges ahead to join GRACE and BRIDIE re-rounding the DAIRY COWS with the WHIPPET still running haywire – still barking its head off unrestrained amidst them all.

We see BRIDIE fix her perceptive eyes on the WHIPPET invading her territory and as the encroaching WHIPPET comes to distance – chin stretched out, BRIDIE streaks forward and sinks her teeth into the WHIPPET'S hind left-quarter. The response is instantaneous.

We see the WHIPPET leap while giving out a high yelp of pain to pincher its tail between its hind legs, fleeing, yelping, straight up the field with BRIDIE chasing after it.

We see grazing DAIRY COWS lifting their heads, sensing the reactionary behaviour, and they too begin to move steadily after the chased and chasing dogs – increasing their speed, which develops into a drumming, galloping race towards the escape route – the open gateway.

GRACE

(panting after the DAIRY COWS)
Ahem, well ... It just goes to show,
Mother. Where the difference lies ...

STELLA

If your confounded whippet causes any
of our cattle to slip their calves ...
I'll sue you for every penny you've
got. Do you hear me?

*Without waiting for a reply, STELLA sheers away after the DAIRY COWS, blowing out her breath as though cooling hot porridge.*

PASSENGER

(shouting alongside STELLA)
<u>By the way, we've not been introduced
in the proper sense. I'm here about
the job vacancy.</u>

STELLA

(angry glances thrown his way)
Vacancy! If you can't exercise
restrain over that whippet of yours,
how can we be expected to believe
you'll come up to scratch?
    (draws breath in and expels it
    noisily)
Have you ever done a stroke of farm
work in your life?

PASSENGER

(jauntily)
I'm able to promise you, I can turn my
hands to most agricultural

>           undertakings, besides ...
>                   *(confidently)*
>           I'd rather have a good job than run
>           the whole show.
>
>                   GRACE
>           In our experience an amateur farm-hand
>           always takes twice as long as a
>           practised farm-man.
>                   *(increases her speed to procure*
>                   *the gate)*
>           And at best ...
>                   *(shouting over shoulder)*
>           <u>A passable job results.</u>
>
>                   STELLA
>                   *(acidly)*
>           If you're really looking for farm-work
>           here, then you'd better stop talking
>           and start shaping.

*We see STELLA and PASSENGER bestride towards gateway as though running in a three legged race.*

*We see the assailing dogs disappear through the gate entrance with the snorting DAIRY COWS in close pursuit - and GRACE only a stone throw behind. We hear the gate crash closed!*

*We see the DAIRY COWS jostling, sweating, wading into narrow stream quenching their thirst. We see BRIDIE and the WHIPPET wriggling under far yard gate to disappear from view.*

>                   STELLA
>                   *(unsuited)*
>           That hound, if it's a dog, spells
>           trouble!

> PASSENGER
> It's called Charlie, and it came to me unasked for, and ...
>
> STELLA
> We, the Asquith women can vouch to having had a stomach full of that!

*We see the hustling DAIRY COWS beginning to move out of the beck, to head for their various cow-houses.*

## SCENE 9
**INT. STOCKDALE FARMS – ONE OF THE PIG-HOUSES – 12:45 PM**

*We hear commotion within the building adjoining bottom yard. A large white SOW being separated from others. PASSENGER angles a door across a corner of the building. STELLA grabs SOW'S tail and twists it. SOW feels pain and lets out a series of ear-splitting squeals as it becomes trapped. SOPHIE holds a tool box.*

*PASSENGER, with deftness not lost upon STELLA and SOPHIE, slips a rope noose into the gaping mouth of the SOW and pulls it tight over the bristling snout, behind the large yellow teeth, to securing rope through hook in the wall.*

*SOPHIE hands PASSENGER a spear-headed pig-ring. He manually forces the spear-head through one nostril. The SOW lets out a long drawn-out scream as he thrusts and twists through the dividing wall of muscle.*

*We see the pointed end of the brass ring emerge through the socket of the SOW'S nostril.*

*The PASSENGER – a meticulous worker – temporarily circles the ring several times before finally inserting the ends into place with tiny screws. Operation over. Rope, then door barricade removed, only now does the large SOW switch off her penetrating scream.*

            STELLA
Job well done. That will eradicate any rooting about in the garths.

## SCENE 10
**EXT. STOCKDALE FARMS - PIG-HOUSES - 1 PM**

*STELLA moves out of a pig-house. SOPHIE follows. The PASSENGER closes door behind him and shoots the bolts across into their couplings.*

           SOPHIE
I'll go see if Grace needs a hand cooking the dinner.

*SOPHIE heads home. STELLA and the PASSENGER inspect each other openly in broad daylight.*

           STELLA
    *(tone business-like)*
When can you start work?

          PASSENGER
    *(turning towards parked Rover)*
My luggage is already in the boot of the Rover.

           STELLA
It's only fair to say, I'll take you on for a year, then we'll see how we all get along ...

                    PASSENGER
                (mind seems preoccupied)
            Thank you for being so frank with me
            ... and with someone you've only met
            an hour or two ago.

PASSENGER heads for Rover.

We hear heavy hob-nailed boots clattering down yard. JAKE corners the pig-houses forcefully.

                    STELLA
                (rebuking)
            What have you been doing all this
            time, Jake?

Suddenly STELLA notices, nestled in the crook of JAKE'S arm – SAM'S double barrelled gun. Switching her stare we see in his other hand, JAKE is trailing a limp bloody body by its hind legs, its head beating a brisk tattoo on the yard flagstones.

JAKE comes to a stilted halt.

                    JAKE
                (snarls)
            Theer! It had a ewe down an' startin'
            on its lamb ...
                (slings the limp, dead WHIPPET
                at STELLA'S feet)
            Nivver seen owt quite like it! A
            bloody whippet runnin' haywire in t'
            countryside!

                    STELLA
                (expostulates)
            I'll tell you where this peculiar

animal came from -

                JAKE
    *(cuts across regardless)*
Ah'd just finished plantin' me wallflowers ...

                STELLA
    *(incredulously)*
Wallflowers!

                JAKE
Aye. Wallflowers. Ollus had soft spot for wallflowers ...
    *(bottom lip droops)*
Ah do an' all ...
    *(mournfully)*
Ah do an' all.

*JAKE, with sudden change of facial and vocal expression is back to his belligerent self.*

                JAKE
Aye, when sudden like, ah heard this bloody barkin' commotion in me front garden, an' when ah looked ovver garden wall ah spotted this bugger wi' our Bridie! Rampagin' an tryin' t' bloody fuck among me newly planted wallflowers! Ah can tell thee ...
    *(spits saliva)*
Ah wore so sodden mad ah went straight for boss's field gun!

*STELLA shudders against his filthy habit.*

                    JAKE

By time I'd found cartridge an' sorted
out gun they'd gone chasin' an' rivin'
about among lambin' ewes in back
fields an' tha knows as well as ah do
consequences ...

*JAKE eyes her banefully, leaning nearer to her.*

                    STELLA
                *(demands)*
Lacerations to the lambs and sheep.

                    JAKE
            *(without taking a breath)*
It had a lamb down an' maulin' it
about, an' dragged ah fair amount o'
wool out o' ewe. If ah could get me
hands on its putrid owner.

*JAKE looks menacing about himself.*

                    STELLA

The dog belongs to the new farm-
worker. He can see to the injured
animals and he can bury ...

                    JAKE

Farm-worker! 'Ere! Is that what tha
just said. Ah farm-worker?

                    STELLA

He's getting his belongings from the
car ...

JAKE

Car! Ah farm-worker wi' ah car? Ah've a good mind to shoot fuckin' dog all ovver again!

STELLA

Mr Holmes gave him a lift and as for the farm-worker, he's very effectual – very thorough and ...

JAKE

*(rasping voice)*

Tha knows nowt about him, lass. He could be anybody, far rather have a word or two wi' this bugger afore he unpacks his bloody bags.

*JAKE strides out, gun wedged under and along his wiry arm. STELLA steps over the prostrate WHIPPET and follows him.*

JAKE

Is yon bugger him?

*We see PASSENGER – a jaunty character now gripping four, if not five bulging suitcases.*

JAKE

Yon merchant looks t' me as though he's here t' bloody well stay!
 *(leans over yard gate)*
Weel! I'll be buggered!
 *(grasps top spar of gate,*
  *squinting in foreboding manner)*
Didta ask him for any introduction or ...

                    STELLA
                (nettled)
    No! My business sense has always been
    sound, and -

                    JAKE
                (snarls)
    Weel! Shall ah shoot t' kill now or
    later?

                    STELLA
    It might be more practical and clearly
    not a disadvantage to allow him to
    bury his dog first. Perhaps -

                    JAKE
    Perhaps me arse ...
                (wheels round to face her)
    Can't t' mek out who yon bastard is?

                    STELLA
                (shocked)
    Bastard! You mean ... as in packsaddle
    ...

STELLA and JAKE'S eyes lock together. JAKE'S sinewy features curl up like the insides of a cracked walnut with hate.

                    STELLA
    Take it easy - now, Jake.

We see the benefactor carefully placing his cases on the side of the cart-road before he swaggers loose limbed back to the Rover to close boot lid.

JAKE fights hard to supress his warped feelings.

JAKE

By Gawd! T' way he moves an shape o'
him tha'd tek him for John Asquith as
ah first knew him ovver fifty years
ago.

*STELLA pinches her cold cheeks to induce a rich-rosy bloom and hide her cold murderous thoughts as he approaches them.*

JAKE

By ... hell! Spittin' image o' his
grandfather, owld John, an' ...
   *(darkly)*
We know what happened t' him!

*STELLA leans onto the gate. All dark signs erased from her features. Her newly animated expression lifts her face with spiritual—like illumination in the warm sunrays.*

STELLA

*(enlightening)*
If I had a farm which I could afford
to lose there is no earthly reason why
I should hand it over to an Asquith
knave ... of spades.

JAKE

Aye. Raither like losin' thee ferret
wi'out catchin' ah rabbit.

STELLA

*(flinches)*
I was thinking more on the lines of
two farms ... two bosses. It would be
like two stools. A woman could come to
ground between them.

                    JAKE
          How d' yah mean, lass?

*JAKE looks knowing all the same.*

*We see the distance between them and him measure, feet away.
They begin to chaff away with friendliness that could fool
the keenest observer. He now stands before them, gripping his
case-possessions self-assertively.*

                    JAKE
          Good day t' thee, lad. Tha's new
          worker then?
                *(extends hand)*
          Ah'm Jake Swales, an' tha'll be ...?

                    PASSENGER
          Spencer. Francis Spencer-Asquith.

                    JAKE
                *(grave deliberation)*
          Tha mentioned Asquith. Weel, now,
          that's ah bloody coincidence ...
          Asquith, eh?
                *(turns to STELLA with mock
                innocence)*
          Noha distant relation o' thine, ah tek
          it, boss?

                    STELLA
                *(struggles to hold onto her
                more placid disposition)*
          Poor Sam. It's at moments like these
          when I can't help being reminded that
          it's three months since he was buried.
                *(smiles bravely)*

Poor Sam. What a way to go ... and he wasn't ready to die ... and -

      JAKE
Tha nivver knew Sam Asquith, then? Nay how cud ta?

*An instant spasm of rage grips JAKE'S throat, while FRANCIS SPENCER-ASQUITH regards them closely from the other side of the gate.*

      FRANCIS SPENCER-ASQUITH
Sam Asquith, was my father.

      JAKE
    *(elaborates)*
Nah then, watch thee tongue.
    *(leaning forward)*
Ah've worked here for ower fifty years an' nivver seen nowt or heard owt about Sam Asquith havin' had ah son, nohow!

      FRANCIS SPENCER-ASQUITH
That's as may be.
    *(voice hardens)*
For my part in this family business, I knew nothing about my real father until I was fourteen years old, but it's no use ploughing the air. Now I'm here.
    *(throws wide glances about)*
Do you know?
    *(half-smiles)*
I already feel as though I've come home.

*We see STELLA and JAKE nodding their heads in a flagellant way. Oh yes - their eyes say, both can believe that all right.*

> FRANCIS SPENCER-ASQUITH

Right!

> *(sounds like his ancestors)*

Shall we get started?

> STELLA
>
> *(gets edge back into her voice)*

Right! Francis. You'll be lodging ... with Jake in the next-door farmhouse, and as you can see they are adjoin ...

> *(pause)*

Adjoining, being the operative word.

> JAKE
>
> *(crudely)*

As long as tha doesn't expect t' share me bed ... Ah'm not inta bugger's delight.

> STELLA
>
> *(blinks explicitly the image away)*

The little corollary Samuel and J. W. Hinchcliffe did not seem fit to clarify at the time of implementing the recent will.

> *(pause)*

Therefore, leaving myself and our two wonderful daughters completely in the dark. Meanwhile, I've instructed John Hinchcliffe to look thoroughly into the business of clarifying which

adjoining farm my husband had in mind
when he wrote his latest will.

*We see STELLA open her beautiful eyes wide with angelic
innocence – which immediately become less innocent.*

          STELLA

So, Francis, until all is rendered
down to some sort of human
understanding – we'll retain the
spoken agreement of one year, farm-
worker contract ...

*We see STELLA gracefully extend her hand. She smiles, her
rosy face beautifying in the spring sunshine.*

*FRANCIS SPENCER-ASQUITH'S hand meets hers half-way. His face
creases into a half-smile as though he wants to shake her
hand all over again.*

          JAKE
      (looks on dolorously)

Weel, ah nivver did. Yah says tha
nivver knew owt about thee father. Tha
knows, it's true what they say, "No
man's lot is known till he's dead".

*JAKE pushes open gate. FRANCIS SPENCER-ASQUITH moves aside
as, STELLA full of vicissitude, passes him without a glance
or another word. She heads for the bottom garden gate,
hearing JAKE'S voice ...*

          JAKE
      (uncouthly)

What ivver tha does, lad. Nivver
grease ah fat sow's back.

**SCENE 11**

INT. STOCKDALE FARMS - STELLA'S KITCHEN - 9 AM

*New arrangements - extended table.*

*STELLA seated, head of the table. SOPHIE sat at STELLA'S left - next to "call me SPENCER". GRACE sits at bottom - facing STELLA. JAKE and HARRY sit opposite side to SOPHIE and SPENCER.*

    STELLA
   (cutting rind off bacon slice)
Tell us a little more about yourself, Spencer ...

    SPENCER
   (sinking his teeth into a wedge of home-cured bacon, tongues it aside)
I was a youngster when my mother married my stepfather ... Morris Spencer. A year later we emigrated to Australia ...

    JAKE
   (heartily)
All ah know about Australia is that they use t' send bloody criminals out theer as a punishment and ...

    SPENCER
   (buttering toast lavishly)
That's true, on the other hand Morris was a qualified joiner and specialised in roof timbers.

STELLA

(*pleasantly*)

And your mother?


SPENCER

(*amiably*)

An auxiliary worker until I left school and sadly, Morris suffered a fatal heart attack. Which threw a spanner into the wheel.

(*pause, takes second helping of scrambled eggs*)

I grew up overnight. Mother took a wager and became a cattle drover and –


JAKE

(*with measured glance*)

I'm not a bit surprised, your mother was a great big –


STELLA

Boned woman. Which I'm sure would have been an advantage.


SPENCER

(*scooping up the last helping of black pudding*)

Mother prided herself that she'd brought it off one season after another. She had every intention of dying in the saddle ...


SOPHIE

(*quietly*)

And did she?

                    SPENCER
        No!

*Breakfast finishes in mannered silence.*

**SCENE 12**
**INT. STOCKDALE FARMS - STELLA'S LIVING ROOM - 10 PM**

*One week later.*

*We see STELLA, GRACE and SOPHIE relaxing after the rigours of their working day.*

                    STELLA
            *(between sips of tea)*
        There's no getting away from Spencer's
        strength of workmanship. The muck-
        leading and muck-spreading has taken
        on a new dimension - we're fields
        ahead.

                    GRACE
            *(chiding)*
        And he has a certain knack with the
        horses, even Jake begrudgingly admits
        that - says he's just like how
        fanatical grandfather was years ago.

                    SOPHIE
            *(a curious lilt to her voice)*
        And, the hand-milking of the dairy
        cows now has all of us on the balls of
        our feet ...

                    GRACE
        Moreover, before breakfast, he's swept

down – shovelled out the manure from all the cow-houses' grips and emptying each barrowful onto the yard middens and there are many ...

*(pours out more tea)*

... and all before Jake returns taking the milk churns to our roadside milk-stand for the daily eight a.m. lorry collection ...

          STELLA

*(pouring milk into teacup)*

And Jake is naturally mortified. He said, "If the bastard's not careful, he'll disappear up his ..."

*(pauses artfully)*

Well ... back passage.

*(stirs tea)*

I believe Jake, for the first time in his life, feels his age.

          GRACE

*(with discern)*

Jake sees Spencer's presence here as the betrayal of the Asquith men, thereby, he must be continually conscious that it's himself who is the outsider.

          SOPHIE

*(thoughtfully)*

I've never seen Jake so, so animated. He's beginning to frighten me a little.

**SCENE 13**

INT. STOCKDALE FARMS - STELLA'S KITCHEN - 12:30 PM

*Two weeks later.*

*STELLA carving leg of lamb. GRACE heaping creamy mashed potatoes, basted potatoes, sliced carrots, turnips and whole sprouts sprinkled with preserved chestnuts into culinary dishes. SOPHIE is sat reading letter from HARRY.*

     STELLA
   *(smouldering with chagrin)*
If anyone, even Aunt Winny had said, four mouths ago that Sam Asquith would be dead and a son, an only son of his that we had never even heard of would be settling under our roof.
   *(clatters utensils into place)*
A half-sharer to all and sundry ...
   *(pause)*
And furthermore, Jake Swales would have his feet under our table ...

     SOPHIE
   *(looking up from letter)*
And Harry every weekend.

     GRACE
   *(placing lids on dishes)*
And the young untrained stallion we bought from Jeff Harrison hoping it will throw Spencer with the aid of Jake's slight of hand.

*We hear voices, boots contacting flagstones, scrapping of boots over iron foot scraper - the door sneck lifts and falls* with a clunk. JAKE struts into kitchen followed by SPENCER.

>           JAKE
> 
> By heck, something smells good, and
> I'm ready for it, whatever it is.

JAKE and SPENCER wash and dry their hands, then take to their seats. JAKE'S in a talkative mood. STELLA eyes him suspiciously.

>           JAKE
>       (to STELLA)
> You remember Jessie Foster from
> Bewerly – always wore a berretta and
> carried a sack with a spare ferret in
> it, and –

>           STELLA
> No!

>           JAKE
> You know ...
>       (picks up knife and fork)
> She married Joe Whatton who use to
> breed rabbits and supplied butchers in
> village, until myxomatosis ...

>           STELLA
> No! You're talking about folk you knew
> years ago.

>           GRACE
> Rather like references to scriptures,
> we don't know either.

> JAKE
>
> Horse chestnuts – which reminds me –

> STELLA
>
> *(places dish of stewed apples on table with a jug of meat gravy)*
>
> Just a little touch we provide here and no questions asked.

> SPENCER
>
> You really do turn a meal into a banquet, 'Ella.

*Silence falls as they tackle the midday meal with enthusiasm. STELLA, GRACE and SOPHIE are aware that JAKE is being unreserved.*

> SOPHIE
>
> *(pouring cream over sponge pudding)*
>
> I'll simply get enormous ... And if I'm not careful, I'll not be able to fit into my new outfit for Cousin Mike's wedding.

> GRACE
>
> *(half-smiles)*
>
> Which took most of our clothing coupons ...

> STELLA
>
> And I'll not be wearing widow's weeds.

*STELLA averts her eyes from SPENCER as he helps himself to more mutton.*

STELLA

Sam would not have wanted that, besides, I've yet to decide between my moss-green or cerise coloured costumes.

SOPHIE

Oh yes, Mummy. Your cherry red suit – looks dangerous rather than sombrous.
    *(giggles)*
That should give Aunt Winny something to talk about next Saturday.

GRACE

    *(keeping the women's talk*
    *going)*
And swagger coats are all the rage now.

STELLA

    *(mouth tightens)*
Ah! Winny. She somehow gets to know far too much about Stockdale business ...

SOPHIE

    *(splendidly indiscreet)*
Harry says Aunt Winny dines most Thursdays with John Hinchcliffe in the Wheat Sheaf while Uncle Abe attends the cattle market in Holbridge.

STELLA

Now, that explains a great deal of Winny's inside knowledge.

*We see STELLA, GRACE and SOPHIE exchanging meaningful eye contact.*

*We hear JAKE'S voice overbearingly droll. We see SPENCER looking as though he can't take much more improvisation inflicted upon him.*

                JAKE
I've just said, off colour-like.

                SPENCER
Yes. I heard what you said Jake, but what's she actually doing?

                JAKE
She's doin' nowt, that's what's botherin' me ...

                SPENCER
It's bothering all of us.

                JAKE
Well, she's only middlin' ...

                SPENCER
How long has she been like this?

                JAKE
Oh, for a good bit ...

                SPENCER
But for how long exactly?

                JAKE
For a good bit ...

SPENCER

And how long would you say, a long or a good bit is?

JAKE

Oh, ever since we bought her ...

SPENCER

And when was that?

JAKE

When she came with t' others ...

STELLA

*(the peacemaker)*

Such a pity to wangle over a pig. Have you both forgotten the veterinary should be here this Friday morning to castrate the young colt I bought from Jeff Harrison, early spring, and while he's here, I'll ask him to check over Ruby -

SPENCER

Casting! Surely not?

JAKE

*(with antic gestures)*

Standin'! I'm in tune with modern methods even if I don't approve o' change.

*We see JAKE shoot able looks to STELLA. STELLA disengages herself from JAKE'S repeated intentional stares. She turns aside to brush imaginary crumbs from her riding breeches.*

**SCENE 14**

**INT. JEFF HARRISON'S STABLES - DAY (JAKE'S MEMORY)**

*We see JAKE eyeing the wild chestnut STALLION with a fanatical expertise eye.*

                JAKE
          *(turns to STELLA)*
    Just t' job! A wild, young untrained
    stallion - or ah standin' castration.
          *(lips curl)*
    This colt wi' ah helpin' hand, would
    soon cause chaos, like it or not,
    looks as though it could go fuckin'
    mad!

                STELLA
          *(to JEFF HARRISON)*
    We'll buy him. He's just what we need
    to take our minds off Sam ... and
    Bonny's demise.

*We see STELLA writing out a cheque, while JAKE makes arrangements for delivery.*

**SCENE 15**

**INT. STOCKDALE FARMS - STABLES - DAY (JAKE'S MEMORY)**

*We see the restless, splendid, chestnut coloured STALLION tethered in BONNY'S stall.*

**SCENE 16**

**INT. STOCKDALE FARMS - STELLA'S KITCHEN - 12:35 PM**

*SPENCER angles STELLA.*

> SPENCER
>
> You know, 'Ella you've got the makings of a magnificent stallion here. More's the pity if you go ahead and have him cut.

## SCENE 17
## I/E. HORSE-BOX - DAY (STELLA IMAGINES)

*We see SAM drunk, and EVELYN RIDGEHOLM Neanderthal-like, thrashing about in coition amongst bedding straw in the back of a horse-box behind the sheep-pens at Holbridge Agricultural show.*

> STELLA (V/O)
>
> And here I am with the end result!

## SCENE 18
## INT. STOCKDALE FARMS - STELLA'S KITCHEN - 12:36 PM

*STELLA suffocates a snarl with a conciliatory smile.*

> STELLA
>
> Castrate! The chestnut colt could otherwise be a handful - too headstrong - too highly strung for horse-drawn implements. He'll take too much reining in ...

> SPENCER
>
> *(drawling, sounding more Canadian than local)*
> Would you reconsider, 'Ella if I suggested to you, I would gladly take him off your hands by way of -

> STELLA
> *(sharply)*
> What is it with you Asquith men, you seem to me to have an unhealthy penchant for risk taking which have detrimental results and a crying shame to those left behind.

*We see JAKE slowly raise his mug of tea, over the rim of the mug his hard-boiled eyes size up SPENCER.*

## SCENE 19
**EXT. STOCKDALE FARMS - DAY (JAKE'S MEMORY)**

*JOHN ASQUITH standing in farmyard. Shorthorn BULL drinking from yard water trough. JOHN ASQUITH, arms spread wide, re-directing BULL back into cow-house.*

*Retaliation: We see JOHN ASQUITH strike the BULL on its bull-ring - (pierced nostrils). BULL bellows, charges, gores JOHN ASQUITH. Witness antagonist BULL shaking its head, vigorously trying to shake JOHN ASQUITH from its horns.*

## SCENE 20
**INT. STOCKDALE FARMS - STELLA'S KITCHEN - 12:37 PM**

*JAKE lowers his mug of tea.*

> JAKE
> I knew John and Sam Asquith inside out - worked alongside them fifty odd years.
> *(raillery)*
> Knowledge you missed, lad. They knew no bounds when challenged. Aye, dreaded for their ferocity.

>               (barely conceals his relish)
>           And I lent them a willin' hand knowin'
>           even friends would shirk t' share wi'
>           each other ...

>                       SPENCER
>                     (drawls)
>           What are you trying to say, Jake?

*SPENCER reaches out and scoops a dessertspoon full of plum jam to go with his portion of sponge pudding, followed by pouring ample custard; and a pool of cream. Four sets of eyes pin-point every move of self-service, without showing a hint of: We hope it chokes him! SPENCER lifts his eyes, taking in all the seated diners – their eyes spontaneously meet his.*

>                       SPENCER
>           Are you implying, Jake that I'm seeing
>           my family, the Asquith family through
>           spectacles with finger-prints on the
>           lenses?

*JAKE, mouth full of food, begins to answer – catches STELLA'S parental frown. He swallows his words with the dessert. The meal is finished in a pleasant enough silence.*

**SCENE 21**

**INT. STOCKDALE FARMS – STELLA'S LIVING ROOM – 1:15 PM**

*STELLA, GRACE and SOPHIE are taking a quarter-hour break.*

>                       STELLA
>                     (sinking into easy chair)
>           We need this midday few minutes to
>           repose ourselves away from the
>           menfolk, and –

                    GRACE
               (pouring out tea)
          Jake has looked too energised all
          morning. He's up to something.


                    SOPHIE
               (reclines attractively on sofa)
          I saw the postman hand two letters to
          Spencer this morning, which didn't go
          amiss to Jake, either ...

*We see them settle down - ruminating.*

*We hear outside kitchen door open, close with a bang.*

                    STELLA
               (rising)
          That's Jake. He's no house pet.

*STELLA swishes back brocade curtain along its brass rod. We hear brass rings clatter disparaging into cluster, as STELLA descends steps into kitchen.*

## SCENE 22

**INT. STOCKDALE FARMS - STELLA'S KITCHEN - 1:16 PM**

*We see JAKE exhibiting vacillations.*

                    JAKE
               (bawling)
          <u>Abe! That fuckin' Abe. He's been</u>
          <u>storin' that bastard's mother's</u>
          <u>furniture in his top barn ever since</u>
          <u>she came home t' die eighteen months</u>
          <u>ago - and now - he's written t' tell</u>
          <u>that young bugger t' collect it and</u>

                         194

<u>cart it here t' Stockdale. Inta my home!</u>

          STELLA

He told you so?

          JAKE

No! I saw him readin' letter this mornin'.

**SCENE 23**

**INT. STOCKDALE FARMS - MORNING (JAKE'S MEMORY)**

*We see SPENCER'S jacket - unattended - hung on hook in the wall of the top cow-house - JAKE takes letter from its inside pocket.*

**SCENE 24**

**INT. STOCKDALE FARMS - STELLA'S KITCHEN - 1:17 PM**

*JAKE looks aggravated at STELLA.*

          JAKE

I can read.
    *(enunciating)*
I can ruddy well read! Old John's missus learnt me and -

          STELLA

    *(nods in agreement, speaks as though to herself)*

That explains many things and suggests more. I know now why Abe smiled so secretively on the day he called, the day Bonny was put down ...

**SCENE 25**

**I/E. STOCKDALE FARMS - WINTER - DAY (FLASHBACK)**

*We see STELLA standing outside BONNY'S loose-box, leading halter in her hands.*

*We see MR DAVIS inside loose-box, holding the humane gun. BONNY, sunken glazed eyes. We hear the sharp crack. See BONNY'S legs buckle, the thudding down, emaciated body.*

*We see drag marks left from BONNY being winched from loose-box into KNACKERMAN'S wagon.*

**SCENE 26**

**INT. STOCKDALE FARMS - STELLA'S KITCHEN - 1:18 PM**

*STELLA centres herself into the here and now.*

          STELLA
Cousin Abe and his family have known of Francis Spencer-Asquith for at least, the last few months, yet never breathed a single word ...

          JAKE
   *(his body vibrates with hatred)*
I'll swing first before I let that bastard flit Eve Ridgeholm's bloody furniture through my front door-hole!

          STELLA
Where did you say these ... these chattels are stored on Abe's property?

          JAKE
Far barn! Top barn! Next t' straw

stacks!

></>

                    STELLA
                *(with conviction)*
        Just leave this local problem to me, Jake. I'll think of a solution while I'm outside muck-spreading.

## SCENE 27
**I/E. ROVER CAR – ON-ROUTE TO CLARENCE'S FARM – 2:06 PM**

*Two days later.*

*GRACE is driving. STELLA and JAKE passengers.*

*We see a farm-dwelling with outer building on outskirts of Holbridge.*

                    STELLA
        Clarence won't mind. He was always sweet on me, still is, and if I'm right, he will be socialising in the Wheat Sheaf after the cattle market closes, and –

                    JAKE
                *(abruptly)*
        Never mind sweetness an' light! We've about two hours before landlord chucks drinkers out o' t' pub.

## SCENE 28
**I/E. ROVER CAR – CLARENCE'S FARMYARD – 2:10 PM**

*STELLA, GRACE and JAKE alight from the Rover and head towards CLARENCE'S wagon, parked next to pig-houses.*

*GRACE pulls woolly hat over her hair, wrenches driver's door open, sees ignition keys, gets behind steering wheel, turns key - little response. Tries again.*

                    GRACE

Flat battery!

                    JAKE

                  *(impatient)*

Clarence nivver had much spark. Gormless bugger.

                    STELLA

Just find the starting handle, Jake and stop chewing the fat.

*JAKE climbs into back of wagon. STELLA follows. We see them on hands and knees routing frantically amongst old jacks, straw and chaff before triumphantly retrieving it. JAKE lumbers out and struts to front of wagon. Inserts starting handle, after several turnings the engine splutters, then stalls. Several more attempts.*

                    JAKE

                  *(shouting)*

<u>Pull bloody choke out, Grace but not over much or you'll flood engine.</u>

*GRACE gently eases the choke on the dashboard below the window screen. After several more turns of the steel handle the wagon splutters into life.*

                    JAKE

              *(pulling handle out)*

Just like a pig in a poke.

                    STELLA
          Less of that talk, Jake. Let's get
          into the back of this filthy wagon.

*GRACE honks on wagon horn. STELLA and JAKE hardly set feet into the wagon and shut the back door before GRACE stomps her foot down on the boards and away they hurtle towards the upper reaches of the Dales.*

## SCENE 29
**I/E. PUBLIC KIOSK - BECKHOUSE HAMLET - 2:40 PM**

*We see GRACE parking wagon outside sub-post office. She enters the public kiosk. Dials number. We hear telephone ringing.*

                    GRACE
               *(places handkerchief over*
               *speaker)*
          Hello, Abe. Mrs Biggerdyke here.
          Edna's changed her mind. The wedding's
          off.

*GRACE appears to be listening to loud response, holds telephone away from her ear. Then lets it fall loose from her hand to let it hang, swinging.*

## SCENE 30
**I/E. CLARENCE'S WAGON - BECKHOUSE HAMLET - 2:50 PM**

*We see STELLA, GRACE and JAKE crouched in the back of the wagon - peering through the side slats.*

*We see ABE driving his Austin 12. WINNY - a big woman, ample breasted with large hips is sprawled out on the back seat. The Austin 12 revs by, to disappear round the next bend.*

                    STELLA
          Crikey! Winny's wintered well. She
          looks as fat as butter, and Abe looks
          blazing mad.
                    (pushes GRACE out of wagon)
          We'd better press forward. We don't
          want to be caught red handed.

                    GRACE
          The only way to find out what is
          enough, is to do too much.

**SCENE 31**
**I/E. CLARENCE'S WAGON - ABE'S FARM - 3 PM**

*We see ABE'S farm dwelling.*

*We hear BORDER COLLIES barking as GRACE drives into the top yard and backs wagon near barn.*

*STELLA and JAKE fluctuate from wagon like last month's beef prices as they jostle for the barn side-door.*

**SCENE 32**
**I/E. ABE'S FARM - YARD - TOP BARN - 3:01 PM**

*JAKE grabs for the inner door's locking arm; swings it back to release interlocking arms of the double barn doors, swings them outwards to reveal at the far end of the building a huge untidy heap.*

*JAKE yanks sacks and hay aside and once the dust and hayseeds settle they survey the cluster of chattels in the dimly lit building.*

*We see one huge oak sideboard; a black over-strung piano with* mother-of-pearl insets that catch the diminished light of day; a mahogany dining table with four matching chairs; an oak bedroom suite; a set of drawers and a sofa with one matching easy chair.

                    JAKE
                (brusquely)
Well – would you credit it! These are some of old John's missus's furniture! I use t' give her a hand t' polish it.

                    STELLA
No! I would not give credit. Not even if anyone offered to pay me with love or money.
                (with chagrin)
Looking at this assemblage, I'm in two minds as to whether I shall attend the family wedding.

                    GRACE
                (quietly)
We'll talk about that later, Mother. For now, lets get the job done.

## SCENE 33
**EXT. CLARENCE'S WAGON – HOLBRIDGE AUCTION ROOMS – 3:45 PM**

We see the loaded wagon rattling into Holbridge Auction Rooms back-yard.

We sight just one old timer – a CARETAKER holding the fort.

                    JAKE
              (getting out of driving seat)
Where's thee boss, mate?

CARETAKER

Just gone t' bank. Should be back soon.

STELLA
(through the wagon slats)
Blitz methods for quick results, Jake. Get rid of him. Quick!

JAKE
(aggressively)
An' I'm short of time, so fuck off an' brown nose thee boss! An' tell him it's no way t' run a business.

CARETAKER
(like for like)
You foul mouthed old bugger, just you try and make me!

*We see JAKE jab out a left-handed punch hitting the CARETAKER plum on the nose. We hear a slight crunch.*

*We see two startled eyes above one blooded nose.*

CARETAKER
(raises a shaking hand to his bleeding nose, enunciating)
You shithouse!

*JAKE grabs the CARETAKER by the collar and frog matches him to the outside closet, opens door, shoves him inside, slams door shut and slides bolt across.*

**SCENE 34**

**INT. HOLBRIDGE AUCTION ROOMS - SIDE-ROOM - 3:57 PM**

*We see STELLA, GRACE and JAKE dumping furniture into a side-room; leaving a message trapped beneath the piano keyboard lid: PLEASE DONATE PROCEEDS TO WORTHY CHARITY.*

**SCENE 35**

**EXT. CLARENCE'S WAGON - HOLBRIDGE AUCTION ROOMS - 3:58 PM**

*We see JAKE spin the steering wheel round to speed out of the back-yard and onto the main street and away.*

**SCENE 36**

**EXT. CLARENCE'S FARM - 4:04 PM**

*We see STELLA and GRACE barely arriving at CLARENCE'S farm by public footpath when they hear shouting and cursing.*

*We hear hob-nailed boots clattering on flagstones, then CLARENCE MOORHOUSE, aged 55, bachelor, large over-bearing man, rounds the corner of the building - expression dark and his teeth barred squarely against his over-riding rage. He's carrying double barrelled gun.*

                    CLARENCE

Where is he? Where the hangman has he misselled t'?
        *(suddenly seeing STELLA and*
        *GRACE he halts)*
Oh! So! There you are! Stellaaa ... love ...

                    STELLA
        *(mock surprise)*
Goodness me, Clarence. What's all this

commotion about?

> CLARENCE
> *(ogling STELLA, he pants)*
> I'll tell you what's bothering me, Jake Swales usin' my wagon t' gallivant about in, engine's red hot. If I catch him, I'll shoot a cartridge charge right up his arse!

> STELLA
> *(smile becomes general)*
> Jake Swales, you say, Clarence. Hardly likely. We left him ploughing the six acre field next to the garths.

> CLARENCE
> *(guttural)*
> He always was and always will be a tricky son-of-a-bitch.

> STELLA
> *(pleasantly)*
> Optical illusion, Clarence. Blame John Smith's ale, not Jake.

*STELLA manages to convert her pleasantness into a state of absence as she distances herself towards the Rover, where GRACE is already seated.*

> CLARENCE
> *(shouting)*
> <u>That's as may be ... but I'll get t' bottom o' this.</u>

*We see CLARENCE shilly-shallying himself over yard wall.*

GRACE drives out of CLARENCE'S yard and travels down main road to park on grass verge. STELLA and GRACE alight from vehicle to lean over stone wall.

We see wafting grasses, intermingling with wild flowers and wide breadth of moorland covered with heathers. See grazing SHEEP and SPRING LAMBS.

We hear curlews haunting cries as they swoop and circle, glancing over the isolated moorland, calling, calling, so resonantly.

> STELLA
> *(emotionally)*
> I don't think I'll ever get use to their haunting cries ...
> *(pause)*
> It's as though they're calling to the dead ... lost children of all ages, the sound scours my heart.

> GRACE
> *(nods, eyes glisten with unshed tears)*
> I can still hear Uncle Abe's voice resounding in my ear ever since I called from the kiosk.
> *(pause)*
> His precise words – "There will not be a bastard in my family, not like our Sam's lot, one alive, one dead!"

We see tears threatening to spill over the rims of GRACE'S eyelids. STELLA places her arm along GRACE'S shoulders - a silhouette gazing out onto the isolated moorland - birds still swooping and calling, defending their hidden nests.

*We hear the interspersion of distant gun shots.*

                  STELLA
              *(alerted)*
        Can you hear gun shots, our Grace?
        They sound to be coming from down
        yonder.
              *(points down road)*
        Come on, lass. Let's see if we can
        spot Jake.

*We see STELLA and GRACE running down road to finally stop and lean over wall.*

*We see green pasture land. GRACE whistles. We catch sight of a flat cap bobbing every now and then over wall top stones.*

                  STELLA
        That's Jake all right. He must be
        injured. He's moving like a hoppled
        sheep, and he's heading for the wall
        junction.

*STELLA and GRACE run back up the road, then scramble up the wall, bend over.*

*We see JAKE at the foot of the wall, staring up at them. Blood running and glistening on his face and neck. They hoist him to the top stones where he hangs floundering, his cursing barely audible.*

*Suddenly, CLARENCE appears round the road bend, waving his gun while directing himself towards them.*

*STELLA and GRACE spontaneously shove JAKE backwards. He gasps air. We hear slithering sounds. Followed by a dull thud.*

*CLARENCE staggers breathless to within inches of STELLA and GRACE, his eyes uneasy for want of STELLA. His gun held as a pointer.*

                  GRACE
            *(has never liked CLARENCE)*
      I always thought that a gun in a man's hand is used as an extension of his penis.

*CLARENCE narrows his eyes, then alters his stand-point and speaks through clenched teeth.*

                  CLARENCE
            *(to STELLA)*
      Have you spotted him? Tha must have ... can't have gone far. Caught him crouching next t' pig-houses.
            *(squares his shoulders)*
      I took a pot-shot at him just as he scaled me yard wall ...

                  STELLA
            *(looks around her in mild surmise)*
      Now that you mention it, Clarence we did spot someone – pouching rabbits.
            *(points downwards)*
      He was running like a kleptomaniac.

*CLARENCE stares from STELLA to GRACE in a state of breathlessness, then a mixture of malice as he looks in the direction of STELLA'S hand, and without another word, we see CLARENCE running ungainly down road.*

**SCENE 37**

**I/E. ROVER CAR - MAIN ROAD FROM CLARENCE'S FARM - 4:14 PM**

*We see STELLA, GRACE and JAKE jostling into Rover. We hear the roar of the car engine as they turn onto the main road.*

*STELLA is driving. GRACE on passenger seat. JAKE on back seat.*

> STELLA
> *(winding car window wide open)*
> I don't think I can endure the pungent smell of pig manure billowing from you, Jake - just open the windows ... or walk ...

> JAKE
> *(riving about on back seat, wheezing)*
> Just set foot outside blasted wagon ... fuckin' Clarence flew out o' his front door like a blue arsed fly ... dived into pig-house ... big sow skittled me onto my backside ... bret gun ... drunkard moron ...

**SCENE 38**

**I/E. ROVER CAR - STOCKDALE FARMS - 4:45 PM**

*STELLA drops JAKE off at the last home gate.*

**SCENE 39**

**I/E. ROVER CAR - LEAVING STOCKDALE FARMS - 5:15 PM**

*STELLA clean clothes, drives out of STOCKDALE farmyard with SOPHIE.*

## SCENE 40

I/E. ROVER CAR - KAYSHAW TOP - BUS STOP - 5:30 PM

*We see HARRY getting into the waiting Rover.*

## SCENE 41

INT. STOCKDALE FARMS - STELLA'S KITCHEN - 6:25 PM

*STELLA, GRACE, SOPHIE, JAKE, SPENCER and HARRY all sat around meal table - it is teatime.*

*SPENCER looks in excellent form, quite unlike JAKE, who sits hunched and tense over his plate of scrambled eggs. His rubicund face is a collage of scratches and gashes. His bulbous nose; skinned and swelling out from between over-bright eyes.*

*We see JAKE wearing different clothes - a jacket too tight across his chest, trousers which appear to cripple him between his legs - with indirect hand movements, he's trying to rearrange his private parts.*

*Five pairs of eyes watch SPENCER as he reaches out for a second chunk of rich, moist ginger parkin. They have the look about them which suggests they're waiting for a sound which they are afraid of missing.*

    SPENCER
 'Ella, you really do turn the simplest
 meal into a feast -

    STELLA
   *(eloquently)*
 Just a ministrative function we
 provide here.
   *(half smiles)*

>           Rather like politics, continuity is
>           vital.

SPENCER smiles back at STELLA, then laughs good naturedly.

HARRY takes an extra portion of apple pie. SOPHIE leans over table and pours a pool of cream around it.

>                     STELLA
>                (innocently enough)
>           You look a trifle off colour, Jake.
>                (fingers a slice of sponge cake
>                 on her plate)
>           Grace or myself could slip you down to
>           Doctor Liddle's surgery after tea.

STELLA averts her eyes from JAKE in a manner that suggests something indigestible.

JAKE pushes and prods the peaked eggs uncouthly around his plate.

>                     JAKE
>                (snarls)
>           Just lost my footin' nowt t' write
>           home about.

SOPHIE looks sheepishly across the table at JAKE as she crunches on a biscuit. HARRY looks sideways at JAKE without obligation.

We see the side-view of JAKE'S cheek peppered black and wetly red.

SPENCER leans back on his chair with a guarded expression.

                    GRACE
               *(ponderously)*
          You look out of sorts, Jake.
               *(reaches out for cruet jar)*
          Are you okay?

*JAKE strains on his chair and instead of answering, he forces a forkful of scrambled egg between split lips.*

                    SPENCER
               *(traces of SAM'S voice filter
                across table)*
          You should take more water with it,
          Jake. I can smell whisky from your
          breath.

                    JAKE
               *(throws knife and fork on plate
                with a clatter, nasal twang)*
          An' what's tha goin' t' do about it,
          lad?

*SPENCER helps himself to a slice of apple pie and a dessertspoon full of grated cheese to accompany it – they note sagely.*

                    SPENCER
          Experience has taught me not to
          dispute with anyone about tastes and
          whims when they've had drink ...
               *(a grin that shows no
                amusement)*
          One might as well argue about what one
          sees in the fire flames. Go to bed,
          Jake. Sleep it off ...

*JAKE rises unsteadily with everything screwed up before him. He lurches across table to SPENCER.*

>STELLA
>*(with ludicrous sternness)*
>Sam would not condone such loutish behaviour at his meal table! Please behave yourselves.

>JAKE
>*(snarls)*
>Let me tell thee something, lad! Nobody tells Jake Swales t' go an lig down on a bloody blanket. I'll remind thee, I've worked here for thee grandfather John an' thee father long before you were born, let alone heard of in these places ...
>*(voice rises)*
>An' I've never had a solid day off work since bein' fourteen years old ...

>SPENCER
>*(coolly)*
>Commensurability, Jake.

>JAKE
>*(blood beginning to trickle among unshaven face)*
>Don't thee get on a high horse with me, lad. We knew nowt about sin until you showed up here ...
>*(chest heaving and straining against smaller jacket)*
>An' just because thou turned up here

at Stockdale reight out o' bloody blue that doesn't give thee any reight t' tell me what t' do! You're not me boss an' never will be ...

                  STELLA
        *(with a look to quell JAKE'S temper)*
That's very loyal of you, Jake. But to my mind, a man in anger rides a runaway horse.
        *(drops voice and her eyes begin to water)*
Poor Sam ...
        *(a tear trickles down her rosy face)*
I'm sure my Sam wouldn't wish us to mourn him indefinitely and he knew pity didn't suit me – it never has and never will – he told me that, years ago ...

HARRY *looks at* STELLA *and frowns, then adjusts his spectacles.*

SPENCER *gives* STELLA *a curious look of countenance.*

SOPHIE *pats* STELLA'S *resisting arm.*

GRACE *looks knowing.*

JAKE *lengthens his braces to lower his trousers.*

                  STELLA
        *(smiles bravely)*
People don't mourn in the way they use

to ...
>   *(dabs eyes carefully with corner of table cloth)*

People can be so ... so ...

SPENCER

Despotic?

STELLA

Peculiar.
>   *(rises unsteadily)*

Rather like arrivals and departures.

*STELLA assumes an elaborate stateliness of demeanour and vacates the kitchen to enter the living room. She leaves an uneasiness, and many preluding glances.*

GRACE

Mother's rather unwilling to speak of the great loss of father.
>   *(she begins siding away tea things)*

This sort of emotion is bound to come out sooner or later.

SOPHIE
>   *(rises from table and begins to lever water pump)*

Yes. Sorrow takes people in so many different ways.
>   *(fills bowl with cold water)*

Some people are able to see things clearly, or at least differently.

*HARRY scrapes his chair back against wall. Rises. Attempts to put his arms around SOPHIE'S waist to cuddle her. SOPHIE brushes him away, eyes flashing dangerously.*

                SOPHIE
Please don't fuss about me, Harry. I'm simply not in the mood.

*HARRY steps back, blinks rapidly against SOPHIE'S capriciousness.*

## SCENE 42
**INT. HINCHCLIFFE'S OFFICE – DAY (HARRY'S MEMORY)**

*We see HINCHCLIFFE seated behind his solid oak desk.*

                HINCHCLIFFE
    *(brusquely)*
You're losing fettle, Harry, and it shows in your work these days ...
    *(lights cigar)*
If the young lady is anything like her mother, she'll take some handling ... and ...
    *(exhales a smoke ring)*
You're no Sam Asquith ...

## SCENE 43
**INT. STOCKDALE FARMS – STELLA'S KITCHEN – 6:29 PM**

*JAKE barges passed SOPHIE and HARRY.*

                JAKE
    *(harshly, to HARRY)*
Respect lass's grief, if you want t' make yourself damn useful come an' give a hand at milkin' dairy cows.

*JAKE and HARRY head outside.*

*SPENCER rises, pushes chair under table.*

>                    SPENCER
>                   *(sardonic)*
> I'll say one thing about meal times
> here, they're never dull. I feel like
> the lost relation of the dying man who
> bent over to catch the last expiring
> words, only to hear him say, "Boo!
> Who?"

>                    GRACE
>                   *(tartly)*
> Theory! Theory to my mind is not very
> sustaining ...
>     *(hands dirty plates to SOPHIE)*
> It's philosophical conjecturing and
> vain speculation ...

*SOPHIE scours plates briskly as though handling a scalded cat.*

>                    SPENCER
> It's always the same – if you hush a
> thing up, all sorts of rumours get
> about which are ten times worse than
> the truth.
>     *(looks from GRACE to SOPHIE)*
> Particularly in a close rural
> community like this one ...

>                    SOPHIE
>                *(indicative mood)*
> Best see if Mummy's keeping her chin

up.

    *(wipes hands, to SPENCER)*
Father and you, must have known things - family things were bound to come out after his death, and Mother has been so courageous and dauntless throughout this difficult time.

    *(makes beeline for living room)*
And explanations, I know, do take a deal of time.

    GRACE

    *(takes over the washing up)*
Compassion I believe is the first cousin to tenderness and it's written all over our Sophie. She's a heart full of sympathy for those in a dilemma -

    SPENCER

The solution to any dilemma, Grace usually presents itself when least expected.

    *(half-smiles)*
In some cases it can go quietly by unnoticed for years ...

    *(he comes to face her)*
Take myself ...

    *(harshly)*
The result of a rare coupling that took less than five minutes of rigorous actions after too many drinks following The Holbridge Agricultural Show.

*We see GRACE startled.*

SPENCER

Yes, Grace I was conceived in the back of a horsebox parked behind the sheep pens! Forty-three years ago.

GRACE

*(outraged, her coolness gone)*

A horsebox! You mean to stand there and blatantly tell me that my father ...

SPENCER

*(his correction is so hearty to be cruel)*

Our father, Grace!

*(pause)*

My mother always said, "Heaven wouldn't take him for love or for money, and hell would be afraid that he'd take control!"

GRACE yanks plug out of sink plughole.

GRACE

*(eyes blazing)*

How dare you be so flagellant!

SPENCER'S half-smile returns. He touches his forelock in jaunty manner.

SPENCER

I am but a farm-labourer, for now, amongst the indigenous rich; but remember, Grace from the egg to the apple, I'm an Asquith.

*SPENCER bows himself mockingly through the outside door. We hear him whistling for BRIDIE, then her joyful barking.*

## SCENE 44
**EXT. STOCKDALE FARMS - 11 AM**

*A beautiful sunny morning.*

## SCENE 45
**INT. STOCKDALE FARMS - STELLA'S BEDROOM - 11:01 AM**

*STELLA is sat in front of her dressing-table mirror. We see her reflection beautified by spring sunshine. She's dressed in a bronze silk costume, now putting on her undated hat, trimmed with three cassowary feathers - to be held in place by two large silver hat pins topped by two black jet knobs.*

              SOPHIE (O/S)
       (calling from bottom of stairs)
<u>Hurry up, Mam. The sun has left the front of the buildings, and if we don't get a move on, the wedding will be over.</u>

*STELLA rises - smooths her two-piece over her body, turns this way and that way. Yes, she knows she's handsome, still in her prime. Reaches into wardrobe, takes out her mink coat, gathers gloves. Leaves room.*

## SCENE 46
**EXT. STOCKDALE FARMS - FORECOURT - 11:15 AM**

*Rover standing on forecourt - valeted. Reflecting images. JAKE climbs out of driver's seat. He flicks chamois leather over polished Rover.*

SOPHIE, dressed in cornflour blue costume, white accessories.
GRACE, wearing red costume, brown accessories. Both looking
grand.

>                    GRACE
>                  (firmly)
>             Come on, Mother. We don't want to be
>             turning up at the last minute looking
>             like lost sheep.

STELLA'S nostrils flute as she tucks handbag beneath her arm.
She strokes her fur coat.

>                    STELLA
>             The local guests will be expecting
>             Spencer, but instead they'll be
>             getting Harry. No doubt that will be a
>             conversational piece, and Winny does
>             have the extraordinary habit of
>             jumping the gun – on Stockdale
>             affairs. Well, at least we now know
>             where she gets it from ...

JAKE coughs a warning. SPENCER, feeding buckets in both hands
strolls towards them – pauses next to JAKE and scrutinises
their appearances with out-front admiration.

>                    JAKE
>                  (grunts)
>             By hell. All this bloody paraphernalia
>             for celebratin' folks gettin' wed for
>             fuckin' pleasure.
>                  (nods knowingly to STELLA)
>             I'd sooner go t' a damn good funeral
>             any day.

GRACE positions herself on the driver's seat.

                    STELLA
                *(detracting)*
      Seems rather unfeeling to talk like
      that, Jake. I'm sure Sam would not
      wish us to wear mourning clothes ...
            *(pulls salubrious coat closer*
            *to her body)*
      And everyone knows how cold these
      Dales churches can be in May.

STELLA and SOPHIE climb into the Rover. Doors slam. STELLA winds down the back seat window.

We see lilac ladened trees, orchard trees in bud, newly mown lawns and in the nearby woods rooks cawing. STELLA closes her eyes, takes in the sweet fragrancy.

                    SPENCER
            *(leans forward and half-smiles)*
      Always remember, 'Ella to create your
      memories carefully because when you
      are old your memories will be your
      best friends.

STELLA opens her eyes and smiles thinly, arching an eyebrow, then rearranges herself on the back seat.

                    JAKE
            *(bawling)*
      <u>So long. Tha can always rely on me.</u>

JAKE touches cap neb while giving STELLA the look of: We'll catch the bugger one way or another! – And then heads to the cooling house.

*SPENCER puts his head through the open window. It unsettles the women.*

> SPENCER
> Jake and I will keep the wheels well-oiled and turning while you're being collateral with the relations.
> *(pauses overtly long)*
> My loyalties lay bare here, 'Ella.

*Three sets of glittering eyes stare back at him. He jerks his head away. SPENCER looks startled, as though he's dived his head into a barrel of rattlesnakes. He blinks rapidly, his sensation gone.*

> STELLA
> *(draws on her gloves coolly)*
> It's no good us sitting idling here luxuriating in a panoply of good intentions.

*STELLA begins to rewind the window, slowly. SPENCER stares at them through the glass partition. We see his reflection transform into an older reflection – his father, SAM – they are one of the same.*

### SCENE 47
**EXT. ALLOTTED PARKING NEAR HOLBRIDGE CHURCH – 12 PM**

*HARRY directs Rover to paddock, 50 yards from church. We see many cars, a bus, two tractors – all parked.*

### SCENE 48
**EXT. HOLBRIDGE CHURCH – 12:10 PM**

*STELLA and GRACE mingle with LOCALS as they head for the*

*porch entry. SOPHIE and HARRY hold back to talk to each other.*

*STELLA looking expansively around inadvertently catches CLARENCE'S frank stare. He comes to her side at once.*

        STELLA
      *(congenial)*
We know the bride's name only because we've seen it printed on the invitations ...

        CLARENCE
      *(amiable)*
She's Ralf Biggerdyke's lass. Tha knows, Biggerdyke's from Rutton? Edna. That's it. Edna. That's her name!
      *(moderates voice)*
Ah hear she's forced t' wed, an' old Ralf's missus is hoppin' mad – well, tha sees ... they had John Beck's lad earmarked for their Edna – an' the Beck's aren't short o' brass by all accounts, whereas, Abe's lad ... tha knows, he's only paid pocket money – an' thy Sam ...

        STELLA
      *(acidly)*
What about my Sam?

        CLARENCE
Well, story goes – he left Abe nowt! Anyway, ah heard tell in Wheat Sheaf, last Thursday ...
      *(looks from STELLA to GRACE and*

>                   back again, lowers his tone)
> If they'd not been allowed t' keep
> bairn, or t' wed, they were goin' t'
> live with Edna's grandmother ovver in
> Mottley ...
>              *(suddenly he laughs)*
> Imagine that, Stella love. Ah mean,
> livin' ovver t' brush! Here in t'
> heart o' Dales!

STELLA and GRACE exchange hollow glances.

>                   STELLA
> A high price to pay for any young lass
> considering ...
>              *(pause)*
> She was caught first time round, and
> according to my source ...
>              *(her lie doesn't show on her*
>              *face)*
> She'd told the midwife that she'd been
> vaccinated slower.

CLARENCE'S eyelids flinch back at STELLA and his swarthy face goes expressionless, then he wheels away to disappear round a conifer tree.

>                   STELLA
>              *(raises a vestigial eyebrow at*
>              *GRACE)*
> That's what Madge and Ruth Holderson
> use to say about Clarence when he use
> to play the goat with the girls, years
> ago.
>              *(laughs good naturedly)*
> He was caught with his shirt flap up

on many occasions.

*GRACE'S face breaks into a smile.*

          STELLA

And another situation I can tell you ...

*SOPHIE and HARRY join STELLA and GRACE.*

*Several LOCALS rake HARRY up and down with their eyes.*

          STELLA
       *(turning to HARRY)*
Oh they know – all right. They know! No flies on the Dales folks, Harry.

          HARRY
       *(easy going manner)*
It could be a case of kill or cure, there was a case down south ...

          SOPHIE
       *(eyes sparkling)*
You mean, polish him off?

          GRACE
       *(firmly)*
Now Harry! You're not one of us, so don't even try to think like us.

          STELLA
       *(murmurs)*
It's unlikely, but not impossible, Harry.

STELLA, GRACE, SOPHIE and HARRY have hardly got to the church entrance when we see the VICAR SIMMS appear on the threshold with the church WARDEN on his heels. The VICAR SIMMS turns to WARDEN. WARDEN hurries back into church.

      STELLA
     (sapiently)
  Nothing's left to chance. Spotting us
  here has jolted Vicar Simms' memory to
  remind the keeper to place monetary
  collection boxes in strategic
  positions ...

We see ABE with WINNY – she is wearing a pre-war navy costume with serviceable shoes and hat - looming behind the VICAR SIMMS, ABE strikes his forehead with his hand.

      ABE
     (to WINNY)
  God help us! You worry about fine
  details, don't you. She said she'd
  turn up - what more do yah want?

ABE suddenly sees STELLA, GRACE and SOPHIE – he drops his hand and voice.

      ABE
     (eyeballing STELLA)
  Nah, then! Ah see tha's been spendin'
  an' splashin' out with our Sam's brass
  already.

We see Abe clumsily kneading his knuckles to ascertain contour of STELLA'S breasts through her mink coat.

                    STELLA
               (livid, she steps back)
          Everyone likes a challenge of life
          transformed Abe and ...

                    ABE
               (waving STELLA'S reply aside)
          There'll be a damn sight less brass
          floating about when thou relinquishes
          that adjoining farm t' prodigal son!

                    STELLA
               (rashly)
          Putting the cart before the horse
          seems to be a family trait, Abe -

                    ABE
          Tha should know all about that,
          m'lady.
               (he juts in alignment with
               GRACE)
          At least my daughter didn't fraternise
          with the fuckin' Germans an' -

We see WINNY pushing ABE aside.

                    WINNY
          We'll have none of that Hitler talk
          here! Not today! This is our Mike and
          Edna's day, and ...
               (dark curls spring out from
               beneath her veiled hat)
          Nobody's going to spoil it with
          derivative talk.

We hear the church bells ringing out loud and clear. STELLA

*raises startled eyes to the bell tower.*

                STELLA
I thought all those cast iron bells had been seized with all the iron railings by the government's policy to make warfare ammunition ...

                VICAR SIMMS
          *(smiles incongruously)*
Not here! I was a conscientious objector ...

*VICAR SIMMS meets their abashed polished stares – likewise.*

                VICAR SIMMS
Yes! A cloak can hide secrets in the Lord's name. Amen!

*Without further ado, ALL FAMILY and GUESTS troop after VICAR SIMMS, murmuring, "So be it."*

## SCENE 49
**INT. HOLBRIDGE CHURCH – 12:14 PM**

*The church interior is decorated with wild heather, laburnum and lilac.*

*We see HIS and HER RELATIONS and GUESTS separating themselves down the opposite pews.*

*We hear stilted talk, habitual coughing, shuffling feet, echoing. Eventually, ORGANIST plays: "HERE COMES THE BRIDE".*

*We see MIKE – early 20s, tall, dark, sinewy appearance, and his BEST MAN – early 20s, well built with rubicund* complexion, turning round near alter thankfully.

We see EDNA - 20 years old, dark haired with delicate features and large expressive eyes which the veil cannot hide and a large bouquet of roses which help to hide her pregnancy.

We see EDNA'S father RALF, 44 years old, his face poker straight and TWO BRIDESMAIDS.

> WOMAN (O/S)
> Her sister and a cousin ...

**SCENE 50**
**EXT. HOLBRIDGE CHURCH - 12:45 PM**

All wedding GUESTS head for Wheat Sheaf Inn further down the road.

**SCENE 51**
**EXT. WHEAT SHEAF INN - CARPARK - 12:45 PM**

We see parked: two Land Rovers - each with attached horsebox, one tractor with cartload of straw attached, and CLARENCE'S wagon with load of squealing PIGLETS with cloven hooves and pink snouts protruding through the side-slats.

GRACE parks the Rover, she, STELLA, SOPHIE and HARRY alight.

> STELLA
> (haughtily)
> It's not quite part of the High Street in broad daylight, but for some, I imagine, not too big a jump.

HARRY

    *(laughs pleasantly)*

You are priceless, Mrs Asquith and not as daunting as I first suspected. I mean ...

    *(catching STELLA'S glittering eyes)*

After all those dreary years I spent studying at university, just to appease my ambitious parents ...

STELLA

    *(raising eyebrows)*

There's nothing wrong with ambition, Harry.

    *(pause)*

Anyway, what exactly are your parents professions?

GRACE and SOPHIE

Barristers!

HARRY

Capitalists!

    *(looks expansively around and speaks rashly)*

Money! Is all part of the conspiracy of social organisation which I feel is essentially corrupt ...

STELLA

What are you insinuating young man?

    *(stares with wild surmise)*

Just what are you hinting it?

SOPHIE
Never mind about all that jingo, Mam.
    *(slips hand through HARRY'S arm)*
We can go into that later.

STELLA
    *(looks HARRY in the eyes)*
Tell me, Harry, in all honesty, what do you make of Francis Spencer-Asquith?

*HARRY, the moraliser - pushes his glasses back into the groove of his nose.*

HARRY
    *(steadily meets STELLA'S eyes)*
I believe, Mrs Asquith, that some people are put on this earth to force us to make choices - pass judgements, take sides and prove or disprove our loyalties!

STELLA
Thank you for being so frank with me, Harry.
    *(tucks handbag under her arm)*
I can see you're going to be a comfort to all of us - given time.

*Boots clatter behind them, and CLARENCE we see is footsteps away.*

CLARENCE
    *(shouting)*
<u>Ah've just had your Abe onta me askin'</u>

<u>if you lot know ought about some furniture?</u>

                    GRACE
          *(coolly)*
Did you say, lot furniture, Clarence?

                    CLARENCE
Aye!

                    STELLA
          *(turns around grandly, crested cassowary feathers curve sublimely)*
You're in the bric-a-brac trade, Clarence, you should know more about articles of curiosity than we do.
          *(turns her back on him)*
Come along everyone, or before we know it, the wedding will be over and done with ...

## SCENE 52
**INT. WHEAT SHEAF INN - RECEPTION AREA - 12:47 PM**

*STELLA, GRACE, SOPHIE and HARRY join the tailback of GUESTS queuing at the reception area. CLARENCE follows.*

                    STELLA
Weddings are all right if you're not tempted during the course of your marriage to stray into affairs with friends of the family or kindly strangers ...

CLARENCE
*(persisting)*
About this Gawd damned furniture. It had only been in place for five minutes, in top barn ...

STELLA
I don't know which attitude to take first?
*(smiles peculiarly)*
It's a pity the going should be so hard, but I need hardly tell you, Clarence, in my family we have had a death, an unfortunate death by anyone's standards – and as a respite, we are here to celebrate a family wedding. Remember!

SOPHIE
*(pats STELLA'S arm)*
We'll love and leave you for now, just don't be late for your seating.
*(turns to GRACE)*
We'll see you inside, okay?

*GRACE smiles in a gesture of amiable separateness. And off SOPHIE vanishes with HARRY.*

CLARENCE
*(overbearingly)*
Ah'll not be staved off, Stella love. This here entangled affair rather implicates this Canadian o' thine ... the one that you women are harbourin' at Stockdale ... an' by my understandin', he gave old Eve's

furniture, tha knows ...

    *(begins to excite salivation)*

Evelyn Ridgeholm - his mother - unwed mother -

    GRACE

Your perfectly natural impatience, Clarence won't wash with us today. We're here to enjoy the celebration of two young people. Our Mike and er ... Edna ...

    CLARENCE

    *(raising his voice)*

Aye. This Yankee bum o' Sam's gave Abe his mother's furniture t' store while he went on t' Lincolnshire wi' a load o' cattle, then he must have had second thoughts because he wrote an' said, young Mike an' Edna could have it for nowt, then low an' behold it all vanished from Abe's top barn ...

    GRACE

What are you trying to tell us?

    CLARENCE

Ah neighbourin' farmer said that he'd seen my wagon headin' towards upper dale on a Thursday. Weel ...

    *(spreads his arms wide)*

Everybody knows that ah go t' Wheat Sheaf after cattle market closes ... an' it was Thursday when you an' Stella pulled inta my farmyard.

*STELLA, after a prodigious intake of breath, dredges up a thin smile.*

                STELLA
Convenience, Clarence. I had a doctor's appointment to attend, Doctor Liddle will confirm that I've been under the weather lately ...
        *(places hand to her temple)*
I really don't know whether to laugh or cry.

*The cursorial plumage adorning STELLA'S hat, swirl and quiver from her inner anger against his arbitrary manner.*

*CLARENCE continues to stare lustfully at STELLA. He has fantasised of bedding her for more years than he can remember.*

                STELLA
        *(too shrewd to be articulate)*
Will you kindly excuse us, Clarence while we join our family.

**SCENE 53**
**INT. WHEAT SHEAF INN – FUNCTION ROOM – 12:49 PM**

*STELLA and GRACE enter the busy function room.*

                GRACE
        *(with asperity)*
Lustful old sod. I mean he maybe a good guy underneath, just misunderstood.
        *(pause)*
I had the same trouble with

                Rumpelstiltskin.

                          STELLA
                I'm more disturbed over all that
                blasted trouble we went to removing
                all the cumbersome furniture, and to
                crown it all, Clarence nearly killing
                Jake ...
                          (postulates)
                It's just the sort of behaviour that
                gave the Victorians such a bad name
                ...


*The rest of the blame is lost among the knowing smiles and handshakes and half-hearted condolences intersperse between hospitality drinks.*

*We see SOPHIE and HARRY laughing. GRACE is beginning to warm up to the occasion.*

*STELLA glassy-eyed, wearing a fixed smile, circulating, cool yet approachable, aware of CLARENCE'S resentful eyes following her every move.*

*STELLA and GRACE reach the receiving door. WINNY, suddenly looms into sight, breathless, but her tone is so smooth to be almost chilling.*

                          WINNY
                Ah! And there you are, Stella dear.
                Yes. You're both late. What a cast
                iron winter. Everywhere. And yes, poor
                Sam died needless than most - a horse
                and cart job, wasn't it! How like a
                man to leave loose ends. And, there,
                there Stella. Thank goodness, Sam was

such a tight fisted, mean old man. How
long, my dear? Sixteen weeks! And you
look so well! And, dear Stella, is it
true behind the sheep pens? Bastard!
And to come raking back to England
from ... where was it? Canada!

*Usurped STELLA and adamant GRACE stomp away to find themselves place-seated opposite CLARENCE and VICAR SIMMS.*

          STELLA
        *(mortified)*
Winny! The fat-arsed bitch, with her
apple-pie wholesomeness to mask her
discontentment of life.
       *(eyes bright with chagrin)*
Well, our Grace, it doesn't wash with
me. That woman's got the inclination
of a bovine cheerleader.

*We see STELLA and GRACE approaching their allotted seating with slow tread.*

          GRACE
By all accounts, it's well known that
these two bachelors don't turn down
free hospitality.

          STELLA
And both men can eat while they talk
which enables them to consume more
than their fare share of food.

*CLARENCE and VICAR SIMMS are in full swing talking, eating, talking.*

> VICAR SIMMS
> *(chewing on a pork pie)*
> People think I can save them.
> *(swallows quickly)*
> I can't tell them how wrong they are ...
> *(takes a large bite)*
> It's written in the good book ...
> *(tongues meat aside)*
> If you must compare life and death ...
> *(chewing)*
> You must know them both ...

> CLARENCE
> *(chewing copiously)*
> Confounded hypocrisy.

CLARENCE reaches out to select for himself, an early, plump, hand-reared pheasant, set amongst several others arranged on large ornamental dishes placed along centre of tables. He sinks his teeth greedily into the roasted fowl – grease trickles down his chin.

> CLARENCE
> *(with his mouth full)*
> No-ha-body risks bein' an outsider by disputin' summat evvery-one knows ...
> *(swallows noisily)*
> Tha couldn't stop a pig in a ginnel!
> *(takes another huge mouthful of tender fowl)*
> Nivver mind helpin' sinner through pearly gates!

**SCENE 54**

**EXT. WHEAT SHEAF INN - CARPARK - 1:49 PM**

*We see STELLA and GRACE meet up with SOPHIE and HARRY.*

*Newly weds - MIKE and EDNA; we see their cases packed, they are ready to leave by public transport. ABE is on the lookout for the local bus.*

              SOPHIE
        *(smiling to STELLA)*
  A buffet and a dance-do has been arranged tonight.
        *(pauses eagerly)*
  Eight p.m. to midnight, here in the lounge - will it be all right if I stay on ...?

              STELLA
        *(returns smile)*
  Make arrangements with Grace, love, I'll just have a quick word with the newly weds ...

*We see STELLA advancing on MIKE and EDNA, standing among a GATHERING of noisy well-wishes.*

*We see ABE toing and froing outside carpark entrance - keeping on watch.*

*STELLA diverts and heads towards ABE.*

              STELLA
        *(with civility)*
  There's no accounting for the things we do for our children, Abe.

                    ABE
              (hard-boiled eyes meet STELLA'S
              stare)
        I want a word with you, m'lady. And
        the word is furniture!

                    STELLA
              (cool and distant)
        This is neither the time nor the place
        to dwell on such mundane matters, Abe.

*ABE tries to swallow his envy and temper against STELLA'S gained wealth and soundness of health.*

                    STELLA
        The Valley Gardens will be a real
        pleasure ground to please the eye,
        especially this time of the year – all
        the wonderful crocuses on the Stray. A
        real treat ...

                    ABE
              (harshly)
        Treat! Yah say. Well, you've noticed.
        Ah know you have. Our Mike's shot his
        bolt!

*STELLA grasps the nettle with both hands – the bus will be here soon.*

                    STELLA
              (rashly)
        Well, I'll be blowed. That's something
        that seems to run in the Asquith blood
        ...

                        ABE
                (he gives an impression of
                SAM'S voice)
        Thou should know all about that,
        Stell'.

STELLA flinches.

                        ABE
        Thee look t' thee own daughter, an'
        old Sam's bastard son.
                (pants)
        By hell! He kept that under close
        wrappings, but let me tell thee this -
        we all knew about thy eldest lass
        being put in family way with a fuckin'
        German Prisoner O' War. An' I'll tell
        thee something else -

We see spittle gathering at corner's of his mouth.

                        STELLA
                (white with anger)
        I beg your pardon - you bamboozling
        swine. How dare you speak so loutish,
        and on your son's wedding day.

                        ABE
                (mortification immense)
        Ah know all about it! The way he was
        strung up over barn beam. Oh! Aye! The
        Gerry Germanic! POW. The young bugger
        didn't put ah runnin' knot round his
        own neck and shout ...
                (cups his hands around his
                mouth and shouts)

<u>"Give us bloody Poland". Before he jumped off pig cratch!</u>

*FLASH – POW hanging nude from barn beam – too raw to be natural – it burns into STELLA'S mind.*

     STELLA
    *(bitterly)*
You Asquith men are all tarred with the same brush.

     ABE
Seeing as we're talkin' about Asquith men – ah hear that Canadian bastard son has been left one o' farms ...
    *(laughs harshly)*
Now! That must have put thee nose out o' joint. Thou'll perhaps be needin' a manual or a user handbook t' see thee way around that one?

     STELLA
You must think I was born on the day after the last of March, Abe. After all, the community knows that you're grieved because your cousin Sam never left you or Winny a single penny – and few egos are small enough to cope with that kind of rejection!

*ABE stands as though rooted to the ground. He's outraged!*

*STELLA turns away from him and looks down the street, seeing HARRY signalling to her to return. Excusing herself disobligingly, STELLA meets HARRY halfway.*

                    HARRY
               *(mixed emotions play on his
               features)*
     There are times when I'm made to feel
     like I'm a true outsider, and just
     when I'm beginning to feel at home ...

                    STELLA
               *(kindly touches his arm
               lightly)*
     Harry, lad. Don't be too quick to want
     to change, we'll all lick you into
     shape soon enough.

                    HARRY
               *(grins amiably)*
     Mrs Asquith, that's the first time
     I've heard you speak ordinary words to
     me.

                    STELLA
               *(smiles benevolently)*
     And you've had too much champagne,
     Harry Bletchford.

*We see the bus pull up abruptly at ABE'S bidding. BEST MAN shoves cases into its boot. MIKE holds his hand out to STELLA, she takes it graciously.*

                    MIKE
     Thanks for coming Aunt Stella. Pity
     about Uncle Sam.

*We see MIKE give STELLA a look as though to say: What more can she want, we've been left nothing.*

STELLA

More than a pity, Mike. Our minds feel
bruised and resentful by the
devastating way poor Sam died.
> (shudders sublimely and gathers
> her mink closer)

One never knows what's waiting around
the corner.

MIKE
> (accentuates)

Well, if it's any comfort t' you, Aunt
Stella, everyone knew Uncle Sam always
treated you as though you were one o'
his prized cows.

STELLA blinks the image away while maintaining her smile.

STELLA
> (gallantly)

Just goes to show, lad. There's no one
way to view a woman.

STELLA turns to EDNA, whose full lips curve into a smile. We see EDNA wearing a dark suit – the buttons would have looked better left undone, her legs are bare and her shoes too given to wear.

EDNA
> (murmurs)

Aunt Stella. I've heard so much about
you.

STELLA presses her lips together to hold back fretful emotions. Playing for time, STELLA opens her handbag and removes a brown envelope.

                    STELLA
                (constrained)
            Shopping, my dear – is a revelation to
            all of us these days after five years
            of wartime scarcity.

STELLA presses the bulky envelope into EDNA'S lean hands.

                    STELLA
                (tone softens)
            Be happy, both of you, and take care
            of yourselves for the bairn's sake.

                    EDNA
                (her eyes appeal in a contrite
                manner as they meet STELLA'S)
            Thank you. You're the first person to
            say that.
                (eyes glistening too much)
            And I thank you, again, Aunt Stella.

                    STELLA
                (kindly)
            Don't overdo the thanking, my dear,
            but know where I live.
                (squeezes EDNA'S arm
                momentarily)
            In my opinion people ought to leave
            things alone more. After all, a woman
            always gives more than her fair share
            of herself into things like pregnancy
            and marriage ...

STELLA'S words bring them to the re-grouping of EDNA'S FAMILY
and IN-LAWS – all watching every movement in a cogitative
manner.

STELLA *inclines her head gracefully in acknowledgement, and turns away, to seek out her own family.*

*Breaking away from the cluster of* GUESTS, GRACE *links her arm through* STELLA'S.

                GRACE

Come on, Mam ...
    *(voice gruff with underlying*
    *emotions)*
Let's head home. I've had enough, what with seeing Edna, you know ...

GRACE *closes her eyes tightly so no eyewash can escape.*

                STELLA
    *(compassionate)*
I know – Edna triggered me off emotionally, she looked kind of lost – reminded me of you when you left home, pregnant, to go and live with my mother, Grandma Blanche.

                GRACE

Don't say another word about that time, Mam.
    *(voice quails)*
I don't think I could take it, still so raw. Let's go home. I've had enough for one day.

                STELLA
    *(parental tone)*
Hold on, our Grace. Don't give the Asquiths any satisfaction through seeing your grief. They'd feed off it

for years.

*STELLA and GRACE head for the tea-room.*

                STELLA

I ordered a pot of tea beforehand, with a brandy chaser ...
    *(mouth droops)*
I'd a feeling something like this would happen, as your father use to say, often ...
    *(eyes flashing)*
"It's a question of who holds the foot of the ladder".

## SCENE 55

**EXT. STOCKDALE FARMS - BUILDING TO BULL-PEN - 11:30 AM**

*We see JAKE putting final twists to capping nuts supporting brackets, through which the sliding bars secure the outside building.*

*JAKE, a half-smoked cigarette dangling indifferently from corner of his mouth - dressed in a khaki loose overall coat hung carelessly over a worn waistcoat and beneath that a frayed washed-out shirt without collar - shabby trousers strung high with faded braces, knee indented, barely touching tops of hobnailed boots.*

*We see STELLA standing embolden on the causeway.*

                JAKE
    *(snarls)*
Theer! That should settle his ash!
    *(shoots bolts back and forth on bottom, then top of dividing*

>           *doors)*
>       Any road, how long can a man be
>       expected t' remain outraged an'
>       affronted?

*JAKE gives the outdoors another vitriolic forward and backward thrust. He squints up at STELLA eyes glittering with asperity.*

>           JAKE
>       Just tha job.
>           *(voice has cutting edge)*
>       Just ah piece o' cake.

*STELLA looking suitably dazzled at the supplementary work.*

>           STELLA
>           *(speaks with deep sincerity)*
>       If that contraption doesn't sustain
>       his gallop, tell me what will?
>           *(she wheels round)*
>       Where is he? He's suppose to be back
>       from ...

>           JAKE
>       Nowt's bloody lukewarm t' yon bastard.
>           *(grinds teeth as though he has*
>           *pinching pain in his bowels)*
>       He's all or nowt. The bugger's
>       approach is typical o' old John's
>       ways.

*JAKE rises from crouching position with stiff exertions, just as BRIDIE appears – noticeably in pup, to join them.*

                    JAKE
                (incensed)
            Theer y' are! Even bloody dog works
            better for him, an' t' cap it all –
            even pups will be more different!
                (stares at STELLA)
            Tha'll never be able t' sell them. Who
            ivver heard o' crossbred whippets!
            She'll be ruined!

JAKE, in two minds, makes an irrational grab for yard brush.

STELLA'S reaction: takes steps towards whelping BRIDIE.

JAKE vigorously begins to sweep wood flakes from between yard flagstones.

                    JAKE
            Whatever Sam Asquith was up t' behind
            them sheep pens, Gawd only knows, but
                ...

SPENCER suddenly appears, light of foot round the corner of the bull house.

We see SPENCER – a clothes conscious man, who always appears infinitely meticulous about how he looks – compared to JAKE. STELLA averts her eyes from the comparison.

                    SPENCER
            He's dead!
                (sternly)
            Yet you both bring him back to life,
            constantly, to face me.
                (lip curls)
            Something he managed to avoid when he

was alive.

STELLA steadies herself inwardly – SPENCER has the habit of unsettling her system.

> STELLA
> (turning to SPENCER in a
> cordial manner)
> We need an extra pair of hands,
> Spencer. It's Duke. He's got foul of
> the foot.

> JAKE
> (back in his stride)
> Aye. Standin' on three legs.

JAKE thrusts bristled brush across apron of loose-boxes.

> SPENCER
> (pleasantly)
> Sounds like Duke has a bacterial
> infection.

We hear SPENCER slip the top bolt smoothly back along its brackets, while toeing bottom bolt to accomplish a coincident in time – to effortlessly swing door open to lead STELLA and JAKE through the loose-box and along the passage to the bull-pen.

We hear an inordinate bellow from the roan champion shorthorn bull, DUKE – in response to their arrival.

**SCENE 56**
**INT. STOCKDALE FARMS – BUILDING TO BULL-PEN – 11:33 AM**

We see DUKE, tethered in the bull-pen – he is stood

*majestically sideways to STELLA, JAKE and SPENCER. DUKE looks uneasy as they lean over the side door - proudly gazing at him.*

*We see DUKE'S back foot knuckled over in extreme lameness - to be almost immediately lifted - then lowered - to an agonised withstand. Giving DUKE an unquiet and brooding presence.*

                   JAKE

Aye. He's got foul o' foot, all reight.
    *(looks SPENCER in the eye)*
Ovver here, we call it foot-rot. Ah don't know what tha calls it ovver water like!

                   SPENCER

Fusiformis neorophorus. The organism usually found invading cloven -

                   JAKE

Aye ... Aye ... That's reight.
    *(no alteration in his droll*
     *tone)*
Tha's put me mind at rest, lad.

                   SPENCER

This isn't going to get us anywhere standing about. I'll sort out the dressing and ointment.

*Without waiting for a reply, SPENCER heads out of the building.*

*JAKE, still gripping sweeping brush, leans against inner*

*wall, ankles crossed, waiting for SPENCER'S return. No words
are exchanged. STELLA'S still observing DUKE'S behaviour.*

*We hear outside door clunk open, then rebound behind SPENCER.*

*JAKE rotates his head in casual way.*

*DUKE breaks the silence with a long drawn out bawl, then
slowly begins scouring the whitewashed stone wall with his
thick horns.*

*SPENCER returns and enters bull-pen - now in the foremost
position, bends down - inspecting DUKE'S hind inter-digital
space between the cloven hoof.*

                SPENCER
It's worse than I first thought. I can
see from here, the redness, the
swollen area ...
       *(thoughtfully)*
Even smell the stinking discharge from
here.
       *(turns to STELLA and JAKE)*
How did we all not notice Duke's
symptoms?

                JAKE
       *(with drollery)*
Too busy muck-spreading, an' Duke not
bullin'.

                SPENCER
The beast will take some holding once
we start tackling the infected area.

                        JAKE
            Nah. Not wi' our expertise, an' thine.

*STELLA solely for the purpose of future absolution, lifts her
chin up by at least two inches.*

                        STELLA
            Duke, was Sam's pride and joy. He's
            sired ...

*STELLA purses her lips seductively in order to spread out the
following alluring words for as long as possible.*

                        STELLA
            Some wonderful, milking daughters.
            Anyone can tell them a mile off. It's
            written all over them.

*STELLA'S brilliant eyes shine and sparkle until they are
beautiful – and they hold SPENCER'S whole attention.*

*SPENCER'S eyes are waiting on STELLA, he leans towards her
smiling.*

*STELLA does what she seldom does – she looks point blank at
SPENCER, appraising him for the last time, and finding little
of SAM in him and feeling glad for that.*

                        JAKE
                  (juts impatiently between
                   STELLA and SPENCER)
            Nivver mind about bullin' doesta see
            that contraption above yon openin'?

*JAKE uses brush handle as a pointer to draw instant attention
to a metal yoke above an opening in the bull-pen, then to a*

stone trough set on the windowsill.

                    JAKE
Nah then, boss an' mesen will collar Duke's head while tha gets on wi' things at this end.
      *(sagely challenging)*
Hasta any idea what tha'll be lookin' fore or even doin'?

                    STELLA
      *(quickly)*
I'll get the feeding nuts to entice Duke to the window.

STELLA instantly turns and is gone from sight.

                    SPENCER
      *(confidently)*
Just make sure you secure his head properly in the yoke, then leave the rest to me.
      *(smiles indulgently)*
Oh, I'm sure I'll be all right, Jake. I've been around livestock most of my life.

                    JAKE
Don't tek ower long, that's all.

JAKE juts his way back down passage, hardly able to believe they've got so far, so easily.

**SCENE 57**

**EXT. STOCKDALE FARMS - BULL-PEN WINDOW - 11:36 AM**

*JAKE is stood by STELLA'S side. Their eyes meet and hold with the look of waiting, anticipating for a sound or movement and afraid of missing it.*

                  STELLA

    Cush, cush ...
        (rattles bucket handle)
    Cush, cush ...
        (scrapes metal scoop against
        inside of bucket)
    Cush, cush. Come on, Duke ... Cush,
    cush ...

*Nimbly, STELLA shakes generous measure of cattle food into stone trough, leaving a few loose nuts in the scoop to rattle - to entice DUKE towards the glassless window.*

*We hear snorting, guttural sounds, then scraping of horns against stone wall. STELLA and JAKE cast wry glances through the empty window space.*

                  STELLA

    Cush, cush ...
        (rattles nuts in scoop)
    Cush, cush ...

*Presently the snorting nose with large brass bull-ring dangling through fluting nostrils appears then the glistening eyes - before the broad mouth delves into the feeding trough.*

*STELLA and JAKE yank the lever and the metal yoke crashes down to trap DUKE'S massive neck.*

                    JAKE
                (shouting)
        All right! We've got him. An' don't
        tek all day!

We see JAKE'S eyes dark and impervious to the rays of broad
daylight - STELLA involuntarily, imitates the same outward
signs that make unknown the inner feelings.

We hear inner door open then close.

STELLA and JAKE grip onto the lever - waiting - then cold as
clean - STELLA turns her head to nod assent to JAKE.

We see JAKE scuttle, weasel-like, lean and mean, back round
the building corner - to slide the bolts - to lock the doors.
JAKE returns breathless - fingers already crooked to grab the
lever.

                    JAKE
                (re-seizes lever)
            Wallflowers!

We see DUKE stiffen - give a tremendous bellow and whips his
head against the window stones, as though aware of the yoke
clamped around his neck.

We see STELLA ducking and squinting along the window edges.

We see a glimpse of SPENCER dressing the infected hind foot,
while hanging onto the thrashing hind leg.

                    STELLA
                (whispers to JAKE)
            I believe Spencer is applying the
            abrasive ointment, and if we don't

> move quick, he'll have the treatment
> cut and dried before we can throw the
> switch.
>> (her eyes meet and hold JAKE'S,
>> she snarls)
> Now!

And just as JAKE let's go of the pressurised lever to bring his clenched fist down on DUKE'S ringed nose, STELLA hears SOPHIE'S voice within the bull-pen, then everything happens.

DUKE lets out a tremendous bellow of pain and lunges backwards, whipping his great head round, getting one horn out from the loosened yoke.

We briefly see SOPHIE handing out to SPENCER an old syrup tin containing the crude mixture of copper sulphate and Stockholm tar.

> STELLA
> (screams)
> Dear God! Sophie! Sophieeeeeeee ...

We see STELLA throwing herself headlong passed startled JAKE - to throw herself outside the loose-box door, she is reciting the Lord's Prayer incoherently. Frantically grappling with the newly fitted bolts which refuse to budge in her trembling hands.

We hear a clang! Then a clatter of the yolk as it hits the stone floor, then the menacing bellows of let loose DUKE.

> JAKE
> (shouting to STELLA)
> What the hell's t' playin' at?
>> (tries to rive her grappling

> hold off bottom door bolts)
> It's a bit bloody late t' start
> changin' thee mind!

JAKE thumps STELLA'S locked fingers free from the sliding bolts then jumps with alarming agility to reach out to re-close the top half of the door.

STELLA - demented - rises from her knees with the speed of lightening, already picturing her beautiful SOPHIE plastered like strawberry jam against the back of the door.

We see STELLA bring her knee up and into JAKE'S groin with all the strength she possesses - lifting JAKE onto his boot caps, forcing his eyes to protrude, mouth fly open, all his breath to expel in one single bellow of pain, then he keels over.

STELLA vacillating - swings top half of door wide open, tears jumping from open eyes.

We see a blurred figure of SPENCER catapulting over the bottom locked door.

STELLA staggers backwards, eyes wavering into vagueness.

> SPENCER
> (shouting)
> Move! Woman! Move!

We see STELLA remaining upright, then she's flat on her back straddled beneath the body of SPENCER.

> STELLA
> (belated howling)
> Sopheeeeeeee ...

We see STELLA fighting wildly to disarrange herself from SPENCER'S pivoted knees.

We hear the thudding of DUKE'S thick horns against the back of the door.

                STELLA
                  (screaming)
<u>Sophieeeeeeee ...</u>

                SPENCER
           (grips STELLA firmly by the
           shoulders, then shakes her)
Sophie's all right! Take a hold of yourself - woman! 'Ella!
           (shouting into her blank face)
<u>She's safe! Look at me while I'm talking to you!</u>

STELLA is unable to grasp his words. She's too distraught to reason.

                SPENCER
           (pronounces each word slowly)
'Ella! Sophie - my - sister - is - still - very - much - alive!

                STELLA
Sis - ter ...

STELLA'S eyes dilate as desperately she fights to overcome shock and the reverberation of the word: sister.

                SPENCER
           (persisting)
Yes! I threw my sister into the manger

and before I'd cleared the inner bull-
pen door ... I witnessed her hoisting
herself over the hayrack and reaching
towards the hayloft trap door.

*We hear DUKE - the ton weight of prime beef - snorting, bawling, pounding unmercifully against the wooden door.*

          STELLA
     *(weeping, she screws up her*
     *face in misery)*
Sophie shouldn't have been there in
the first place.

*SPENCER pulls STELLA to her unsteady feet. STELLA sags against his lean body.*

          STELLA
So-rry ... I'm so-rry ... my mind can
do nothing but announce its distress
to itself.

*JAKE unnoticed by them - drops his trousers, then slowly, painfully, dangles his private parts under the yard's trough cold water tap.*

          JAKE
     *(cursing)*
By Gawd ... as thrang as onny woman's
tongue ... by Gawd ... as thrang as
...

          SPENCER
Come along, 'Ella.

*SPENCER wipes STELLA'S wetly cold come hot cheeks dry with the palm of his hand.*

>                    SPENCER
>           I'll take you home.

>                    STELLA
>           Oh! No!
>                 *(lugubrious laments)*
>           Not all the way to Canada!

## SCENE 58

**INT. STOCKDALE FARMS - STELLA'S KITCHEN - 9 AM**

*STELLA, off-colour, is going through a religious phase after the bull-business - she recites a little prayer of thanksgiving.*

*Meanwhile - GRACE clunks cups onto saucers.*

*SOPHIE is wearing a surgical collar from whiplash injury, and one wrist is resting in a sling - she looks sheepishly at STELLA.*

*SPENCER seems invigorated - toned up.*

>                    JAKE
>                *(eats greedily)*
>           By gum, ah slept like ah new born
>           bairn last night.

>                    STELLA
>                 *(acidly)*
>           People who say that usually don't have
>           one in the house.

*STELLA pours herself a cup of tea while casting a covert*

glance at SOPHIE – who looks as fresh as a daisy, eating unperturbed.

               JAKE
           (voice grating)
     Tha never knew thee father, did ta, lad!

SPENCER'S routine half-smile vanishes. He fixes eyes onto JAKE.

               JAKE
     He never said out t' me about thee. Not a blind word in forty odd years ah worked fore him.
           (looks rancidly at SPENCER)
     Aye. Not ah single bloody word!

JAKE shoots a reserved glance at SOPHIE – questions to himself: Is she softening towards big brother? – Then switches his eyes back to SPENCER.

               JAKE
     Aye!
           (crunches and grinds on bacon rind)
     We knew nowt about sin or thee until tha showed up ... Aye, reight out o' bloody blue!

               SPENCER
           (leans back on chair, gaze truculent, impersonates JAKE)
     So nah tha knows. An' now tha can bloody well let it drop!

STELLA meets GRACE and SOPHIE'S eyes fleetingly. She makes a gesture barely indicating, signifying care from now on.

> JAKE
> (determined to have the last word)
> Thee father wore a Christian. Aye. Ah real Christian t' me thee father was ...

> GRACE
> (pushes her half-finished breakfast to one side, voice gruff)
> My father may have been a Christian to you, Jake, but to me he was a murderer!

> STELLA
> (alerted)
> Mur ... der ... er? I don't like the sound of that, Grace. Whatever your father's faults in life were, you really shouldn't call him one of those.

STELLA tries to signal to GRACE to hold her tongue or leave the table. GRACE remains seated, ignoring STELLA.

> GRACE
> (clearer voice)
> Yes! Father, my Christian father, hung Hertz in broad daylight.

GRACE'S facial expressions change in many ways – that JAKE and SPENCER find difficult to take in.

                    SPENCER
               *(he looks quizzically from
               GRACE to STELLA)*
Hertz?

                    SOPHIE
One of our German Prisoner Of War
soldiers. They worked on the farms ...
          *(looks beseechingly at GRACE)*
He was fatally besotted with our
Grace. He was young, blond ...

                    JAKE
          *(knowingly)*
An' cun't speak ah bloody word o'
English t' save his life, never mind
owt else.

*STELLA, unprepared for this turn of events, bites hard on her back-bacon, again trying to catch GRACE'S eyes.*

                    GRACE
Our only crime was, we simply fell
truly in love.
          *(eyes shine brightly)*
And there's a language of thoughts and
feeling, Jake ...

*GRACE sights each in turn, and they stare back at her waiting – anticipating – her voice penetrates their ears anew ...*

                    GRACE
I became pregnant –

                    JAKE
Another bastard!

*JAKE'S eyes swivel around the kitchen and across the ceiling as though to discover it lodging somewhere amongst the hanging side bacon and cured hams.*

> JAKE
> Wheer t' hell is it? Wheer did ta put it, lass?

> SPENCER
> *(quite naturally)*
> The child ... Grace ...

*STELLA takes another stab at her bacon and eggs and chews, waiting.*

*GRACE looks as though she can't trust herself to answer. Abruptly she rises from the chair, unexcused, and vacates into the living room.*

> SOPHIE
> *(rises and gives one of her calm looks)*
> I'm sorry, our Grace doesn't fit in too easily with folks who stick out too much. She's naturally reticent ... excuse me.

*SOPHIE follows GRACE.*

> STELLA
> *(makes shushing noises)*
> Well, it just goes to show, one's children never cease to astonish one, and they somehow never quite tell their parents everything.

                    SPENCER
            *(vacates chair and heads for*
            *outside door, pause, turns to*
            *STELLA)*
    Is it true what Grace said about my
    father?

                    STELLA
            *(not looking at SPENCER)*
    Women use generalisations in order to
    get across the depths of emotions they
    feel ...
            *(reaches for a slice of toast)*
    The trouble with men, they take what
    we say so literally.

                    SPENCER
    You surely can't call the accusation
    of murder a general inference. It
    means just one thing – murder!

                    JAKE
            *(scraping legs of his chair on*
            *the flagged floor, rises)*
    Aye. It's ah job that only needs doin'
    once.

JAKE stares at SPENCER in his sapient way of: I taste ... I know ...

SPENCER stares back at him as though he incenses him.

                    JAKE
            *(thrusts himself forward)*
    Tha should see theesen.

*JAKE'S eyes sweep SPENCER up and down with vigour which breathes new fire into SPENCER'S belly.*

>              JAKE
> Tha stands theer like ah bloody
> gristly bear wi' ah gurt sore prick.
> Anybody a mile off could guess tha
> nivver even acquainted wi' thee
> father.
>     *(lips curl cruelly)*
> If tha'd known him like ah did, tha
> wouldn't even have t' ask!

>              SPENCER
>     *(coldly)*
> And what's that all suppose to mean?
> What are you trying to tell me, Jake?

>              JAKE
> Mek of it what tha likes. Ah've
> forgotten more about goin's on at
> Stockdale over years than tha'll ivver
> begin t' know.
>     *(scours SPENCER with his eyes)*
> Nah! If tha stands theer much longer,
> lad, ah'll begin t' suspect tha'll be
> beggin' me next t' kiss thee arse an'
> call thee Peggy Martin.

*SPENCER jerks up a warning hand, without a glimmer of welcome on his face.*

>              SPENCER
>     *(he steps aside)*
> Would you kindly excuse us, Jake. I
> would like a private word or two with

'Ella.

JAKE is not to be hurried out of the kitchen. He turns to
STELLA shaking his head.

>               JAKE
>                 (morosely)
>           It's ah funny business this here
>           family business ...

>               STELLA
>                 (pontificating)
>           Never mind the funny business, Jake.
>           Just get on with some farm work.

>               JAKE
>                 (looks at her as though she's
>                 given him a compliment)
>           Ah'll be off then, boss.

JAKE charges out of the kitchen to slam the outside door
behind himself.

>               SPENCER
>                 (demanding)
>           About my father, 'Ella?

>               STELLA
>           What about your father?

>               SPENCER
>                 (with a strained smile)
>           I don't want every anecdote, just the
>           basic facts. That's all I'm asking
>           for. Surely that's not asking too
>           much.

                    STELLA
              *(raises a defiant eyebrow)*
          How typical of a man to look for a
          sudden solution without the
          intervention of interest in discussing
          all the particulars before hand.
                *(she begins to spread marmalade
                 onto a slice of toast)*
          It's my experience, men and women use
          the same words, but that doesn't
          necessarily mean the same thing ...
          Besides ...
                *(takes bite out of toast)*
          I find it impossible you should know
          nothing about your father, on the
          other hand ...
                *(swallows toast)*
          It would be no exaggeration to say,
          Sam found it easy to discard anything
          or anyone who proved something of a
          disappointment ...

*STELLA'S voice breaks off – memories become too clear.*

*The corners of SPENCER'S mouth twitch, pushing back arguments.*

                    SPENCER
              *(bitterly)*
          One can never get away from being
          illegitimate, not even for one day.
          It's worse than being tied daily to a
          herd of dairy cows!

*Hugging his shoulders to his ears, SPENCER involuntary reseats himself opposite STELLA.*

*They sit in silence over the remains of breakfast, eyeing each other wearily.*

*SPENCER tortured by circumstances.*

*STELLA burdened by duty.*

*Both scraping butter over cold toasted bread, and clinking cups as they pour and re-pour cups of tea in a way they have not intended. Eventually SPENCER breaks the silence ...*

                SPENCER
My mother – a woman of few words. She made her own pattern independently and without guilt.

                STELLA
      *(rises and begins to clear away breakfast placings)*
Sam always thought guilt was an indication of psychosis.

                SPENCER
      *(leans back on his chair)*
The Prisoner Of War. Tell me about him, 'Ella.

                STELLA
Tell you what?

                SPENCER
The circumstances ...

                STELLA
What circumstances?

                    SPENCER
            The surrounding state of conditions
            relating to the incident ...

                    STELLA
            Incident.

*With a neat movement STELLA picks up a tray and begins to collect the dirty dishes into well-chosen stacks, then rearranges them in another way.*

                    SPENCER
                  *(offers)*
            Insidious - then.

*STELLA swings back round to the sink and deliberately drops the loaded tray from the height of several inches.*

                    STELLA
                *(smile fixed)*
            I think most people feel like that
            from time to time.

                    SPENCER
                 *(unabated)*
            'Ella, if I am to come anywhere close
            to understanding my family background,
            I need to have some insight into their
            paternal behaviour and habitual
            practices.
                *(half-smiles)*
            Surely I'm entitled to that.

*We hear STELLA clattering cups and plates about in the sink, then slowly she turns and trains her eyes, bright with intensity upon him.*

STELLA

They made him stand on the pig cratch
– you know the ones I mean.
> (pause)

The table-like frames with flat rungs
and stumpy legs – most farms have one
for dressing the pigs down at pig
killing time ...

*STELLA turns aside to stare out of the kitchen window – as though distancing herself.*

STELLA
> (low flat voice)

Do you know what I remember most? I
remember.

*STELLA falls silent.*

*SPENCER moves uneasily on the wooden chair, but he's watchful.*

STELLA

I remember most vividly the way Sam
and Jake kicked out ... to strike out
the pig cratch from beneath his bare
feet. And the way his toes had curled.
Whited between and around the slatted
concaved surfaces ...

SPENCER

This is barbaric!
> (shoots up from seat to affront
> her, voice rasping metallic)

Next thing you'll be telling me is
that they created a eunuch!

                    STELLA

You speak and sound like a true
Asquith. Take your father as he was,
with all his calculated methods and
quick results. They were all he knew
or wanted. Sam Asquith was never one
to accept defeat or compromise, and
when he was wronged he was ruthless
and callously cruel.
     *(smiles thinly)*
He never asked for anyone's
commiserations. He didn't see the use
for them.

                    SPENCER
     *(anger is fuelled by outrage)*
I can't have you explaining him
through me. From what I'm hearing
you've marked him down as an innovator
with a ruthless perpetrator of his own
original parsimony schemes.

                    STELLA
     *(snaps back)*
Dress him up as you like ...
          *(drying off knives and other*
          *edged crockery collectively)*
But kindly give me the acknowledgement
of knowing your father, besides being
married to him for nearly thirty
years, he was ...
     *(slams cutlery draw shut)*
Very nearly a virtuous man. A man
whose greatest fault was that he could
not abide any form of betrayal ...

SPENCER

Betrayal! He betrayed all his family!

*SPENCER waits wrathfully for STELLA to break her silence – as she rattles one after another breakfast things into the kitchen cupboard, then swings the door shut with a loud bang.*

STELLA

Do you really think that we womenfolk need more earth shattering events and insistents to loosen up our senses? All things taken into consideration, I feel, we've taken more of our fair share of encumbrances and cessations over the last two or three years.
    *(voice quails)*
There was a time when we all wanted to be at least a little bit dead.
    *(unties pinafore strings and*
    *wrenches garment off, hurls it*
    *aside)*
So, Francis Spencer-Asquith, if you feel the need to persist on these peremptory family matters then let me suggest, you tattle J. W. Hinchcliffe!

SPENCER

Hinchcliffe!

*STELLA, thrusting her feet into wellington boots and slotting her arms through the sleeves of her mackintosh.*

STELLA

Yes! If you take the trouble to draw that man out, you don't know what you might find!

FADE OUT.

END CREDITS ROLLS TO SONG BY IDA BARKER, "I FORGOT TO FORGET".

END OF EPISODE 2.

Episode 3

# Summer

## EPISODE 3
## SUMMER

**SCENE 1**
**I/E. ROVER CAR – SUMMER RURAL LANDSCAPE – 2 PM**

*We see long view of abounding Dales countryside bathed in summertime. We see LIVESTOCK grazing on Stockdale Farms' pasture land. We see wild roses blooming in hedgerows – yellow gorse fading.*

*We hear from over the northern moorland, pewits and curlews defending cries, as swooping, wheeling, protecting their nests hidden amongst rush-grasses and rigorous heathers.*

*We see STELLA driving Rover, SOPHIE (wearing neck brace and an arm-sling) and BRIDIE are passengers. They are motoring up the cart-road towards meadows.*

> STELLA
> *(expansively)*
> To think, everything was behind schedule due to the austere winter, but somehow we effectively managed to finish off ploughing, and sowing the row crops ...

> SOPHIE
> And attended to land draining ...

> STELLA
> And mucked out all the loose-boxes and scrubbing them down.

>           *(pause)*
> Whitewashed the lot – and cleared the middens from the yards – at the same time, leading it out to spread over the land.
>           *(turns head to look at SOPHIE)*
> Farming is no job for anyone with a glass back ...

           SOPHIE
>           *(laughing)*
> And dear Harry almost passed out with surprise and pleasure when he got the knack of hand-sheering the sheep.

           STELLA
>           *(finding it hard to avoid SOPHIE'S smiling eyes)*
> Yes. It has to be said, Harry has blossomed – your father would have been suitably impressed with him, if nothing else.

*We see the Rover stop on the edge of the moorland. STELLA and SOPHIE step out of the vehicle with BRIDIE – open and close field-gate to view the meadow fields, to calculate the growth for summer haytime.*

           STELLA
>           *(shudders positively upright)*
> It's moments like this, our Sophie, when it dawns on me that for nearly thirty years, I've always inspected the meadow crops coming up to June with your father, which now I come to think about it ...

>           *(places hands to midriff)*
> gives me the feeling of almost painful sensations in the pit of my stomach.

>                   SOPHIE
>           *(compassionately)*
> Poor old Mummy.
>           *(by impulse)*
> Sometimes when I hear Spencer talking, I think it's Daddy.

>                   STELLA
>           *(swings round to face SOPHIE*
>           *with fierce eyes)*
> I'll have less of that kind of talk, my girl, and seeing as you've just mentioned blasted Spencer – whatever was you thinking about when you placed yourself into danger by entering the bull-pen?

>                   SOPHIE
>           *(self-consciously runs a hand*
>           *over the neck brace)*
> I was too upset with Harry to be able to think of our riddance plan – I mean, Harry said he had plans to visit his parents, usually conspicuous by their absence from his life by all accounts. And added to that ...
>           *(looks vulnerable)*
> Harry didn't even think to include me – after all he's had, and gets, a shed-load of hospitality from my family.

STELLA

(scolds)

You have a disgraceful charm dear Sophie, and a mother is more susceptible to your sort of charm than a husband or lover can ever be – but I have to remind you that your sentimentality could have cost you your life – and you my dear ...

(glares)

was not the one on our hit-list! Remember!

SOPHIE

I do regret my misdemeanour, and especially when Harry reversed his decision to forgo his home holiday to help with the sheep dipping and shearing which caught up with the wool prices, and Spencer did say –

STELLA

(sharply)

Never mind the wool prices, the bull-business knocked me sideways.

(places hand to temples)

By jingo, the giddiness, the constipation and all that endurance of insomnia. It's not as if I'm indulgent towards myself ...

(grips SOPHIE by the shoulders and shakes her firmly)

We will not always tolerate your lackadaisical behaviour Sophie, it's a luxury which we cannot afford these days. At this rate, we'll be running out of riddance plans while, Francis Spencer-Asquith will be as unrestrained as a wild horse on a Canadian prairie.

          SOPHIE
Sorry, Mummy. But I have to say ...
    *(catches STELLA'S hand)*
Jake's beginning to frighten me, more than Spencer.

*STELLA squeezes SOPHIE'S hand in response, then turns her head away so SOPHIE cannot see her dark expression.*

          STELLA
    *(changing the subject)*
Promise me you don't utter one word of our riddance plans to Grandma.
    *(letting go of SOPHIE'S hand)*
Come on, lass. You can walk back home with Bridie, while I go, as promised, to collect Grandma Blanche.

          SOPHIE
    *(murmurs with delicacy)*
I know Grandma Blanche will take a shine to Spencer because she's partial to scintillating and attractive men, and women who understand men are unreliable aides.

          STELLA
    *(instantly alert, looks sharply at SOPHIE)*
For an instance, Sophie, I'm not quite sure if I don't resent such insight

>           from you.
>                   *(pause)*
>           Those sort of remarks are disturbing,
>           even alienating – you're beginning to
>           sound like Grandma Blanche.

*We see them retracing their steps along the edges of the lush fields, see tall grasses brushing their bare legs.*

>                   STELLA
>           Yes. Another week to ten days Sophie,
>           and we'll be ready to start three
>           months of haymaking – and Kit
>           Sullivan, will be arriving any day
>           soon.

## SCENE 2
**EXT. STOCKDALE FARMS – WATER-SPLASH – 4 PM**

*We see SOPHIE crossing the water-splash by the stepping stones. She is happy and laughing as she turns to SPENCER.*

*We see SPENCER dismounting from chestnut stallion – NELSON. He gives the horse a slackened rein while it drinks.*

*We see BLANCHE (mother to STELLA) aged 74, motherly figure. Down-to-earth person with waspish humour, though soft hearted. She is standing on the forecourt with STELLA.*

>                   BLANCHE
>               *(her tone is easy going)*
>           So, that's him – Francis Spencer-
>           Asquith.

*STELLA refuses to be bated as they watch the DAIRY HERD leisurely amble from the beck towards their own stalls in the cow-houses for their second milking of the day.*

                BLANCHE
        *(observing)*
There's no denying, the man looks right at home here ...
        *(pause)*
As right as rain, if you ask me. And it's a pity Sam didn't have the decorum to come clean about the affair years ago.
        *(turns to STELLA)*
It's not as though it happened haphazardly during your marriage.
        *(looks at STELLA more closely)*
You don't mind me going on about this do you?

                STELLA
        *(feistily)*
There are times since Sam died when I remember to remember he did not always please my mind ...

                BLANCHE
Sam was a man whom you have history with – more than I ever had with your father ...

                STELLA
Sam Asquith was domineering, rough and apt to jeer and sheer in ways that have left my mind bruised and crushed.

**SCENE 3**

**I/E. STOCKDALE FARMS - BOTTOM COW-HOUSE - 4:02 PM**

*We see STELLA push the quarter glass windowed cow-house door open to stand reflectively on the forecourt.*

*BLANCHE is talking in-between chaining each DAIRY COW by the neck to the individual side pole.*

> BLANCHE
> Talking about men ...
> *(pause)*
> Knowing Jake, he's bound to feel his nose has been pushed out of joint with a son - and a bastard one at that ...
> *(laughs good naturedly)*
> I mean, a son suddenly being willed onto Stockdale Farms ...
> *(eyes hold ironical expression)*
> Jake will know as well as we do, that sons spell out new methods which will eventually produce modern changes sooner than later.

> STELLA
> *(with pungency)*
> Are you saying Mother, sons give a bit more of themselves than wives and daughters?

*STELLA is chaining up RHODA, whose standing contently in her stall.*

> BLANCHE
> I may be wrong on what is right or preferable, but I've always had the

> strong impression that Jake Swales
> feels he had the covenanted agreement
> from the Asquith family that the
> adjoining farmhouse was and is his
> home until the day he dies.
>> *(her smile comes and goes)*
> I've not forgotten Jake's distorted
> reaction towards me when you wanted me
> to move in next door when I retired!
>> *(steps over the grip channel to
>> stand on the centre causeway)*
> And what's this I hear?
>> *(pause)*
> Jake's got his feet under the same
> table ... dear me! What would Sam say?

## SCENE 4
**EXT. STOCKDALE FARMS - GARDEN BOUNDARY WALL - 4:12 PM**

*We see STELLA and BLANCHE rounding the garden boundary wall leading to bottom yard - BLANCHE'S cogitations are cut short as they see JAKE sat astride POLLY, a mare, already in season, being watered at yard trough.*

*We see SPENCER unexpectedly come into sight riding the charged neighing stallion, NELSON, who is advancing through bottom yard gateway.*

*We hear NELSON whining loudly, he lungs forward, rears aloft, throws his forelegs onto and around POLLY'S rump to overlap JAKE. NELSON surges forwards and backwards without an ounce of friendliness.*

*We see JAKE catching a glimpse of SPENCER'S assailing expression before JAKE somehow throws himself to the flag stoned yard - regardant - until NELSON suspends his activity with forefeet thudding to the ground.*

*SPENCER is very good about it.*

*JAKE confounded to silence, judders upright, face grey-pallid, turns away and hobbles off in the direction of the bottom barn.*

*BLANCHE looks expressively around herself.*

>           BLANCHE
> Well! That was a sight for sore eyes!
>      *(turns to look at STELLA with a
>      bold eye)*
> Do you remember, our Stella -

>           STELLA
> No!
>      *(avoids SPENCER'S eyes)*
> But I could do with a good stiff drink
> to get me off the ground.

**SCENE 5**

**EXT. STOCKDALE FARMS - STELLA'S BACK GARDEN - 4:35 PM**

*We see STELLA and BLANCHE sat beneath plum trees in back garden with a bottle of homemade bilberry wine placed between them.*

*We see GRACE, she drops a dripping wet hessian sack down before them - it bears the impression of a large stone.*

>           GRACE
> Jake!

                    BLANCHE
          (regards the sack)
     I told you so! Jake is a malicious old
     man.
          (smacks glass down on garden
          table, heads for farmhouse)
     I'll go and prepare our teatime meal.

STELLA empties wine bottle and passes last glassful to GRACE.

GRACE sits down on vacated chair and slowly takes sips.

                    GRACE
     I saw Jake throw this sack over the
     arched bridge top-stones, but I was
     too late to recover it alive.
          (continues drinking the wine)
     Who's going to tell our Sophie?

STELLA rotates her head to look GRACE in the eye, niggling doubts plain to be seen.

                    STELLA
     Womenfolk speak as we find and feel,
     and men would be simply devastated
     forever if they took everything we
     said to them literally.

                    GRACE
          (gives her a sharp glance over
          rim of glass)
     I suppose the logical reasoning to
     that would be the compensation - that
     men think women operate in the same
     way, so women are expected to forgive
     and forget the devastating things men

say and do to them.

          STELLA
    (mutters)
Dear Lord, if only Sam had, sometimes, shown more of his heart.

          GRACE
Father's dead. Jake's alive, and we must never lose sight of the fact that Jake's as ruthless as he is devious ... it crossed my mind as I dragged the sack out of the beck, there might be a more sinister purpose to Jake's motive.
    (grips STELLA'S arm)
You must have noticed our Sophie has softened towards big brother since the bull-business – and ...
    (tightens her grip to emphasise
    her words)
And – Spencer is now giving driving lessons to Harry when he takes him back to Holbridge, each Sunday night.

          STELLA
I have noticed, more than once, that Jake's attitude to Sophie has noticeably changed. A durable change since the bull-business ...

          GRACE
Yes, and I suspect he believes Sophie, who is as promiscuous as a snowdrop, rather like Grandma, will let the cat out of the bag – so Jake's testing her

reaction, and Spencer's.

          STELLA
       (*points to the contours of the sack*)
Who doesn't know about this?

          GRACE
Sophie and Spencer ...

*We see BLANCHE looking out of a back window of the farmhouse.*

          BLANCHE
       (*calling while pointing to the back fields with a bread knife*)
<u>Jake's coming!</u>

*We see a black dot moving awkwardly down through the meadows, to gradually become larger and larger.*

*STELLA seizes the sack and thrusts it back into GRACE'S hands.*

          STELLA
Take Bridie's drowned pup back where you found it. We don't want to feed his prejudices, I've had pre-knowledge of Jake Swales' cut and thrust methods – and I believe what you say, Grace.
       (*collects bottle and glasses*)
The question, we the Asquith women and Grandma must ask ourselves is, how safe are we in killer hands?

**SCENE 6**

INT. STOCKDALE FARMS - STELLA'S KITCHEN - 5 PM

*We see STELLA, JAKE, GRACE, SOPHIE, SPENCER and BLANCHE present.*

*BLANCHE is seated in SOPHIE'S place. SOPHIE on HARRY'S chair. We see STELLA placing large piece of boiled ham in the centre of the table, slices already cut.*

          STELLA
       *(pleasantly)*
Help yourselves to ham ...
       *(sits down)*
It needs to be eaten up, and feel free to make up your own sandwiches with raw salad or savoury between ...

          SPENCER
       *(helping himself generously)*
I'll be testing the implements ready for haytime - don't want any hold-ups particularly if the weather holds up.

          STELLA
Yes, indeed. As you all know, Sophie and I inspected the meadows this afternoon.

          SOPHIE
       *(looks at SPENCER)*
We usually start haytime on the first Monday of June.
       *(smiles)*
Weather permitting ...

JAKE
*(stabs his fork into slices of ham)*
Aye. We can always tell weather by formation o' clouds.
*(spreads butter over bread)*
Aye, clouds movin' higher an' whiter inta blue sky we call them fair weather signs ...
*(places ham onto bread)*
Old John always said, clouds were weathermen of the heavens, but then ...
*(pauses to looks at SPENCER in a baleful way)*
We don't expect thee t' know owt about thee family. Weel ... tha nivver knew ought about Asquiths.

BLANCHE
*(peacemaker)*
And they're dead and gone and God only knows where ...
*(turns to STELLA)*
What I want to know is, are you and the girls going to Mottley Show this Monday?

STELLA
I don't see why not, but of course, it won't seem the same without Sam being there –

SOPHIE
This year we've not entered any livestock into any local agricultural

                    shows, Grandma, as a mark of respect
                    to Daddy.


                              STELLA
                         (pats SOPHIE'S arm)
                    I'm sure your father wouldn't condone
                    us, anyone of us, to stay at home, and
                    it would be simply churlish not to go.
                    Everyone knows that.


                              GRACE
                    I'm not too fussed about going, so
                    Grandma can have my ticket.


                              SOPHIE
                    And it's Harry's day off, so we're
                    going into town, shopping.

They all settle down to eating - except STELLA aided by the
bilberry wine cruising hither and thither through her veins
with soothing and deceptive mildness.


                              STELLA
                         (sublimely)
                    I've been thinking ...

STELLA brushes bread crumbs from her curved mouth - all stop
eating to stare at her - each seeing a link coming between
that moment and things that have happened earlier in the day.


                              STELLA
                    Yes! My mind's made up ...
                         (smile hovers on her lips, her
                         gaze covers extended family)
                    I've decided to go ahead and place an
                    order for a milking machine.

*Silence deepens around the table, each knowing these machines operate by electricity.*

*BLANCHE has an involuntary coughing fit – then peers around the seated ones without showing any signs of comprehension – so helps herself to another thick slice of boiled ham.*

>                    SOPHIE
>                   (kindly)
>        Gracious me, Mam. That will suit Grace
>        and myself right down to the ground.

*SOPHIE helps herself to a second helping of new potatoes.*

*SPENCER nudges butter dish to SOPHIE'S reach, while he casts a favourable glance at STELLA.*

>                    GRACE
>           (with her hand round the pickle
>            jar, speaks with feeling)
>        Well! I can see before haytime is
>        over, between us, we can expect to
>        learn much more than a few dance
>        techniques, and some of us may even
>        learn to fly!

>                   SPENCER
>        Petrol! A petrol milking machine,
>        that's what 'Ella's talking about.

*JAKE looks conspiratorially from SPENCER to STELLA and back again, then his eyes flicker unfavourably on SOPHIE'S neck brace and limp wrist.*

*We see JAKE take another stab at the ham, then plaster it with mustard.*

JAKE

Petrol! Ah petrol machine?

    *(darts accusing eyes at*
    *SPENCER)*

Tha'll be tellin' us next tha brought it all t' way from bloody Canada!

STELLA

    *(squares her shoulders, raises*
    *her head haughtily)*

Sam had it all in-hand before he left us, I'm merely carrying out his wishes, besides, he felt it was time Sophie and myself had a rest from tugging and pulling about beneath the dairy cows' udders, and ...

BLANCHE

    *(earnestly, while reaching out*
    *for another cup of tea)*

There's nothing like feverish activity to rid the mind of brooding.

STELLA

    *(with effluence)*

The principals are ...

*STELLA takes quick little sips of tea – curling her little finger accordingly.*

STELLA

Petrol engine – all copper pipes laid throughout all cow-houses. Rubber tubes. Four suctional teat tubes attached to each unit per cow ...

*STELLA looks expansively around the seated diners – her eyes bright with purpose, she holds their attention.*

          STELLA

But here I go again – talking – and talking away.
    *(rises swiftly from her chair)*
There's nothing I'd like better than to stay here and keep talking to you, all, about this marvellous machine, but as you know, we simply do not have the time.

          SOPHIE
    *(excitedly)*
When can we expect this milking machine to arrive? And when will it be installed?

          STELLA
Wednesday. And all going well the equipment should be properly erected and working by Friday.

*STELLA'S smile is refined from sensuality. She looks almost angelical.*

*SPENCER leans forward and grasps the remains of the ham by the hind part of the thigh bone and salutes STELLA with it.*

          SPENCER
To the future of Stockdale and to the Asquith women for being so tolerant and so well intentional, and with no earthly sense of the impossible ...
    *(looks at each in turn)*

                    And I guess, will dare almost anything
                    once.

SPENCER laughs. He looks attractive - freewheeling and
wickedly magnetic. The women feel almost drawn to his
scintillating personality.

                              STELLA
                    I think a celebration would be in
                    keeping, how about Saturday or Sunday
                    night?

JAKE sits perfectly still, expression dead-pan, as the diners
smile - then laugh - BLANCHE picks up her dessert spoon and
taps the table surface repeatedly, in high spirits they pick
up a utensil and beat out a random tune.

SPENCER rises gracefully from the table and heads for outside
door. STELLA'S cheeks look rosy - inviting - she's sheds ten
years in a flash. GRACE finds it hard to avoid STELLA'S
smiling eyes. SOPHIE, thrilled to bits - abandons her arm-
sling as they jostle for the kitchen outside door.

                              SPENCER
                         (leading the way out)
                    To my way of thinking, England
                    compared to the developing countries
                    is well behind intensive farming
                    methods. It has to catch up or it will
                    surely be left behind ...

BLANCHE and JAKE remain seated, as the lively voice fades
from earshot.

BLANCHE studies JAKE'S expressions over the rim of her teacup
- a dark face. Dark with bitter resentment. A face riddled

with jealousy and ill-feelings, yet he's sat so still ... so unlike him.

                   BLANCHE
You know as well as I do, Jake, that given time, a proceeding son has to be followed in a case of the like-kind ...

JAKE'S silence is unyielding.

                   BLANCHE
             (conversationally)
And it's so unlike you to be so wooden - so still - so quiet ...
             (casts another coveted look at
             JAKE)
You rather remind me of the grandfather clock I had for years and years. I'd become so accustomed to its ticking that I only noticed it when it stopped ...

BLANCHE rises from the chair and begins to clear away the tea things. JAKE stays mute.

                   BLANCHE
             (mildly as though talking to
             herself)
About our Stella and Spencer ...
             (slips cups and saucers into
             washing-up bowl)
It may take more than dovetailing Stockdale Farms to make two such impervious individuals communicate without causing a deal of problems ...

BLANCHE swishes soap flakes amongst crockery.

JAKE grim faced, moves to take a stubbed out cigarette and spare match out of waistcoat pocket. He strikes match against underside of table. He gulps smoke away deep down into his lungs.

> JAKE
> (voice rasping)
> Bastard! The fuckin' bastard!

BLANCHE flinches and clatters tea things in sink to mark her disapproval.

> JAKE
> Let's hope t' mongrel bastard doesn't get t' bloody greedy an' feel need t' grab thee daughter's share as well as his own, then buggers off leavin' only big drag marks outside Stockdale's main gateway.

JAKE scrapes his chair back against kitchen wall and elevates himself upright to affront BLANCHE. She stares back at him.

> JAKE
> (he bawls straight into her face)
> <u>An' where t' hell would t' start bloody lookin' for him?</u>
> (through clenched teeth)
> In some sodden foreign developin' country?

JAKE charges out of the kitchen doorway, cursing – unheard of words to BLANCHE – she knows what he is getting at.

> BLANCHE
> *(mutters to herself)*
> That old man is setting seeds ... I remember Sam Asquith saying, "Murder's always best when it imitates natural causes".

## SCENE 7
**I/E. VALETED ROVER AND HUMBER CARS - STOCKDALE FARMS - 8 PM**

*Saturday night celebration, and both the Rover and the Humber cars are standing on the forecourt, engines ticking over.*

*We see SPENCER settling as smooth as cream onto driver seat of Humber. JAKE begrudgingly scrubbed down - determined not to be left out - sits in passenger seat. SOPHIE (without neck brace) and HARRY climb happily onto the back seat.*

*We see GRACE arranging herself on the driver's seat of the Rover, and BLANCHE settling herself on passenger's seat. STELLA positioning herself on the back seat.*

*We hear the slamming of car doors.*

*We see SPENCER winding down front window - thrusts his head out with celerity.*

> SPENCER
> *(shouting across to Rover car)*
> <u>See you all in the Wheat Sheaf in half an hour.</u>

*We see SPENCER press his foot on the accelerator and speeds through the water-splash.*

*GRACE drives some distance behind.*

                    STELLA
                (repositions herself on back
                seat of the Rover)
            Good to tell it's not his car, and
            he's not footing the petrol
            arrangements.

                    BLANCHE
                (leans back contentedly on seat
                and lights cigarette at
                leisure)
            You know ...

BLANCHE, squinting through veil of smoke discharging from rear-end of Humber car.

                    BLANCHE
                (speaks slowly)
            I can't help feeling that a thing that
            has been hidden away for so long, and
            left quiet about for so long ...
                (exhales cigarette vapours)
            Then there's a damn good reason and a
            damn good case for leaving it right
            there.

STELLA smooths her fine wool rustic suit about her shapely legs.

                    STELLA
                (snarls)
            It's a family trait! And we've no
            telling how much perverse pleasure Sam
            got from raking up the past and
            throwing it right back onto our
            doorstep!

STELLA raises her eyes – resisting eyes – just in time to see the Humber round the bend on the cart-road.

                    STELLA
After all, Mother, by producing and now exhibiting a son – even an illegitimate son into our female midst, Sam knew he had a real chance of passing the Asquith name into yet another generation ...
          *(pause)*
Quite unlike his own daughters who will submerge his identity into other men's families ...

                    GRACE
The price of belonging to a patriarch.

GRACE keeps a keen eye on SPENCER as she swings the car out of the main gateway.

                    BLANCHE
It's strange when one comes to think about it ...
          *(climbs out of Rover to close last gate behind them, then returns)*
Sam must have been about seventy years old last year. You married an old timer, our Stella.
          *(pause)*
Even worse, he wasn't ready to die.

STELLA eyes the back of BLANCHE'S head, retrospectively.

STELLA

*(speaks in such a way to mean more than just farming)*

Of course Sam was starting to get on a bit in years, not that it seemed to slow him down at all.

STELLA looks discontented.

BLANCHE

*(looks over her shoulder at STELLA)*

Never mind, lass. I can't help feeling that some sides of marriage tend to be overrated ...

*(frowns)*

After your father was killed in the First World War, I had more than one relationship over the years, and after making some physical and mental calculations, I came to the conclusion, I'd rather settle for a good cup of tea and a good cigarette, any day.

STELLA

*(mutters)*

That puts it into a nutshell. Women are impelled by duty and loyalty, all at the price of a seven and six licence.

GRACE takes the bend at Kayshaw top with unmaidenly velocity.

GRACE

Hertz was wonderful. So wonderful it

>           all seemed too natural – too natural
>           for words.

And before discontented STELLA and BLANCHE can put into words: Just as well, when he could not string together half a dozen English words! – They find themselves at the top of Kayshaw Hill.

>                       STELLA
>               (stares down the ascending
>               hill, shouting)
>       For God's sake, Grace, slow down!

We see a strange faculty of vision – we see, GRACE no longer GRACE, but a newly-risen image of SAM.

>                       STELLA
>                   (screaming)
>       I'm going to hell!

>                       BLANCHE
>               (looking pettifoggery)
>       Hell's bells – our Grace ...
>               (clamps hands to her ears)
>       I can hear my past sins making
>       personal acquaintance ...
>               (screws eyes up tightly)
>       Their almost a bewildering pain ...

We see the Rover speed down the steep banked hill – speed needle no longer registering.

>                       GRACE
>                   (painfully)
>       I still remember Hertz with profound
>       enduring love ...

We see a flash of the railway station coming into view at the bottom of the hill – village store – public ale house, smoke coming from its chimney – row of terrace houses – hump-backed bridge.

>                    GRACE
>                (desperately)
>     I still feel ... love ... I taste ...
>     smell ... I knew Hertz ...
>                (pause)
>     So well ...

We see the Rover speeding through the village – buildings all a blur.

>                    GRACE
>     Hertz had a terrible tenderness which
>     was both joy and anguish ...
>                (pause, voice breaks)
>     And from what I read in his eyes ...

We see STELLA and BLANCHE'S staring eyes switch from the speed clock on the dashboard to affix GRACE with hot pricking eyes.

GRACE, oblivious to their disorders – nods to her own view of mind, she's smiling lovingly.

>                    GRACE
>     I've never before or since felt so
>     strongly in the wonderful, magnetic
>     power of the attraction of a man ...

STELLA looks unnerved at GRACE'S bold confession.

BLANCHE stares at GRACE'S profile with strained intentness.

*We see the village behind them as GRACE stops being emotional as quickly as she started.*

                GRACE
        *(blinks herself back to the*
          *present, moderates her driving)*
I don't quite know what came over me – I hope my outburst will be taken with good faith.

               BLANCHE
        *(pats GRACE'S knee in a*
          *disorderly way)*
You know, flower. I didn't really mind the war years at all. The blackouts were dreary, but on the whole people seemed to be more friendly and more wholesome than they were before the war ...

               STELLA
        *(her over-bright eyes dart*
          *everywhere for want of clarity)*
War! I'm profoundly glad to see I'm still on planet earth.
        *(clears throat)*
War! The upshot of it all was Hitler and Mussolini, Lord Woolton and ration books, and not forgetting all the frugal war-efforts.
        *(pause)*
Those men! All those fathers, brothers, sons and cousins – all used as fodder for the War Lords!

GRACE

*(abruptly)*

People who live in glass houses shouldn't throw stones.

*(pause)*

Remember! Father had a hand in the fodder war-effort!

STELLA

*(recovering)*

You're saying it, Grace, not us, but you're right, only don't put the full blame on your father. Hertz and Jake had a hand in the matter too, and Hinchcliffe ...

GRACE

*(resounding bellow of a she-bull standing her ground)*

<u>No! No!</u>

*GRACE again drives fast to foreshadow tears and torment of mind.*

BLANCHE

No wonder nasty Jake Swales has his boots planted so firmly under the Stockdale table – I need another cigarette before I can think straight.

*BLANCHE lights up, inhales, exhales smoke.*

STELLA

*(gritting her teeth)*

It's amazing what you can stomach if you have to.

>           *(rearranges herself)*
>
>     Bloody amazing.

*STELLA quaffs up her hair – opens handbag – removes gold powder compact and powders her face, pinching pallid cheeks, applies ruby red lipstick to moving lips – pops cosmetics back into handbag – closes clasp with a lucid snap!*

>                  BLANCHE
>           *(wantonly generous)*
>     In the war years, everything was cut
>     and dried. I mean, some men I had the
>     acquaintance of – briefly – an
>     American service man who was like a
>     house on fire – I had to curb his
>     enthusiasm with, "Is this going to
>     take long or have you finished?"

*The women smile knowingly.*

>                  BLANCHE
>     And another rather blatant Home Guard
>     – whom I found out later – was a
>     jobbing chimney sweep ...

>                  STELLA
>           *(mutters)*
>     Oh ... Mother ...

>                  GRACE
>           *(murmurs)*
>     Grandma ...

>                  BLANCHE
>           *(good naturedly)*
>     Well, men were scarce in the war years

>           – anyway – to cut a long story short,
>           he didn't look at the mantle-piece
>           when he poked the fire.
>                   *(pauses to light another*
>                   *cigarette)*
>           And do you know? I don't think men do
>           ... they think women prefer a large
>           member ...
>                   *(laughs good naturedly)*
>           When really women would rather have a
>           smaller busier one ...

*BLANCHE'S comments lift STELLA and GRACE'S spirits up no end. They smile and look humoured.*

>                           BLANCHE
>                   *(happily)*
>           I blame the war ...
>                   *(pause)*
>           It seemed to encourage and inspire
>           such propensity.

## SCENE 8
**EXT. WHEAT SHEAF INN CARPARK – 8:35 PM**

*We see the Rover heading down ancient high street of Holbridge, GRACE swings the steering wheel into the Wheat Sheaf's carpark, to immediately spot the Humber. BLANCHE stubs out her cigarette.*

*We see SOPHIE and HARRY waving, smiling, walking to meet the Rover. SPENCER stands looking ready for anything within reason. JAKE contrived to look benevolent, keen, hearty, bland but knowledgeable.*

*STELLA steps out of the Rover, throwing wide glances towards* all.

> STELLA
> *(exaltation in her voice)*
> Hello again. Let's see how the other half live.

## SCENE 9
## INT. WHEAT SHEAF INN - BAR-ROOM - 8:36 PM

*We see STELLA, SOPHIE, HARRY, GRACE, BLANCHE, SPENCER and JAKE trouping into the bar-room, they're met with a noticeable silence as they head for the high-backed wooden settles arranged against whitewashed walls with oak tables and John Smith's beer place mats.*

*We see a DOZEN MEN, mainly farmers and farm-workers, sitting, drinking from pint glasses.*

*We hear sportive comments intermingling with clicks from domino games at the far end of the room.*

*We see an enormous black leaded fireplace with polished horse-brasses hung from leather straps adorning the range firesides.*

*We see long brass fire-irons laid before cast iron fender.*

*We hear a large log hissing and sparking in fire grate.*

> FARMER
> *(not over friendly)*
> Nah then, Mrs Asquith, an' how's t' keepin'?

*This comment brings forth baleful assents and knowing nods as the DOZEN MEN'S alert eyes pass stoically from one visitor to the next to alight with the power of perception upon SPENCER.*

*We see LANDLADY walking across to STOCKDALE fraternity, who are seated.*

> LANDLADY
> *(placing drinks in front of them)*
> Your food and drinks are on the Stockdale account, so enjoy the celebration.

> STELLA
> *(extolling to DOZEN MEN)*
> Good value for money. Sam and I always held our occasions here without any complaints, so don't hold back on Stockdale hospitality, you're all welcome ...

*We see the DOZEN MEN drinking, talking, drinking, laughing, talking.*

> FARMER
> *(passing on way to bar, speaks in drollery tones to SPENCER)*
> Ah thought I'd recognise thee close-up. Aye. Ah can see now tha's tarred wi' same brush ...

> SPENCER
> *(lip curls)*
> Catch-words used without self-consciousness ...

FARMER
*(boldly droll)*
Aye. Ah remember Eve Ridgeholm, by gum, she was an overgrown sort o' woman.
*(drains his glass)*
Ah'll bet thee father, old Sam must ah put solstice umbrage an' oospy-la-la between straw bedding an' horse muck ...
*(laughs)*
Aye, ah almost feel as though I've been there myself.

SPENCER
*(acting macho)*
According to impeccable sources, I'm the end result of the divided ribbon of poverty and privilege.
*(smile aims to scold)*
Yet, everyone seems to like a tale of a life transformed ...

BLANCHE
*(impressed by SPENCER'S jocular attitude and shrewdness)*
You know ...
*(nudges STELLA)*
I don't know whether to condole or condone the ability Spencer has to bypass emotional obstacles, and so quickly ...
*(smiles)*
He can separate feelings from facts with such razor-sharp skill.

                        STELLA
                    (snaps)
                An inbred peculiarity.

STELLA charges off with GRACE to finalise the evening meal arrangements, and check if ABE and WINNY have arrived, leaving BLANCHE to marvel over SPENCER.

## SCENE 10
**INT. WHEAT SHEAF INN - BAR-ROOM - 9 PM**

We see SPENCER catching hold of STELLA'S arm as she sweeps into the bar-room.

                        SPENCER
                    (pleasantly)
                There's something that I'd like to
                show you, 'Ella, before we have a bite
                to eat.

                        STELLA
                    (turns on SPENCER, smooths her
                    hair and smiles bountifully)
                I can't for the life of me imagine
                what you have to say or show me right
                now that can't wait, Spencer.

## SCENE 11
**EXT. WHEAT SHEAF INN - 9:02 PM**

STELLA'S cogitations are cut short as SPENCER steers her through the outside door; across Wheat Sheaf carpark; down the street; over the main town bridge.

We see a fork road sign-post: ST JOHN'S WALK. BECKHOUSE. THE OLD TOWN.

We see SPENCER retrieve STELLA'S elbow and direct her towards The Old Town.

We see an archway branching off from the roadway.

SPENCER
Follow me! 'Ella!

We see SPENCER leading down a dark narrow passage.

STELLA unprepared, lurches from and into a cobbled inner causeway.

We see a row of small houses - windows mostly boarded up. Doors have planks of wood nailed across rotting doorways, others hang insecurely on a single hinge - paintwork peeling.

SPENCER turns to STELLA, his lips curled with efficacy - then he turns away, carrying her whole attention with him as slowly one by one he scans each abandoned house.

SPENCER
I want you to see, 'Ella, where your husband - my father - allowed my mother to live for the last few years of her life ...

SPENCER kicks a front door open. It slams against an inner wall to rebound back and hang relinquished from one rusty hinge.

We see SPENCER marshalling STELLA forward and into the living room. A room straight off the inner street pavement.

### SCENE 12
### INT. EVELYN RIDGEHOLM'S HOUSE - LIVING ROOM - 9:06 PM

*We see damp invading worn out linoleum and rotting skirting-boards; wallpaper hanging from dampened patches - fireside cupboards half-open revealing dishevelled, yellow newspaper linings - a black leaded fireplace where a fall of soot fills the grate to overflow onto the hearth below.*

*We see a deep windowsill - a glass vase marked with a dank waterline containing a bunch of decomposed flowers.*

### SCENE 13
### INT. EVELYN RIDGEHOLM'S HOUSE - KITCHEN - 9:07 PM

*We see STELLA moving slowly into the kitchen. The only thing standing is a chipped earthenware sink with dripping tap.*

### SCENE 14
### INT. EVELYN RIDGEHOLM'S HOUSE - BEDROOM 1 - 9:08 PM

*We see an empty bedroom.*

### SCENE 15
### INT. EVELYN RIDGEHOLM'S HOUSE - BEDROOM 2 - 9:08 PM

*We see a room furnished singularly with chipped enamel bedsteads and discoloured bare mattress.*

*STELLA, white-faced, eyes large, mouth small. She is appalled.*

### SCENE 16
### INT. EVELYN RIDGEHOLM'S HOUSE - STAIRCASE - 9:09 PM

*We see SPENCER standing, waiting at foot of stairs.*

*We see STELLA taking each downward stair slowly. Body erect.*

              SPENCER
You'll probably know John Asquith paid the annual rent and when he died that obligation passed over to Father.

*We see STELLA, for once in her life, lost for words.*

              SPENCER
       *(with rising truculence)*
Eighteen months after I was born, Mother married a local joiner, and before we emigrated to Australia, Grandma Ridgeholm moved in with us to hold this property for anyone of us – if and when we decided to return home ...

*We see SPENCER move aside as STELLA'S feet touch the ground floor. STELLA grips the banister's carved knob for support.*

              STELLA
The Asquith business was often, a closed book – even to me.

              SPENCER
       *(harshly)*
A small price to pay for keeping our mouths closed.
       *(pause)*
Would you not agree, 'Ella?

*STELLA stifles the need to escape – to avoid any altercations. She reverts from present, to previous way of thinking.*

                    STELLA
               *(speaks with caution)*
          Sam was very meticulous, very exact in
          regarding facts.
               *(coughs dampness away)*
          Small gifts gave Sam a great deal of
          pleasure - and - at the same time, I
          believe - helped him to paper over his
          conscience.

*STELLA does not smile, instead gives an apologetic gesture.*

## SCENE 17
**EXT. EVELYN RIDGEHOLM'S HOUSE - BACK-YARD - 9:11 PM**

*We see STELLA staggering outside for fresh air to sanitise her senses.*

*We see a back-yard with outside toilet - door ajar - washed grey.*

*STELLA averts her eyes and steps into the garden. A long and narrow strip of land.*

*We see entangled grasses and weeds beneath the walls, gooseberry and blackcurrant bushes, almost overcome by nettles and thistles.*

*We see an old lean-to green-house has a mountain ash tree thrusting its boughs through the window-less centre. A clothes line, dirty and weathered hangs forlornly between a leaning post and a gnarled branch growing from the single apple tree.*

*We see STELLA turning uneasily away.*

                        STELLA
                (muttering to herself)
            How long can a woman remain outraged
            and affronted ...?

*We see STELLA retracing her steps slowly back through the garden and yard, back into the house.*

## SCENE 18
**INT. EVELYN RIDGEHOLM'S HOUSE – LIVING ROOM – 9:13 PM**

*SPENCER is watching STELLA.*

                        SPENCER
                (abruptly)
            Not too dull for you, I hope, 'Ella. I
            know you and I have not always
            harmonised and I don't expect we'll
            always agree in the future.

                        STELLA
                (swings round to face him,
                speech is hesitant)
            Spencer ...
                (she gives him an exquisite
                troubled but brilliant smile)
            You have no idea how much all this
            squalor has disturbed me.

*We see STELLA'S hair illuminated by the saffron light rays shafting through the open front door, giving her a brightness to behold.*

*We see SPENCER staring back at STELLA. Remembering ...*

SPENCER'S MEMORY – The first day SPENCER met STELLA, when

she'd leaned against the bottom yard gate – the smiling face – her undiluted beauty illuminating in the spring sunrays – remembering again – how strongly she had appealed to his favoured complexity in love.

We see SPENCER suddenly blinking himself alert, as STELLA walks through the living room door, heading for the outer-front door.

>                    SPENCER
>               (shouting, sprints over damp
>               linoleum)
>          Just a minute, 'Ella.

## SCENE 19
**EXT. EVELYN RIDGEHOLM'S HOUSE - 9:14 PM**

We see STELLA poised on front door step. She turns.

>                    STELLA
>                 (composed)
>          You mean, there's more?

SPENCER edges himself out of the doorway to gesture with a sweep of his arm along the breath and length of the terrace houses.

>                    SPENCER
>          Yes, much more. These cottages were
>          all under Compulsory Purchase Order
>          when I returned home for Mother's
>          funeral. Father had the order lifted,
>          and whatever his reasons being – he
>          then bequeathed them to me ...

STELLA begins to shake with emotional shock.

                    STELLA
                 *(turns paler)*
            Lifted! Bequeathed!

*While SPENCER talks, STELLA looks as though she could faint.*

                    SPENCER
            Yes. Lifted and willed to me.
                 *(casts a cold eye about his*
                 *forbearings)*
            In the 1930s I understand Father
            bought them lock, stock and barrel in
            the slump.
                 *(lips twist)*
            Mother said at the time he had reasons
            behind reasons, keeping the last
            reason to himself.

**SCENE 20**

**INT. HINCHCLIFFE'S OFFICE – DAY (SPENCER'S MEMORY)**

*HINCHCLIFFE is reading out SAM'S will.*

                    HINCHCLIFFE
            Woodclose ... Ah ... Yes ...

*We see HINCHCLIFFE lighting a fresh cigar. His voice fades to a soliloquy of five words as though offering drinks and his facial expressions disappear behind clouds of emitting smoke.*

                    HINCHCLIFFE
                 *(repeating in a loop)*
            Two ups and two downs ...

**SCENE 21**

**EXT. EVELYN RIDGEHOLM'S HOUSE - 9:16 PM**

*SPENCER looks forthright at STELLA.*

                  SPENCER
              *(sedulously)*
        The way I see things, I have one and another option open to me.

*STELLA moistens her dry lips while anticipating. SPENCER slowly spreads out his fingers, thoughtfully.*

                  SPENCER
        As I'm financially embarrassed right now, due to our gentleman's agreement.
              *(pause)*
        I could sell these properties as a whole to the Borough Council for demolition, as Father intended to do - I believe the council were proposing to build bungalows here for the elderly, or, I could sell my share of Stockdale Farms, next spring, so the proceeds would naturally go to renovating the whole row of cottages back to their original state.

*We see STELLA suddenly clutching at the rotting door-frame for support, struggling to conceal her fury and renewed murderous thoughts - turning her head away from him and with sheer willpower she rearranges her deadly thoughts to feign gormlessness.*

                  STELLA
    Sell?!

                    SPENCER
                  *(sternly)*
          Stella! Did you hear a single word
          I've just spoken?

                     STELLA
          I was wondering ... transiently ... do
          they have dinner at teatime in Canada?

## SCENE 22
**EXT. WHEAT SHEAF INN - CARPARK - 9:21 PM**

*We see STELLA over-hastily returning, alone to the Wheat Sheaf. She is charging up to the Humber car, she heaves the car bonnet up and over - peering into the mechanics, rummaging in handbag for gloves.*

*We see STELLA fingering oily plugs - untwisting bolts - pulling wires while issuing confounded orders to an imaginary mechanic.*

*We see STELLA close bonnet - whip off gloves with action of finality.*

## SCENE 23
**INT. WHEAT SHEAF INN - ENTRANCE - 9:23 PM**

*We see STELLA entering the Wheat Sheaf, to be met by HARRY.*

                     HARRY
                  *(concerned)*
          Mrs Asquith. We've all been waiting
          for you to start the meal off ...
                  *(looks beyond her down the
                  passage)*
          Have you seen Spencer?

               STELLA
          (trying to recover memory)
     When did you last see him?

We see SOPHIE hard on HARRY'S heels, she sees STELLA'S
distress.

We see STELLA'S face looking grey in electric light and a
muscle twitching peculiarly in her left cheek.

               SOPHIE
          (concerned)
     Don't move an inch, Mam. I'll get you
     a good stiff drink.
          (pause)
     You look keyed-up and washed out.

We see SOPHIE hastily disappear from view.

We see HARRY re-adjusting his spectacles. He looks carefully
at STELLA.

               HARRY
     Your friends from the Bridge Club ...
          (pause)
     Sorry, I didn't catch their names,
     they've arrived and ...

We see SOPHIE breeze back into sight. She's holding forth a
noble offering of brandy. She thrusts it into STELLA'S
crooked fingers.

               STELLA
          (gratefully)
     Thank you, dear Sophie ...

We see and hear STELLA gulping the ardent spirit down her
throat with pronounced noises, before she vacillates down the
passage towards dining room, trying to hold onto herself.

We see ABE advancing towards STELLA.

                    ABE
               (sardonic quality)
          Don't want t' butt in, like - but did
          missus and mesen see thee an' that
          Canadian slippin' up t' Old Town about
          half an hour ago?

We see ABE standing in STELLA'S pathway, encumbering her
vision.

                    STELLA
          I really don't know what you saw, Abe.
               (makes gesture of defiance)
          But it's a chastening thought though.

STELLA elbows ABE aside.

We see WINNY suddenly bob out from behind ABE.

                    WINNY
          Ah, there you are, Stella, dear.
               (she looks friendly enough to
               please, but not at any price)
          You're late as usual, Stella, and some
          foods don't stand well, and yes, Dick
          Yates could only come for a drink, so
          he's gone and ...
               (eyes rake STELLA up and down
               with diligence)
          Oh yes, where did you and that Spencer

>                    abscond to? The Old Town ... his
>                    mother's place ... Tell me, Stella
>                    dear, is it true, Sam bought the whole
>                    lot for a song in the thirties slump?
>                    Crafty old sod! And Stella, dear what
>                    shameful reasons ...

*We see STELLA'S lips tighten to WINNY'S inference.*

>                              STELLA
>                    I think it's a great deal more
>                    shameful to be riddled with envy of
>                    others while believing in your own
>                    pretence of liking them ...
>                              *(takes a prodigious breath and*
>                              *dredges up a thin smile)*
>                    And more to the point, Sam would not
>                    have condoned these derogative scraps
>                    of inside knowledge leaking out and
>                    into the location.

*WINNY'S head gives a little wobble of discontentment.*

>                              WINNY
>                    Mere conjecture ...

*DR LIDDLE, aged 72, suddenly appears and aligns himself to STELLA.*

>                              DR LIDDLE
>                              *(gravely)*
>                    Now, now, Stella, lass.
>                              *(gives STELLA'S arms little*
>                              *absurd pats, smiles radiantly)*
>                    In my long experience there are two
>                    kinds of women. Those whose pleasure

would become less if they knew they had to share a privilege with the family, and those whose pleasure would be all the more greater ...

                    STELLA
              (fends DR LIDDLE off)
In my experience, so many women in our farming families seem to be judged mainly on their working ability, and I can't help thinking – often – if Sam had lived me out, when commiserated, he would have said without batting an eyelid, "Aye, she was a grand old worker". Not – I loved her.

                    ABE
           (with no apparent absence of
              mind, speaks earnestly)
Ah feel that way mesen.

*WINNY takes possession of the situation – she is hungry.*

                    WINNY
How can you men expect women to take you seriously when you have willies? And stiff willies have no conscience!

*With these homely philosophical words, WINNY leads the way into the dining room.*

## SCENE 24
**INT. WHEAT SHEAF INN – DINING ROOM – 9:26 PM**

*We see JAKE already seated and helping himself generously to food and drink.*

>           ABE
>       *(repellently)*
> By hell!
>       *(plonks himself between STELLA*
>       *and BLANCHE, turns to STELLA)*
> That Jake Swales goes well beyond the
> ordinary bounds o' the farm-man. His
> insolence stands out like a bloody
> sore thumb in ah poke. Sack him!

## SCENE 25
## INT. WHEAT SHEAF INN - DINING ROOM - 11:40 PM

*We see the remains of a splendid meal set out with fourteen people dining and wine drinking, talking - smiling - eating - laughing. The meal is rounding off with coffee, brandy, cigarettes and cigars.*

*STELLA manages to collar GRACE in a furtive half-minute, and GRACE listens because STELLA wants to her listen.*

>           STELLA
>       *(snarls)*
> Selling his Stockdale share ...
> inherited unknown cottages ...
> interfered with Humber brakes, don't
> let Sophie ride home in Humber ...
> twist her arm if you have to ...

## SCENE 26
## EXT. WHEAT SHEAF INN - CARPARK - 11:59 PM

*We see the party break up - rain has set in for the night. We hear the midnight chimes.*

*DR LIDDLE and his resplendent WIFE leave first - followed by*

STELLA'S BRIDGE CRONIES, who look excited rather than gratified or dismayed by SPENCER'S free-wheeling attention and bachelor status.

ABE, with bilberry complexion is bombastically cranking away at his Austin car until he's breathless, giddy and soaking wet – WINNY, over-fed and inebriated is slumped, snoring on the back seat – finally the engine ticks over.

ABE in tardiness, shakes a few hands, heaves himself onto driver's seat, puts his foot down and heads home.

## SCENE 27
**INT. WHEAT SHEAF INN – GENTS – 12.01 AM**

JAKE – not a big drinker – we see is shadow fighting and cursing imaginary people in the gents.

SPENCER and HARRY marshal JAKE out.

## SCENE 28
**EXT. WHEAT SHEAF INN – CARPARK – 12:02 AM**

SPENCER and HARRY frogmarch JAKE onto the back seat of the Humber car – where JAKE collapses – trumping and belching.

We see SOPHIE spluttering and coughing, staggering off back seat of Humber.

>SOPHIE
>Contemptible old man ...

We see STELLA and GRACE conducting hard on SOPHIE'S heels. They grab her and bungle her head-first into the Rover.

> STELLA
> *(snaps)*
> Sit on our Sophie if necessary, Grace!

> SOPHIE
> *(gulps down a sob and sobers up quickly, to GRACE)*
> Don't treat me like a child, I'm already reminded of the feelings I use to have when our parents quarrelled in front of me - and you.

*We see GRACE climb onto back seat next to SOPHIE. They hold hands.*

*We see BLANCHE, tiddly, bumping her way clumsily onto passenger seat of the Rover - a damp cigarette dangles from her moving lips.*

> BLANCHE
> *(happily)*
> I'm determined not to miss anything good or happy that comes my way, now or in the future.
> *(slams car door shut, throws cigarette out of window)*
> Thank God, my Stella's not short of brass ...

*We see STELLA flanking the driver's side of the Rover. She is fired with the black-market brandy and ruthless demeanour. She dives onto driving seat and slams the door shut against the pouring rain and outsiders.*

*We hear the Rover and Humber's engines running.*

We see SPENCER pulling out of Wheat Sheaf carpark - he pips the motor horn jauntily, then turns the wheels right.

STELLA turns the Rover's wheels left.

## SCENE 29
### EXT. STOCKDALE FARMS - WATER-SPLASH - 5 AM

The rain has subsided - thunder in the distance.

We see GRACE and BRIDIE herding DAIRY COWS through water-splash. The cattle leisurely head for their known cow-houses. We hear the petrol machine engine's frequency - loudly.

## SCENE 30
### INT. STOCKDALE FARMS - BOTTOM COW-HOUSE - 5:05 AM

We see STELLA and GRACE wiping down COWS' udders and teats with hessian cloths, to start milking commencement.

          STELLA
       (alert)
No signs of Spencer or Jake - even Harry - anywhere.

          GRACE
       (vigilantly)
No. Spencer would have been up and about by four-thirty, herding the dairy cows out of pastures, and Jake ...

          STELLA
Would have been hard on his heels. That's been his job for the last fifty years.

                    GRACE
          I know. Jake, only said the other day,
          that he never knew what heart-burn was
          until Spencer showed up ...
                    *(picks up milk unit from*
                    *causeway)*
          Only he didn't say Spencer, he said -

                    STELLA
          One filthy expletive after another.

*STELLA emerges from behind LUCILLA'S hind-quarters, and reaches for the bristle brush.*

                    STELLA
                    *(with diffraction)*
          These petrol milking machines are a
          blessing in disguise. If only we'd
          known this option to an electric one
          ...

                    GRACE
          Is Grandma still in the dark about our
          riddance plans?

                    STELLA
          Yes! There would be ructions if she
          knew.

*We see STELLA manoeuvring the brush bristles down the cow-house grip to separate animal urine from faeces, so that the discharged liquid can run down into the draining system.*

                    STELLA
                    *(adamantly)*
          I can see already that Grandma has

turned round to Spencer's way of
thinking - and ...
>   *(swills brush head under
>   causeway tap)*

Our Sophie, I noticed lately, is
bonding with her half-brother -

                    GRACE
Yes! And I've notice, Jake has noticed
our Sophie's leaning towards him too -
Jake needs watching.

## SCENE 31
**I/E. STOCKDALE FARMS - COW-HOUSE NEXT TO FARM - 7 AM**

*We see STELLA and GRACE entering the last cow-house situated to the adjoining dairy milk cooling department.*

*We hear the distinct sound of a vehicle arriving above the hissing and suction of the teat tubes. We hear BRIDIE barking a warning.*

                    STELLA
                *(vigilant)*
Not Jake's driving. I can tell his
riving at the gears a mile off ...

                    GRACE
                *(listening attentively)*
And the sounds aren't Spencer's speedy
composition, and Bridie would not be
barking so intensively.

*We hear two doors slamming shut - the front and the more distant sound of a far back door.*

                        STELLA
                So one has returned!

*STELLA and GRACE exchange a signalling look, and instantly
return to attending to the business of milking the DAIRY
COWS.*

*We hear boots pounding outside on the stone flagged yard –
then approaching footsteps, outside half-closed cow-house
door, followed by a pause – then door thrust open.*

*We see policeman's helmet protruding, then the whole figure
framed in the doorway.*

                        CONSTABLE
                Mrs. Asquith?

*We see STELLA, partly emerging from behind MARIGOLD'S
hindquarters. She is carrying a spare milk unit.*

*We see GRACE playing for time, as she bends the rubber air
pipe to cut the suction power off – so she can busy herself
refitting the milking cups back onto DAISY'S pendulous teats.*

*We hear the CONSTABLE snapping his fingers together
authoritatively for general attention.*

                        CONSTABLE
                    (repeating louder)
                Mrs. Samuel Asquith?

*We see STELLA lurching across the manure channel, moving as
countryfolk do with animals – at right angles – to the
CONSTABLE'S line of approach. He turns.*

STELLA
(with civility)
I'm Mrs. Sam Asquith.

We see STELLA gripping the moving fingers of the CONSTABLE.

STELLA
What brings you so far out into the Dales, and so early, Constable?

CONSTABLE
(speaks slowly)
Are you the present owner of a maroon Humber vehicle - registration number ...

STELLA
(sublimely)
My dear late husband's. Poor Sam. He was so partial towards Humber cars -

CONSTABLE
(brushes her laments aside impatiently)
One thing at a time, please.

We see his fingers flip through a pocket note book. STELLA stands at bay.

CONSTABLE
The accident was reported by a Mr. Clarence Moorhouse of Sedgefield ...

STELLA
(lively)
Clarence! What's Clarence got to do

with it?

                  CONSTABLE
              *(remonstrating)*
A great deal!

STELLA and GRACE brace themselves.

                  CONSTABLE
On closer inspection Mr. Moorhouse discovered an old man incarcerated in the car boot, smelling heavily of drink and oblivious to his surroundings.

We see the CONSTABLE run his thumb along the ridge of his tongue to turn a page.

                  CONSTABLE
Mr. Moorhouse then found on further ascertain, one of his Swaledale sheep had been run over – killed – and was still lodged beneath the motor car – incidentally, bringing the car to a halt near the edge of Sedgefield stone quarry.

                  GRACE
Quarry!
        *(joins STELLA on the causeway)*
Well. The Humber does goes well uphill, if you push it!

                  CONSTABLE
        *(flicks over to another page)*
Jake Swales ...

>           *(looks from STELLA to GRACE)*
> Do you know a Mr ... Mr. Jake Swales?
> He appears to have lost his memory, or
> at least – perturbation of mind.

*STELLA and GRACE look at each other in mock surprise.*

>             STELLA
>           *(friendly)*
> Know Jake Swales. He's been working
> here at Stockdale Farms for the last
> fifty years ...
>           *(smiles)*
> I can remember as if it was only
> yesterday when Jake –

*The CONSTABLE maliciously decides to impair her reminiscence.*

>             CONSTABLE
> A Francis Spencer-Asquith and a Harry
> Bletchford ...
>           *(consults note book)*
> Driver and passenger of the vehicle
> were earlier found approximately ...
>           *(glances down)*
> One-thirty a.m. wandering injured and
> confused on the Linton to Holbridge
> Road. They were later ambulanced into
> hospital ...

>             STELLA
> Consternation!

*STELLA pants in vain for more words to come to mind, she's finding it impossible.*

                    GRACE
              *(takes control)*
About the extent of the men's
injuries? Could you kindly and quickly
shed some light on this family matter,
Constable, as you can see ...
              *(spreads arms wide and her eyes
              hold their ironical gleam)*
We're very short of man power and well
behind the milking-schedule this
morning – and we don't want to be late
for the milk collecting lorry, or
we'll be chasing the driver from one
neighbour's milk-stand to another ...

                    CONSTABLE
              *(not to be ousted easily by any
              women's talk, proceeds)*
There was only one animal fatal
occurrence. The two men in question –
one I believe to be a close relative
of yours ...

*He looks at them in an intractable sort of way. STELLA and GRACE acknowledge this only with their eyelids.*

                    CONSTABLE
Francis Spencer-Asquith stated that
they – he and Harry Bletchford, left
the car to relieve themselves behind
the wall-back and when they turned
round the vehicle was moving on its
own accord down Linton Road – they
pursued the motor, but in the poor
visibility, they were hit by a passing
motor – the driver refused to stop.

                        GRACE
                (turns to STELLA slowly)
        Would you credit it?


                        STELLA
        And Jake?

*As though well-rehearsed – JAKE appears and elbows passed the CONSTABLE and into the cow-house. He darts glances, not directly at anyone, but between them.*

*We see JAKE gripping a milk bucket in one hand and a three legged milking stool in the other hand. He charges unchallenged to the bottom end of the building – kicks the hock of MURIEL – a robust roan cow – she let's out a surprised bawl, but side-steps neatly as JAKE, lobs himself over the manure channel, to plonk the stool down by her hindquarters.*

*JAKE takes seat – rams bucket between his legs – resting the bottom rim on his cocked boot heels – shoves his head against MURIEL'S flank, while endeavouring to pull away, rhythmically on her pendant teats.*

*We see three sets of shrewd eyes watching JAKE'S precise movements.*

**SCENE 32**
**EXT. STOCKDALE FARMS – FORECOURT – 1:30 PM**

*We see CLARENCE'S wagon pulling up on Stockdale's forecourt.*

*We see STELLA inviting CLARENCE into the farmhouse – she is dressed in riding breeches, close fitted jacket and long leather riding boots.*

**SCENE 33**

**INT. STOCKDALE FARMS - STELLA'S LIVING ROOM - 1:31 PM**

*We see STELLA leading CLARENCE graciously into the living room, where he settles down on an easy chair next to the fire range. STELLA produces two bottles of ale and two glasses.*

> STELLA
> *(pleasantly)*
> Make yourself at home, Clarence, while
> I make you a bite to eat.

**SCENE 34**

**INT. STOCKDALE FARMS - ENTRANCE TO CELLAR - 1:32 PM**

*We see STELLA disappear down into her cellar, to quickly reappear carrying a tray - we see a piece of cooked beef, bread loaf, butter and cheese dish, with a round cake tin balanced above provisions.*

**SCENE 35**

**INT. STOCKDALE FARMS - STELLA'S LIVING ROOM - 1:33 PM**

*We see CLARENCE watching STELLA'S every move as she enters room carrying the loaded tray.*

*We see CLARENCE'S vagary fantasies slowly begin to take expression as he leans back in the easy chair, lulled by the warmth of the fire and nutty brown ale.*

**SCENE 36**

**INT. STOCKDALE FARMS - DAY (CLARENCE'S FANTASY OF STELLA)**

*We see CLARENCE, gazing into the flickering fire flames in STELLA'S living room - a playing field of strategies and exaggerated games as the flames curl and lick away at the* back of the logs like recriminations and sudden reversals of affections.

We see through CLARENCE'S eyes – the fantasist – STELLA clad in soft leather breeches and polished mirroring jackboots – a dashing full-length calfskin Hitler style greatcoat draped carelessly across her bare tanned shoulders.

CLARENCE leans forward, reflectively and makes a series of small enunciating – appreciating sounds – then to enhance vagaries, he tops his image of STELLA with a military hardhat, with a long unicorn horn ... rising from ...

We see CLARENCE'S swift blinks in STELLA'S direction – he sees her nimbly opening the cake tin lid.

            CLARENCE
       (mutters to himself)
  No jumping rails, Clarence ... nothing too lavish ...

We see CLARENCE'S whetted perverse appetite get the better of him, so much so, that we hear him wincing and see him quivering.

            CLARENCE
           (mumbles)
  Don't come now ...

We see through CLARENCE'S fantasy his desperate attempt to transport his mind and body onto a brass hook nailed into diagonal wall to counteract.

We see Holbridge cattle market – we see day old, to week old CALVES enclosed in narrow open pens.

We see AUCTIONEER on platform aiding and abetting FARMERS and BUTCHERS to baiting uppermost prices for veal, and out of the heat-haze, frugally, CLARENCE recalls last week's high prices.

> CLARENCE
> (inaudible)
> By hell ... calfskins' prices will rocket ...

**SCENE 37**
**INT. STOCKDALE FARMS - STELLA'S LIVING ROOM - 1:35 PM**

We see CLARENCE flounder and flounce into a half-lolling position and when the red haze of volatility begins to evaporate, CLARENCE is conscious of blessed STELLA bending over him, showing her teeth like a wild eyed mare looking over a five barred gate.

We see CLARENCE ogling crazily back at STELLA. He makes wild self-defensive motions while struggling to garble gewgaw.

Silence! Intense silence.

We see BLANCHE bustle into the room. She's clearly taken aback to see CLARENCE sat so untidily on SAM'S chair.

> BLANCHE
> Crikey! Give me magpies by the dozen any day! I suppose you've come enquiring about that unfortunate sheep.

CLARENCE does not reciprocate. His mood does not match hers. We see BLANCHE lift boiling kettle off hob and busy herself brewing a pot of tea.

STELLA excuses herself abruptly and leaves the room.

## SCENE 38
**INT. STOCKDALE FARMS - CART-SHED - 9 AM**

We see JAKE checking the horse-drawn cart ready for haytime. His appearance is disreputable. His clothes look slept in and he is unshaven - dead cigarette butt wedged on his lower lip.

We see STELLA entering building forcefully.

>STELLA
>*(firmly but slightly overdone reasonableness)*
>About this accident business, Jake. You're trying my patience. It's high time you gave an explanation or an apology instead of worrying us unduly.

JAKE'S expression becomes forbidding.

>STELLA
>The girls told me yesterday, Spencer said he would be out of hospital by next week, earlier than anyone expects.

>JAKE
>*(snarls)*
>Don't make ah fuckin' hero out o' him!

JAKE stares at STELLA like a dog pointing a game bird, then shoves passed her to check hay-cart's wheel-spokes and felloes. We hear him tapping them roughly with hammer.

                    JAKE
              (gnarls between and through
              striking the hammer down)
        Ah should've cracked open yon
        jackaroo's skull wi' crowbar instead
        o' fartin' about wi' that blasted car
        startin' handle - carried no weight -
        no weight at all!

                    STELLA
        Well! It's not like you to take a
        cavalier attitude toward him.
              (pause)
        And it won't be all that pleasant
        facing Spencer - you'll have to work
        your way around that, Jake. But then,
        things are always slack at this time
        of the year.

*Back in her stride, STELLA marches purposely out of cart-shed.*

## SCENE 39
**INT. STOCKDALE FARMS - BOTTOM COW-HOUSE - 9:03 AM**

*STELLA enters cow-house, where we see GRACE giving a top-coat of whitewash to the walls.*

                    GRACE
              (looks up at STELLA, voice low)
        You look as though you've been saved
        from yourself, Mother.
              (raises eyebrow)
        Such expressions belong to women
        who've upgraded their wardrobes.

STELLA

I've just been trying to quiz Jake about the circumstances surrounding the accident.
   *(looks GRACE straight in the eyes)*
No mention about faulty brakes – thank God, and –

GRACE
   *(edge to her voice)*
Let that be our keepsake, Mam, because if either of us confesses to your demeanour, Jake could suspect you'd been freelancing, and he would automatically jump to the conclusion that we – the Asquith women – were out to rid ourselves of Spencer and himself, leaving Harry to face the music.

*STELLA turns to look out of the mistal window.*

STELLA
   *(slowly)*
Yes ... that's sound advice, lass, our keepsake.
   *(pause)*
And if I'm honest with myself, Jake is beginning to feel rather like a rope round my neck, and, if I allow him to manipulate me, he could, if suspecting any ulterior motive ... on our part ... he would ...

GRACE

(dunks brush into whitewash bucket)

Start with Grandma because every now and then she never lets a thought go unsaid.

STELLA

(nods)

They've never liked each other ever since Grandma retired, when I told your father that I'd love my mother to live much nearer to us, and Grandma agreed she'd love to be settled in next-door ... next to her grandchildren.

(turns away from window)

Jake was incensed, and Sam – your father – in his usual judicial mode, said, "No! Not while Jake Swales is still alive". So that was that.

GRACE

(swills the lime-wash off the brush under indoor tap)

Our Sophie, she's warming up to Spencer. He was the first person she showed Bridie's pups to. And ...

(comes to stand next to STELLA)

she called her chosen pup, Brov'.

STELLA

(coldly)

An abbreviation of brother. No wonder Jake drowned her pup ... Yes ...

(tightens her voice)

> An understatement just to let us know he knows ... A small, but partial change to his way of saying, wild horses will not drag him away from Stockdale Farms.

## SCENE 40

**EXT. STOCKDALE FARMS - FORECOURT - 10:30 AM**

*We see STELLA wearing outlandish hat. She and BLANCHE both in summery style, crossing the forecourt towards the Rover.*

*We see SOPHIE following with BRIDIE. SOPHIE is carrying wicker food basket.*

> BLANCHE
> (to SOPHIE)
> Put the basket in the car boot, flower – and while we're visiting Mottley Agricultural Show, don't stray too far from our Grace, because that nasty old Jake is almost completely inarticulate these days.

> SOPHIE
> (acquiescing)
> Grace and I thought we'd walk into Kayshaw, seeing as it's such a lovely day to see if Mr Holmes will lend us another vehicle while the Humber is being repaired.

*SOPHIE places basket in car boot – STELLA and BLANCHE thank her with a smile.*

*We see STELLA and BLANCHE seating themselves in Rover –*

*STELLA winds down window.*

                    STELLA
                (to SOPHIE)
        We should be back before the cows come
        home – and before Jake finishes
        checking over all the implements ready
        for tomorrow's start to haytime.

*We hear the car engine rev and see the Rover slowly move off the forecourt.*

*We see hands waving and smiling faces before STELLA drives over water-splash to disappear up the cart-road.*

**SCENE 41**

**EXT. MOTTLEY AGRICULTURAL SHOW – SHOW-FIELD – 11:10 AM**

*We see show-field – vehicles of sorts, parked in rows. We hear various sounds of animals bawling and lull of voices. We see YOUNG FARMERS washing, curry-combing, brushing down restless beasts of various breeds, tied by their halters to outside posts.*

*We see STELLA and BLANCHE strolling leisurely in the show-field.*

                    STELLA
                (sociably)
        This is the first time in years that
        we've never shown any livestock here
        at Mottley ...
                (pauses in front of farm
                animals being groomed)
        The girls and I just didn't have the
        heart to enter – that was Sam's

department.

*STELLA and BLANCHE continue to stroll.*

          BLANCHE
     *(links her arm through STELLA'S)*

It seems to be one thing after another since Sam died.
     *(pause)*

I remember the last time I saw your father during the war years, I couldn't bring myself to put the toilet seat down for weeks – I felt so lonely.

          STELLA
     *(kindly)*

Housework always bored you Mother, perhaps you was only making less work for yourself.
     *(smiles)*

On the other hand, you have always been mawkishly tender.

          BLANCHE

Which is more than we can say for Jake.
     *(gives STELLA a measured glance)*

Somehow, I wasn't surprised when you told me while driving here, that he'd tried to kill Spencer – instead he maimed him.
     *(eyes widen)*

Now, that will take some explaining

when the two men are discharged from
hospital.

          STELLA

Moderate embarrassment does no longer
outrage my moral sensibility.

          BLANCHE

I was thinking of your sensibility.

          STELLA

I was thinking purely of me. Right
now, Mother, I fancy bovoroise with
raspberries.

*We see STELLA and BLANCHE come to a halt alongside the bandstand, they're scanning through the show's catalogue.*

*We see The KIRKDALE BRASS BANDSMEN in shirt-sleeves and braces, unpacking, beginning to warm up musical instruments in discord – tuning and retuning.*

*We see BLANCHE turning to face them in anticipation.*

          BLANCHE
            *(turns to STELLA)*

I feel as though I'm standing in front
of a coal-box with a fire-shovel in my
hand.

*STELLA and BLANCHE move on.*

          STELLA
            *(testily)*

If I had to speak disparaging of Sam
Asquith, it would be to say there

should be a conscience clause in every will made, which would impede the person making it from having last minute, conscience pricking feelings towards a hidden family cock-up!

>                    BLANCHE
>                 (supportively)

Now you come to mention cocks, that rather puts me in mind of a chap I once met just after the First World War. He played look-at-me, so proud of his enormous penis-chaffer that I was left sore for days and couldn't walk straight for a week – I've said it before and I'll say it again – if only men knew women in reality prefer a man to have a little busy one rather than a big lazy one! There wouldn't be so much discontentment.

**SCENE 42**
**I/E. MOTTLEY AGRICULTURAL SHOW – MARQUEE – 11:20 AM**

*We see STELLA and BLANCHE making their way towards the crowded Home Produce Marquee.*

*We see displays of forced rhubarb – various brands of onions – marrows – carrots – parsnips – different lettuces and diverse assortments of home-grown fruits and plants – familiar varieties of potatoes and turnips all artistically arranged in clusters of complimentary sizes and colours – all to gain attention and prize money.*

*We see further down: voluntary flower arrangements – embroidery and knitting section.*

We see frugal DALESWOMAN demonstrating how to unpick woollen garments. The DALESWOMAN catches STELLA and BLANCHE'S eyes and STELLA'S remark.

>           STELLA
>       (nudges BLANCHE)
>   That woman over there, has been coming
>   here for donkey years unpicking
>   woollen garments to pieces ...
>
>           DALESWOMAN
>   Tha wraps unravelled wool round a
>   bottle, any bottle as long as it's
>   full o' hot water, an' the heat will
>   do the trick ...

We see STELLA and BLANCHE wandering further down marquee where another DEMONSTRATOR is showing how to cottage-spin raw fleece into yarn, and the degrees of extracting natural dyes from vegetable waste.

>           BLANCHE
>       (soulfully)
>   I blame the wars. It incited all these
>   poverty traps and punitive ways – all
>   those penny-pinching war-efforts! All
>   deliberately designed to encourage
>   women to make do and mend with bugger
>   all!
>       (comes to a stand-still and
>       looks at STELLA)
>   Remember, out Stell', all those
>   careless word slogans, being splashed
>   about everywhere.
>       (eyes fierce)
>   The watchword should have been: "While

>           they are silent, they cry out!"

We see BLANCHE'S tears behind the eyes - STELLA links her arm through BLANCHE'S.

>                    STELLA
>           You were always a campaigner of lost
>           causes with a marshmallow heart -
>           although on second thoughts ...
>                 (laughs)
>           You're rather like a snowdrop, very
>           promiscuous.

## SCENE 43
**INT. MOTTLEY AGRICULTURAL SHOW - WI MARQUEE - 11:57 AM**

We see STELLA and BLANCHE enter the Women's Institute Marquee.

We see sections of homemade jams - pickles - wines - honey and bottles of mead - cakes - bread loaves and teacakes with hardly a current showing.

We see farmhouse pork pies and savouries - a class for cooked pig trotters and pig brawn - all placed to best advantage to catch JUDGES' sagacious eyes. We see STELLA and BLANCHE pointing to and murmuring their interests.

We see WINNY suddenly blossom forth, dressed in an ill fitting home-made dress, taken from a Women's Institute home-pattern package.

>                    WINNY
>           So you made it, Stella, dear, and
>           Blanche!

*WINNY stands ample and plentiful, directly in front of STELLA and BLANCHE. Her dark curls bobbing about her rose-plump face, as she darts quick meaningful glances about her.*

> WINNY
>
> And where are the girls? Not in hospital! And how is poor Spencer? And that nice young man ... What's his name ...? Such a crying shame and what a close shave. Oh, yes, my dear, the unfortunate Swaledale ewe – not fit for human consumption! And what with all that rain ... so, they were knocked down by God only knows ...? And that dreadful old man, Stella, dear ...

*We see STELLA'S eyes grow large and her mouth go smaller.*

> WINNY
>
> How did he manage to lock himself away in the car boot? Dirty old man! And Clarence. You must have compensated him ...? Everyone knows he's always carried a candle for you – nothing like Sam of course, but Sam is dead! And now you have Spencer!
>
>> *(her eyes go smaller and her mouth larger)*
>
> The more one comes to think about it, and I'm sure Sam did. One begins to realise there's no blood relation between the pair of you. Crafty old sod! Keep it all in the immediate family. How like an Asquith!
>
>> *(smiles)*

> There, there, Stella, dear. You look
> quite pale – so ... drained of colour,
> so ...

*As WINNY pauses for breath, we see STELLA having great pains to think of something pernicious to spring back with.*

*BLANCHE, in spite of seeing notices prohibiting smoking, lights up a cigarette and rallies round obstructively well.*

> BLANCHE
> *(crudely)*
> My goodness, Winny dear, you're every
> bit as homely – yet, parsimonious as
> the man who looks overtly at the penis
> of the man urinating next to him in
> the public latrines – and is then
> deeply envious if he sees it to be
> bigger than his own!

*We see WINNY mournfully shaking her head from side to side and clicking her tongue loudly on the roof of her mouth.*

> STELLA
> *(finding her voice with a smile*
> *to scold WINNY)*
> All these bombarding eulogies, Winny,
> require some explanation. I believe –
> and I stand to be corrected, all this
> prying into Stockdale business comes
> from sheer discontentment of Sam not
> leaving a single penny to Abe in his
> will – and furthermore ...
> *(eyes fierce)*
> I'll wager that you are the most
> aggressive listener J. W. Hinchcliffe

has ever known!

                    WINNY
                *(splutters)*
Poh ... pooh ... You - Yooouu ... vain snoot ...

*We see BLANCHE lick a thumb and turn a page in the catalogue.*

                    BLANCHE
                *(parental tone)*
Come along our Stell', the Shire horses are about to be paraded in the centre ring ...

## SCENE 44

**EXT. MOTTLEY AGRICULTURAL SHOW - WI MARQUEE - 12 AM**

*We see STELLA and BLANCHE leaving the WI Marquee via the exit canvas flap and into the mid-day sunshine.*

                    STELLA
                *(panting)*
All we need now is to bump into Abe - I can well do without him lobbing the occasional hard-ball, and so soon after Winny's soft-balling ...
              *(dredges up a smile)*
Well, at least we know where she gets all her inside information from ...

                    BLANCHE
And a free lunch most Thursdays. Well, I do remember Sam mentioning that Winny and John Hinchcliffe courted for a number of years in their younger

days, and your Sam repeated what John
Hinchcliffe told him ...
>  (salivating)

Winny had the disconcerting habit of
knocking him off his stride by not
sucking, but crunching boiled sweets
while in bed.

*We see the refreshment tents have queues a mile long.*

> STELLA
>
> Do you feel capable of queuing for an
> hour in the sun, Mother, because I
> don't ...

> BLANCHE
>
> The beer tent - perhaps ...

> STELLA
>
> No! I don't think I could stomach the
> possibility of seeing Clarence there.
> Let's take a short-cut to the parking
> lot.

**SCENE 45**
**EXT. MOTTLEY AGRICULTURAL SHOW - PARKING LOT - 12:20 AM**

*We see STELLA and BLANCHE climbing over the nearest stone wall to emerge breathless and dishevelled from behind a group of rhododendron evergreens - a mere stone throw from the parked Rover.*

**SCENE 46**
**I/E. ROVER CAR - MOTTLEY AGRICULTURAL SHOW - 1 PM**

*We see STELLA and BLANCHE seated on the back seat of the*

Rover. Food basket between them.

BLANCHE is unpacking the billy-can – still piping hot, from the hay-box. BLANCHE proceeds to pour – STELLA unscrews bottle of whisky and pours noble measure into each cup of tea.

We see them settling back and slowly relaxing.

We hear the surrounding sounds – the devout KIRKDALE BRASS BANDSMEN playing a rousing medley of favoured war time songs, interspersed by COMMENTATORS' amplified voices relaying relevant information over ringside loud speakers – intermingled with the spontaneous bawling from the show BEASTS being paraded by their anticipating OWNERS and SONS from inside temporary judging show-rings.

Then every now and again, we hear the rippling applause travel through the warm air from mulling CROWDS – several rows deep, gathered around individual ringsides – awaiting winning results – then applauding the WINNERS circling the border of each ring.

> STELLA
> It's hard to believe sitting here, that last year we were all at Mottley Show as a happy family. And we'd won several prizes with our shorthorn beasts – and Sam walked away with the Champion Bull Trophy.

STELLA shoots a swift glance at BLANCHE – who is concentrating on her ham sandwich – and side salad.

STELLA'S plate is empty.

                    STELLA
                (*suffering tones*)
            And just look at us now! Sam is dead.
            Jake attempted murder. We're all
            having to budge up to make room for
            that Spencer. Then there's Harry!
            Harry who knows a good thing when he
            sees it – and where do we find him?
                (*voice quavers as she answers
                her own question*)
            We find him flat out alongside the
            bequeathed son, in hospital like a
            pair of bugbears, while my daughters
            have their noses knocked out of joint
            over this will business – and it's
            bloody well obvious, Winny and Abe are
            enjoying it all a bit too much for our
            comfort.


BLANCHE raises an arched eyebrow – then places a consoling ham sandwich onto STELLA'S plate.

We see STELLA bite deeply into the sandwich, then tongue it aside.

                    STELLA
            And now Francis Spencer-Asquith has
            the audacity to propose selling off
            his share in Stockdale Farms to
            subsidise the renovations of Woodclose
            cottages ...

                    BLANCHE
            That speculation was already being
            circulated and summarised in the Wheat
            Sheaf on Saturday night after you and

Spencer were spotted walking towards Woodclose ...

*(helps herself to a chicken sandwich)*

You're forgetting, Lamley, the local builders were about to sign the contract just after Spencer's mother's funeral, but somewhere amongst the deadlines, Spencer turned up looking the spitting image of John Asquith – Well!

*(eyes open wide)*

As you can imagine, the cat was out of the bag!

STELLA and BLANCHE sit silently – eating noisily.

     BLANCHE
*(speaking between swallowing mouthfuls of moreish food)*

If you took the trouble to widen the aspects of friendship, Stella – you don't know what you might find – and if I'm anyone to go by ...

*(facial expression becomes inviting)*

I always loved a man with broad shoulders and a tight bottom ... it's surprising how often this searching for the essence of a man has its uses ...

     STELLA
*(voice strident)*

Mere supposition! And you know it's merely supposition.

BLANCHE
(placates with ease)
Frankly, my dear, if you really had to think about it logically, Spencer could turn out to be as good as any insurance policy.

STELLA refills their china teacups, she holds her tongue.

BLANCHE
(earnestly)
Jake Swales has been at Stockdale too long to be got rid of easily, and it's not as if you're poor, thank the Lord.

BLANCHE sinks her teeth into a large portion of sponge cake filled with fresh cream and bottled raspberries.

STELLA
(grunting)
I'll have the same. I need something to fill the hollow in the pit of my stomach.

BLANCHE
You know ...
(solemnly)
Stell'. The more I think about it, and knowing your Sam over the years, the more I can begin to understand his logic. Simple, imagine, Stell'. If two young ambitious men had their impecunious eyes firmly fixed on Stockdale enterprises, rather than on his daughters' hearts or welfare – just imagine – two grabbing son-in-

>               laws – having the same pretensions or
>               claims – both standing in competition
>               for gain and superiority. Imagine,
>               Stell'! All that gruelling, striving,
>               manual years – day in – day out with
>               never a holiday between you all ...

*BLANCHE pours out two more cups of tea, then a dash of whisky.*

>                         BLANCHE
>               Just imagine – again – all that sweat
>               and hard labour going west, to line
>               two son-in-laws' calculating pockets!

>                         STELLA
>                    *(mutters)*
>               That's just what Sam said about Hertz.

*STELLA passes cake knife to BLANCHE.*

>                         BLANCHE
>               Ah! Ah, that explains much – on the
>               other hand ...
>                    *(raises head from food basket)*
>               The lassies could wed and leave home,
>               and where would that leave you?

*BLANCHE cuts large triangles of curd pie – STELLA stares, waiting for the answer.*

>                         BLANCHE
>               Well, I'll tell you, my girl. It would
>               leave you with that old master
>               pighead, Jake Swales – and even he
>               can't last forever – now ...

>           *(swallows hastily)*
> Take this reasoning another step
> further. What if you decided to
> remarry?

>                STELLA
>           *(eyelids flicker rapidly and
>           eyes water)*
> I must confess, I've harboured the
> thought that perhaps I could still
> conceive another child ...
>           *(voice trails away)*
> Maybe a son ...

BLANCHE stops reaching out for food long enough to grasp STELLA'S hand affectionately.

>                BLANCHE
> Don't you ever think you're on your
> own, lass. Everyone hurts and yearns
> sometimes. Everybody ...

>                STELLA
> Kindly don't sympathise with me,
> Mother.
>           *(pulls hand away)*
> Or I'll be simply gone.

STELLA'S lips quiver, and her eyes brim over – tears begin to trickle down her rosy cheeks. She dabs them away with a napkin.

>                STELLA
> Sam couldn't for the life of him
> understand what was bothering me.
> Believe me, Mother – after seasons of

hand and mouth resuscitation, you give
up trying because it just doesn't
happen.

>           BLANCHE
> Men can be so hapless. So
> disappointing, so ...

*STELLA and BLANCHE exchange mournful glances expressing human broodiness of expectations beyond their reasoning.*

*We see BLANCHE rummaging in her handbag for packet of cigarettes, she lights up and inhales deeply, then breaths out trickles of smoke.*

>           BLANCHE
> I've always felt closer to you than
> our Mable.
>      *(coughs)*
> Perhaps if she hadn't left home so
> early to work as a live-in scullery
> maid for the local gentry ...
>      *(pause)*
> Persevering with that cold eye of
> her's to graduating to the position of
> housekeeper – then mistress ...

>           STELLA
> Sam never did take to our Mable, or
> Lord Farquhar – particularly his
> Lordship, because his ancestors had a
> very large dove-cot and they'd
> released those doves daily, and as a
> consequence, the birds ravished the
> farmers' crops, causing much
> hostility.

BLANCHE

Hostility! Jake's the open enemy here, and God help us if things get out of hand!

STELLA
*(sits upright)*
Out of hand!

BLANCHE

Yes. Out of control! It's as plain as the nose on your face that he's greenly envious of Sam's son, and you don't have to be blind to see he feels supplanted by the rival of Spencer. Two-fold, so, when he has to share the accommodations he considers solely to be his home ...

*BLANCHE draws heavily on her cigarette, then tosses it out of the car window.*

BLANCHE

And we've not heard Spencer's side of the story yet - remember! And by all accounts ...

*BLANCHE unwraps a couple of glasses, pours generous measure of whisky into each and thrusts one into STELLA'S moving fingers.*

BLANCHE

It's all a question of being sensitive to any wrong doing. Honest to God, why risk your own and my grandchildren's future for Jake Swales' incessant

jealousy and ceaseless selfishness.
After all, it's not as though he's a
blood relation ...

              STELLA
       *(splutters convulsively on her*
       *drink)*
Blood relation!

              BLANCHE
You never have been one for settling
for half-measures, have you, and
nobody knew that better than Sam.
       *(touches STELLA'S arm lightly)*
But sometimes, every once in a while,
one has to compromise a combination or
rival systems or principles in which
something of each is sacrificed to
make the combination possible.

              STELLA
Combination!

*STELLA'S eyes open wider and her generous mouth tightens, showing the beginnings of a quarrel.*

              BLANCHE
       *(taking parental control)*
Yes. Combination! Stella! Don't be
blind or too bound by loyalty as far
as Jake is concerned. I've seen the
peculiar way he looks at our Sophie.
He sees she's becoming closer to her
half-brother each day ...
       *(pause to take gulp from glass)*
While our Grace gives rise to not

trusting the old man anymore.
>   *(compelling)*
I strongly believe it is my duty as the only elder parent within your family – my family – to have my voice heard within Stockdale affairs – not Jake!

*STELLA, not getting her lips wet with raw whisky – wedges her body into the seat corner – assigns herself to BLANCHE'S wisdom and useful silences.*

BLANCHE
Don't put Jake's welfare before your own family, Stell'. Remember, you was always proud and loyal to Sam before this will business – and if it's any consolation to you, my dear, I personally believe Sam gave his son scarcely a second thought until he set eyes on him, when he returned from Canada for his mother's funeral.
>   *(shakes finger at STELLA)*
At least, he acknowledged his son, even if it was late in the day.

*BLANCHE lights another cigarette, then views STELLA through fine screen of smoke.*

BLANCHE
Whether Winny intended by design or not to cause mischief, she's right. There's no related blood between you or Spencer – so – wed him before someone else does, and get that son you so dearly desire before it's too

late.

> *(BLANCHE'S disarming smile is
> her defence)*

That way you'll guarantee an even stronger hold over Stockdale ...

### STELLA

What you're really saying, Mother ...
> *(pause)*

And I don't know whether to laugh or cry – to get over someone, you have to get under someone.

### BLANCHE

What I'm saying, among other things, is that you need someone to comfort that restless mind of yours. I know leadership becomes you, and this decision-making position is so crucial to your bones, but you have to let go and trust another ...

### STELLA

Asquith!

### BLANCHE

Spencer is part of the Asquith web, Jake is only a strand, but that strand has already begun to effect the whole of our family. Remember – Stella – how he assisted Sam in the Hertz business, and while you're remembering to know again, stop opposing Spencer. He may be more like his father than you give him credit for?

*We see STELLA'S face grey-green caught in the shimmering shafts of sunlight reflecting on the cigarette smoke as it filters through partly open windows.*

*We see BLANCHE close her eyes on STELLA; done with advice for one day.*

> STELLA
> I remember that fateful day, when my instincts led me to the open side-door in the barn door, more to close it than to step through it ...
> *(puts hand to throat)*
> I can still see Sam and Jake standing there – Sam looking so cold – so cruel – while Jake seemed fresh, toned up somehow? I remember struggling to find words, workable words and my feet felt as though they'd taken root – words and movement impossible – yet distinctly I could hear Jake's voice – so metallic – so rasping, and so very wide aware: "Tha's not come ta tell us yon Gerry-boy would look a damn sight tidier hangin' from t' other corner o' barn hasta?"

## SCENE 47
**I/E. ROVER CAR – MOTTLEY AGRICULTURAL SHOW – 4 PM**

*STELLA and BLANCHE leaving the show ground and drive home.*

## SCENE 48
**I/E. ROVER CAR – STOCKDALE FARMS – 4:30 PM**

*We see STELLA and BLANCHE'S unexpected reactions as they*

sight HINCHCLIFFE'S Wolsey car parked on forecourt as they drive over the water-splash.

STELLA with outlandish hat slightly askew - her face uninviting beneath it. BLANCHE cigaretted and slightly tiddly - toned down.

                STELLA
            (asperity)
      The bother-breeder! I believe John
      Hinchcliffe would prefer women to
      appear to be as flat and one
      dimensional as a child's drawing.

                BLANCHE
            (mellowed)
      Oh, take no notice of him, Stell'.
      He's the type who makes a toasted
      teacake go a long way.

STELLA, speeding too fast, skids passed the frontage on locked brakes and stalls car - wiper scrapes against the glass window screen.

We hear car doors slamming - we see BRIDIE barking and wagging her tail. We see SOPHIE running from kitchen to meet them - abashed without loosing charm.

                SOPHIE
      Thank goodness you're home ...
         (relieves them of empty food
         basket and disarranged hay-box)
      I have just ran out of conversation
      with Mr Hinchcliffe. He's so full of
      unaccountable silences that don't half
      take some filling.

                    BLANCHE
              *(kindly)*
    Calculated silences are the most
    eloquent portions of nothing. Never
    mind, girl ...
              *(places arm round SOPHIE'S
              shoulders)*
    In my opinion, being with a solicitor,
    or a doctor, is rather like going to
    the lavatory - necessary, but
    something to forget as soon as
    possible.

**SCENE 49**
**INT. STOCKDALE FARMS - STELLA'S KITCHEN - 4:33 PM**

HINCHCLIFFE'S eyes alight on BLANCHE as she and SOPHIE enter kitchen first.

                    HINCHCLIFFE
              *(brusquely)*
    Good day, to you, madam. I can see you
    are an oasis of sanctity in a family
    peopled by increasingly difficult
    women.

                    BLANCHE
              *(pleasantly)*
    A lovely day indeed. The sun is bright
    enough to dazzle, and not quite hot
    enough to dampen our spirits ...
              *(contagious laugh)*
    But I've had to pull my cotton dress
    down to shade my winter white legs ...

BLANCHE and SOPHIE breeze passed him, and through to the

*living room and beyond.*

>                    HINCHCLIFFE
>            *(turns to STELLA, voice*
>            *overbearing)*
>    Young Harry, will not be back working
>    in the office for at least four weeks!
>            *(puffs hard on cigar)*
>    He's received a broken leg, a hair-
>    line fracture and cracked two ribs.
>    His parents – barristers you know ...

*STELLA gives him one of her cold blank stares – which he ignores – she stalks into the living room – he follows.*

### SCENE 50
**INT. STOCKDALE FARMS – STELLA'S LIVING ROOM – 4:34 PM**

*STELLA takes a seat on the sofa.*

>                    HINCHCLIFFE
>    They'll be visiting this weekend. They
>    want to get to the bottom of the
>    accident!
>            *(silence falls)*
>    The doctor expects the young man to be
>    discharged from hospital in ten days –
>    and Mrs Hinchcliffe and I have never
>    believed in fraternising with any of
>    our staff. He'll have to stay here!
>
>                    STELLA
>            *(pugnacity aroused)*
>    We're not running a convalescent home
>    here at Stockdale! We women, don't
>    have time to mollycoddle infirmary

men. We'll all be working! We always
work. We've never given up working,
not even when poor Sam was laid out
cold in the parlour for a solid week.

              HINCHCLIFFE
Talking of Sam ...
    *(exaggerated receptivity)*
And your family business - I need
immediate decisions from you and
Spencer's impending business, and also
...
    *(dashes cigar onto the open*
    *fire)*
the overdue settlement of Stockdale's
current accounts - quite unlike Sam
Asquith.

*STELLA takes off her hat and runs her fingers through her hair.*

              STELLA
If there's one thing I dislike, it's
being bamboozled! And being cornered -
particularly in my own home - so why
this displacement activity? A letter
or a bill would be sufficient - this
badgering is quite uncouth.

              HINCHCLIFFE
    *(raising his hand)*
Patience. Please hear me out ...

*And at that moment the kitchen door slams shut!*

*We hear shuffles - then low and behold, SPENCER looms in the living room doorway.*

*We see STELLA, caught on the wrong foot. She looks quite thunderstruck.*

## SCENE 51
**INT. ROVER CAR - MOTTLEY SHOWGROUND (STELLA'S MEMORY)**

*Earlier in the same day - STELLA and BLANCHE on back seat of the parked Rover car.*

     BLANCHE
    *(lighting cigarette)*
There's no related blood between you or Spencer - so - wed him before someone else does, and get that son you so dearly desire before it's too late.
    *(BLANCHE'S disarming smile is*
     *her defence)*
That way you'll guarantee an even stronger hold over Stockdale ...

## SCENE 52
**INT. STOCKDALE FARMS - STELLA'S LIVING ROOM - 4:36 PM**

*STELLA gathers herself together with difficulty.*

     STELLA
Spencer! We've been so worried about you - and I must confess ...
    *(places hand over heart)*
I've been unable to sleep properly for having dreams of you laying between two brass handles - and - quite out of reach - just like your father.

*SPENCER considers her response gravely before he proceeds to move up the last step and limps across to a dining chair and lowers himself down.*

                    SPENCER

    Nah!

*STELLA and HINCHCLIFFE'S inquisitive eyes latch onto SPENCER'S every move. We see SPENCER'S dark straight hair almost at centre parting, hanging thickly like unclosed curtains along each side of his head.*

*STELLA and HINCHCLIFFE'S prying eyes see below the wedges of hair – SPENCER'S face looks grey – and yes – greenish-bluish – a muscle in his right cheek twitches – lips lost colour – drawn back into thin ribbons across his teeth – all his teeth.*

*They further notice the grimace he makes as he pushes his feet back to sit wide-kneed at right angles in the centre.*

## SCENE 53
**INT. DR LIDDLE'S SURGERY – DAY (STELLA'S MEMORY)**

*STELLA is sat, gaining confidential information from DR LIDDLE.*

                    DR LIDDLE
              *(with solemnity)*
        I visited Spencer in hospital, and I
        can confirm he has head injuries
        resulting from Jake Swales striking
        him over the head, repeatedly – with
        the motor-car starting handle –
        causing mild concussion ...

**SCENE 54**

**INT. DR LIDDLE'S SURGERY - DAY (HINCHCLIFFE'S MEMORY)**

*HINCHCLIFFE is sat (gaining the same confidential details as STELLA in previous Scene, 53 from DR LIDDLE).*

>           DR LIDDLE
>        *(with solemnity)*
>    ... also - my patient is enduring
>    fervent pain coming from a cavity in
>    the muscle of his right thigh - the
>    point of impact where a massive
>    haematoma will rapidly spread across
>    the whole limb - that injury, Spencer
>    confirmed was caused by the careless
>    driver whom we have no trace of ...

**SCENE 55**

**INT. STOCKDALE FARMS - STELLA'S LIVING ROOM - 4:38 PM**

*We see SPENCER aware of STELLA and HINCHCLIFFE'S scrutiny to him - he folds his arms and gradually his perpetual half-smile becomes evident - jaunty almost.*

>           HINCHCLIFFE
>        *(ostentatiously)*
>    In my long experience - one might as
>    well compare a hit and drive-away car
>    accident to a prototype example of an
>    argument with a quarrelsome woman.
>    There's no rational bearing or
>    explanation ...
>        *(flashes a glance at STELLA)*
>    No logic order of succession ...

*We see HINCHCLIFFE'S eyes seemingly pin-pointing the*

*inflicted contours upon SPENCER'S large skull – as though he can read the initials of JAKE SWALES branded upon the cluster of informant bumps.*

                HINCHCLIFFE
      You know where you can find me,
      Spencer, when you need me. Your father
      and I went back a long way – you know
      ...

*HINCHCLIFFE avoids meeting STELLA'S eyes and gives SPENCER a man's knowing look before we see him edging himself towards the door.*

                HINCHCLIFFE
         (abruptly)
      Tell me, Spencer, how did Jake Swales
      come to be locked inside the car boot?

*He looks suspiciously from SPENCER to STELLA for some conspiratorial glance to pass between them – and he's not persuaded by its absence.*

                STELLA
      Gentlemen!

*STELLA gives full range to her Dales dialect to remind them that she belongs right here – even if they don't.*

                STELLA
      Ah'm noan t' wiser mesen, Jake keeps
      blackin' owt, but will insist theer's
      nowt matter wi' him, only, don't keep
      on about it. An' Harry! Weel, it's
      hard t' mek owt whether eh feels
      rewarded or punished, an' Spencer ...

*SPENCER meets her glittering eyes - STELLA remains sat on the sofa ensconced amongst cushions - suddenly she smiles at him as if there is some beautiful secret between them.*

>                SPENCER
> People ...
>      *(runs shaking hand through his*
>      *damp hair)*
> Do a lot of things they oughtn't to
> do. My feelings are ...
>      *(creates a diversion by leaning*
>      *forwards towards STELLA)*
> Do you remember, 'Ella, the first day
> I came home to Stockdale?

*HINCHCLIFFE edges himself back into the room. STELLA, wears an illusive expression, nods from depth of sofa.*

>                STELLA
> You mean, the day Jake shot your
> whippet dead for worrying my sheep.

*HINCHCLIFFE rivets his attention on SPENCER.*

*We see SPENCER place moving fingers to his perspiring forehead - he painfully shifts his weight on hard-backed chair - remembering ...*

## SCENE 56
**INT. HARROGATE HOSPITAL - DAY (SPENCER'S MEMORY)**

*We see SPENCER sat beside HARRY'S hospital bed.*

>                HARRY
> I'll never forget Jake's words to me
> after he'd had a few too many at the

Wheat Sheaf celebration for the milking machines ... he said ...
>(impersonating JAKE'S jeering voice)

"Tha should have seem him, lad, eatin' that theer meat stew ah made fore his homecomin' supper – dozy bastard thought eh wore eatin' stewed rabbit!"

**SCENE 57**

**INT. STOCKDALE FARMS – STELLA'S LIVING ROOM – 4:40 PM**

*SPENCER swallows with difficulty and curses under his breath. He's now unprepared to disclose the car accident details.*

>HINCHCLIFFE
>*(impatiently)*

I'll tell you what I think, Spencer. There's nothing more irreconcilable than a man who does not feel he's getting his dues in life. Small grievances, you might think, Spencer, but this accident could be construed as you trying to rid yourself of a long term farm tenant. A tenant with strong assurances from John and Samuel Asquith that the Stockdale farmhouse is Jake Swales' home for life, and ...

*STELLA opens her mouth to speak – SPENCER, with hand gesture stops her at once.*

>SPENCER
>*(slowly with cold precision)*

Jake Swales and I have not always agreed, and I don't expect that we'll always agree in the future.

*We see - they see - SAM'S sardonic image superimposed upon SPENCER'S face - STELLA sways to her feet.*

                    STELLA
        I always think ...
             *(puffs up cushions and repeats*
             *her words)*
        I always think that departures and
        arrivals tend to emphasise people's
        peculiar personalities.

*Without a backward look STELLA staggers out of the living room. We hear the kitchen door slam shut.*

## SCENE 58
**INT. STOCKDALE FARMS - STELLA'S KITCHEN - 5 PM**

*We see STELLA, GRACE, SOPHIE and BLANCHE seated around the table - both SPENCER and JAKE'S chairs pushed under the table.*

                    BLANCHE
        No menfolk. I hope that's not a bad
        sign, but at least we can slacken off
        and make the most of the time while it
        lasts.

*We see GRACE cutting portions of rhubarb pie and placing a share onto serving dishes - BLANCHE pours pool of cream onto hers - each, in turn, help themselves - eating, not talking - until their silence is broken by the loud rattling of the door sneck - then the kitchen door bursts open, and SPENCER lurches right into their space.*

SPENCER

(harshly)

I'm afraid it's bad news!

STELLA

Bad news?

(pushes dessert about in her
dish, dredges up a thin smile)

Bad news for whom?

*We see SPENCER shift the hampering weight from his injured leg onto the other. We see the women's expressions of: Can't it wait until we've finished? - They return to concentrate on their meal.*

SPENCER

(abruptly)

No. It can't wait! The animal is deeply distressed, and I know Jake is fully responsible for its painful condition.

GRACE

Which animal are you referring to, Spencer, and what has Jake to do with its suffering?

STELLA

Just a moment.

(pushes her dish aside)

We can't have you fratching with old Jake. He's still suffering blackouts since the accident ...

SPENCER

Accident!

> *(inclines head judicially)*

Jake Swales has already caused ructions – furthermore, he knows as well as Harry Bletchford and myself, that we perceive with certainty, the dark side of his nature.

          BLANCHE

> *(shivers)*

A chill invades if one lingers too long ...

> *(touches STELLA'S arm)*

And what can never be said out loud – can still surely be thought ...

          STELLA

> *(swivels round on her chair to face SPENCER)*

Where is all this animal business leading to, Spencer?

         SPENCER

> *(with severity)*

I'll tell you where it's leading to for now. It's leading straight to Nelson. Jake has the audacity to try and tell me, the horse's thick leg is due to Nelson standing idle over the weekend ...

> *(bars his teeth against his impending pain)*

I'm well aware this condition does occur, but in this case it's sheer vindictiveness on the old horseman's part.

                    STELLA
              *(bold front)*
Vindictiveness!


                    SPENCER
Yes! Vindictiveness. He's deliberately
over-fed the stallion with corn,
straight after a belly full of cold
water, which severely dilutes the
digestion juices ...
              *(pause)*
I've been around horses and cattle all
my life, so give me credit, 'Ella!


                    SOPHIE
Harry said, yesterday, when Grace and
I visited him in hospital that Jake is
a dangerous old man, and we should not
be complacent towards him - at all
times.

*SOPHIE leaves the table and hands SPENCER a comforting mug of tea - it's plain to see a bond has grown between them.*

                    BLANCHE
Dear - winsome - Sophie.

## SCENE 59
**EXT. STOCKDALE FARMS - FORECOURT - 5:25 PM**

*We see SPENCER stood on forecourt - GRACE and SOPHIE via Rover.*

                    GRACE
              *(calling to SPENCER)*
<u>We shouldn't be long before we're back</u>

from telephoning the veterinary.

**SCENE 60**

**INT. STOCKDALE FARMS - STELLA'S KITCHEN - 5:26 PM**

STELLA enters the kitchen - she's changed into blouse and dungarees.

                  BLANCHE
Leave me to clear away the tea things, Stella. I'm looking forward to later, pulling my feet up and having the farmhouse to myself if only for a little while.

**SCENE 61**

**I/E. STOCKDALE FARMS - STABLES - 5:27 PM**

We see STELLA accompanying SPENCER to the stables.

                  SPENCER
Tell me, 'Ella, in all honesty. Why do you give Jake so much leverage? He's hardly family.

SPENCER opens and closes stable door behind them, leaving the top half open.

                  STELLA
And you are?

STELLA lunges towards the yard brush and begins to stomp the bristles across the already swept down stalls.

                  SPENCER
Is that so hard to swallow, 'Ella?

SPENCER hobbles to the restless stallion - NELSON, tied by its halter in the wooden partitioned stall. He bends down to run an exploring hand over the inside of the massively swollen hind leg. We hear NELSON snort and begin to plunge clumsily about within the restricted area.

We see SPENCER slowly straighten up from massaging NELSON'S thick-set limb and turn to STELLA.

     SPENCER
    (voice cool)
 I don't know which is the worst, 'Ella
 - to see all and say nothing, or to
 see nothing and say too much?

     STELLA
    (uneasy)
 Same difference.
   (she eyes the swelling with
   harassed eyes)
 Monday Morning Disease, Sam use to
 call it, and yes, by a horse working
 all week, then to stand idle on a
 stone floor all weekend ...
   (places brush in corner)
 We had a case like this a few years
 ago, and it was heavy going all week -
 Sam and Jake massaging the legs on and
 off, day and night before the horse
 was classified sound.

     SPENCER
    (looks intently at STELLA)
 You may not like what I'm going to
 say.

*A colossal silence follows his words, as STELLA stares back at him.*

> SPENCER
> First – while I was detained in hospital, I felt I needed and wanted to be right here in the centre of Stockdale action – aware that I was enjoying, perhaps too much, the down-to-earth Asquith women's company – that's why I'd arranged a lift back home with John Hinchcliffe ...

*SPENCER eases his weight onto his sound leg and swallows his pain.*

> STELLA
> *(narrows eyes)*
> You're going to tell me something else you regard as too obvious to be noticed as proof.

*SPENCER takes his time to move back into NELSON'S stall, to rummage about in the HORSE'S trough before returning to her. He holds his hand wide open to reveal a mound of grain corn.*

> SPENCER
> *(curt and impersonal)*
> I'm fully aware if cart-horses are suddenly withdrawn from their daily drag of work, then given to standing idle on flagged floors over the weekend develop Monday Morning Disease. And I'm also aware, horses overfed with corn and then allowed to drink excessive cold water – this –

> can add to many other ailments,
> including digestive upsets –
> furthermore, I'm also aware a good
> horseman never gives water to a horse
> immediately before or after its been
> fed!

SPENCER limps towards windowsill and reaches for dandie brush and begins to groom NELSON.

STELLA stands at bay – not ready to be generous.

> SPENCER
> Horsepower! There's gradually a change
> taking place, particularly in
> Lincolnshire where tractors and oil
> driven machinery are driving a lot of
> the draught horses from the land.
> *(turns to STELLA)*
> Something worth thinking about, here
> in the Yorkshire Dales.

We see STELLA listening to him – he steps away from NELSON.

> SPENCER
> But for now ...
> *(walks lamely to stand by her side)*
> As you can see, 'Ella, this is a
> matter of deliberate, inflicted
> behaviour on Jake's part. Now, shall I
> have it out into the open with him, or
> will you?

Before STELLA can open her mouth, JAKE'S head juts over stable half-door. He throws wide glances about him and over them, before he yanks the inside bolt back and shoves his way into the building, a bucket is nestled in crook of his arm.

                  JAKE
Noan! That's what ah call a bloody bobby-dazzler!

We see JAKE eyeing NELSON'S massively distorted limb in a reproachful manner – then he spits out a measure of saliva.

STELLA radiates stiff disapproval at JAKE'S bad habit.

                  SPENCER
            (enunciating)
Not another bucketful of corn for Nelson!

JAKE incited, furrows his brow as he protrudes his chin, but his weather-beaten face remains impassive and his tone droll.

                  JAKE
Tha might feed horses wi' bloody corn in Canada, lad, but here wi' allus give them oats an' meadow hay.
            (turns to STELLA dolefully)
He'll be tellin' us onny minute next t' put ah cowshit poultice on yon thick leg!

We see SPENCER walking stiff-legged over to the open stable door and dash the grains out of his hand, still glaring at JAKE with grim distrust.

                  SPENCER
You call yourself a staunch horseman! Well, a good horseman worth his salt

                    would never overfeed with corn, nor
                    make determined mistakes with a
                    horse's diet. You know as well as I
                    do, Jake, that water dilutes the
                    digestive system, and -

                              JAKE
                    Here! Here! Thee watch tha tongue,
                    lad! Onnybody would think t' hear thee
                    talk tha'd bought half o' Stockdale
                    Farms, not just ah half-share interest
                    in yan fuckin' horse.

*We hear a throttled gurgle emanating from the throat of SPENCER as he fights with his mental rigidity, hinged on and against his bastardy.*

                              SPENCER
                    You may not agree with myself being
                    here, Jake, but I have every right to
                    be here, much more than you.
                              *(lips curl cruelly)*
                    After all, I am my father's rightful
                    son -

                              JAKE
                         *(harshly)*
                    Ah bastard son!

                              SPENCER
                    I didn't ask t' be born -

                              JAKE
                    By Eve Ridgeholm, ah so-called
                    housekeeper who looked like ah bloody
                    Neanderthal man - she had thighs as

           big as Brimham Rocks. It's a fuckin'
           wonder she didn't crack Sam Asquith in
           half like a bloody walnut!

We see STELLA remaining silent, moving only her eyes from
JAKE to SPENCER. We see JAKE making moves that suggest he's
about to massage NELSON'S distorted limb.

                    SPENCER
               (with ludicrous sternness)
           No! You don't!
               (limps forward to block JAKE'S
               way)
           I find your construed behaviour
           difficult to comprehend, and your
           insidious actions offensive to the
           mind and moral taste of mankind ...

SPENCER shoots penetrating glances to make sure JAKE'S not
lost his memory.

                    SPENCER
           Right now, Jake, I'm referring to the
           rights and wrongs as determined to
           duty. Working duties!

                    JAKE
               (incensed)
           Don't thee start preachin' moral
           etiket t' reights an' wrongs t' me,
           lad. We knew nowt about fuckin' sin
           till tha came here, never mind thee
           father, fuckin' away in back o' thee
           grandfather's horsebox ...

SPENCER gives out an articulating roar of unshielded rage,

and lunges at JAKE.

We see SPENCER land a blow over the neck and shoulder of JAKE'S body, causing JAKE'S eyes to bulge out more conspicuously from the rest of his grisly face.

We see JAKE enraged, juddering round to throw a wild punch which strikes SPENCER'S nose and mouth; bluishly-redish with mottled blotches.

                STELLA
            (mutters)
        Just like an exotic orchid ...
          (finding her voice, shouting)
        <u>Stop this noxious behaviour – at once!</u>

We see STELLA blindly thrusting and elbowing herself between JAKE and SPENCER.

                STELLA
        Can't the pair of you see that work is
        already piling up – and I've had
        rather a disturbing day?

Unabated the raucous exchanges of blows continue, with each man trying to place her aside.

We see STELLA buffeting against their hard unyielding bodies – and her feminine senses over-reacting to the generating testosterone hormones.

These long remembering noises escape from unguarded lips as we see STELLA staggering out of the tight compression.

                STELLA
        Ohh ...! Uhgg ...! Ooohh ...!

And it's too much for her to bear – when NELSON chooses that precise moment to strike out, and catch STELLA with a metal rimmed shoe.

We see STELLA buckling to slither into a moaning heap onto the stinking stable floor, only a breath away from a pile of smouldering horse faeces.

We see STELLA quavering to her knees – she's trying to brave it out.

> STELLA
> (gasping)
> I'm so lucky ... to have ... kept so sane ... thank goodness ... I've always had a certain spiritual force ...

We see SPENCER hovering over her.

STELLA screws her eyes tightly closed, to hold back any glitters of salty tears.

SPENCER does just right without belittling her – she rapidly blinks moisture away.

> SPENCER
> Say what you like, 'Ella. People tend to lose their tempers with truth, and you don't have to be a bastard to work that out.

We see STELLA drop her disquiet gaze from SPENCER'S bashed nose and loosely split lip, and wearily eye the newly discharged heap of horse excrement.

                    STELLA
               (mutters mournfully)
          Sam's death came too soon ... He
          wasn't ready to die.

Silence.

When SPENCER speaks, his voice sounds as normal as anyone
could or ought to, under the circumstances.

                    SPENCER
          God help us all.

We see JAKE crouched with his balls tucked between his
thighs.

                    JAKE
               (snarls)
          I'm capped tha ivver fuckin' asked ...
               (screws his head in her
               direction with suspicious
               willingness)
          What ivver happened, lass t' mek thee
          feel fit t' sit among horse's shit?

STELLA holds up her hand, palm outwards so to silence them.
Proudly she holds up with everything about herself, from her
nose to her posterior, both appearing higher than usual. She
draws in deep breaths – then noisily expels them – before she
sways one way and another to find her feet.

We see SPENCER thrusting out his hands to lift her from
stable floor. We see STELLA being launched to her feet – she
swoons.

We see STELLA looking at SPENCER as though she's discovered

*something wonderful by accident – so she works in a couple of extra moves.*

*We see SPENCER eyeing STELLA longer than intended, searching her gorgeously wholesome face – he eases his body close to hers in response and when he speaks, it's as though he's alone with her.*

                SPENCER
        For the first time in my life, I'm
        exceedingly glad that I've never known
        my real father ...

*We see JAKE leaning back against the wall – he's keeping watch for the purpose of self-interest. We see by his expression a slow dawning of suspicion that STELLA and SPENCER have started to iron out their preferences and difficulties.*

                JAKE
             (snarls)
        Weel! Let's not start the home-fires
        burnin' yet!

*We see STELLA removing herself from SPENCER'S arms – to assume an elaborate stateliness of demeanour as to be expected from a fallen woman.*

*Her eyes glaze over JAKE as though she's not heard or seen him.*

                JAKE
            (enunciates broadly)
        Weel! Weel! Ah'd nivver ah believed it
        in ah bloody month o' Sundays.

                    SPENCER
          *(seeming pleased enough to be
          agreeable)*
     You have hit the nail right on the
     head ...

                    JAKE
     Aye, but what puzzles me, like ...
          *(rubs a hand artfully across
          his throat with joyless wonder)*
     Whose bloody half-share was it that
     kicked out at thee, lass?

*STELLA'S eyes open wider and her mouth goes smaller.*

                    STELLA
          *(expostulating)*
     I will not be reduced to taking sides.

*We see STELLA, in a fit of reverie, take her leave from the stable and head towards the bottom garden gate. We see STELLA walking through the cultivated grounds ... talking to herself ... inspecting herself. We see the angular indent of the iron horse-shoe on the back part of her leg muscle. She opens her mouth wide and lets out a silent scream.*

**SCENE 62**
**I/E. ROVER CAR - HAYFIELDS - ONE WEEK LATER - 9 AM**

*We see STELLA driving the Rover car slowly up Stockdale Farms cart-road, approaching the hayfields.*

*We hear the click-clicking sounds coming from the mowing machines as the bar catch drops into the teeth of the ratchet-wheel, indicating JAKE and SPENCER, each with a HORSE and cutting machine coming to their corner of the divided field – and yes – there again – the click-clicking sound carries in the hot summer air by the warm breeze, as the MEN back HORSES and implements before releasing the detend to start mowing the next line of cut.*

*We see GRACE and SOPHIE are already raking back the newly cut grass swaths at each corner, in readiness for the oncoming machines.*

*We see STELLA driving nearer to the closed gate which separates moorland from meadows.*

## SCENE 63
**I/E. STOCKDALE FARMS – STABLES – 7PM (STELLA'S MEMORY)**

*One week ago.*

*We see SPENCER in the stable – massaging NELSON'S hind leg.*

*We see the veterinary, MR DAVIS pulling into the yard. We see STELLA, with BRIDIE closing gate behind MR DAVIS – they enter the stables.*

*We see MR DAVIS inspecting NELSON.*

          MR DAVIS
       *(instructions concise)*
    Yes, I can confirm the massive
    hymphangitis is due to this horse
    having been fed – yes, overfed on corn
    – an oversight ...? And yes, certainly
    continue massaging the hindquarter and
    exercise Nelson regularly – including
    throughout the night – for the best
    results.

*We see MR DAVIS administer injection. We see him shake hands with SPENCER, while giving STELLA a head-nod.*

> MR DAVIS
> I'll be around this way, Mrs Asquith, so I'll revisit Nelson on Wednesday – and, please – no more grain – with water.

*MR DAVIS takes his leave.*

## SCENE 64
**INT. STOCKDALE FARMS – LOOSE-BOX – 7:10 PM (STELLA'S MEMORY)**

*One week ago.*

*We see SPENCER moving NELSON into loose-box – both walking lamely.*

*We see in TIME-LAPSE, STELLA, GRACE and SOPHIE taking it in turns to assist SPENCER with NELSON.*

> STELLA
> *(pleasantly to SPENCER)*
> The first time you met your real father, what was your first impression?

*We see SPENCER persevering with steady rhythmic massaging movements over NELSON'S gross swelling – he straightens up stiffly and looks at her keenly.*

> SPENCER
> The first reference I heard of my real father was at my step-father's funeral – when my mother confessed to tossing

a mental coin as to whether we should come home to England or to move to Canada – she said, "At least we'd get a welcome with our Connie which is more than we would ever get from that cold, tight-fisted artisan ..."
>  (he grimaces)

Only my mother made the word sound like arseisan! She said, "That man was so mean – and drunk, how you came about was a proper marvel".

*We see STELLA and SPENCER sitting down on a pair of three legged milking stools with a billy-can of hot tea between them. STELLA pours out two mugs of tea – they puff and blow over them – almost in a companion way.*

>               SPENCER
> If I really had to think about my life. From then on – I mean – learning that Morris Spencer wasn't my father – my life became a roller-coaster ride – and if I'd to boil it all down ...
>   (sort of laughs)
> I felt I must keep re-stablishing, re-inventing myself as having adequate power, equal or at least proportionate as the primogeniture son of Samuel Asquith, to complete myself.

*SPENCER raises hot tea to his healing lips – STELLA raises her cup and sips.*

>               STELLA
>     (demurrers)
> Sam was a task-master, but he did

practice what he preached.

SPENCER

Mother was more succinct. When I saw her off to England after the letter arrived informing us that her mother had been taken into Harrogate Hospital with a broken leg and malnutrition – her parting words were, "She may be ninety but she's still my mother – and no! I won't be coming back." And with these last words ...

*(gulps tea down)*

Mother turned away and meandered ...

*(wipes mouth with back of his hand)*

in that fallen arched way of hers.

STELLA

*(thoughtful expression)*

The splayed tread of a woman who has spent a deal of time on the prairies ...

SPENCER

*(a leakage of unhappiness in his voice)*

And, not once did she look back – and that was the saddest thing to bear.

*(pause)*

I can still remember continuing to watch my mother amble away – gripping in each work-swollen hand a battered suitcase, until she squeezed herself small through the turn-style to disappear from my sight ...

SPENCER throws the dregs from his mug into the corner of the loose-box.

> STELLA
> (face lengthens)

I well remember – at the time – how devastated I felt when Sam died – and – for us left behind, it was the cruellest of the long, unsaid, goodbyes.

> SPENCER
> (replenishing their drinking mugs)

I arrived back in England, fifteen years later, from British Columbia, with a flight load of young Hereford bulls – later transported by road into Lincolnshire – where I received a telegraph message ...
> (his voice sounds split between exasperation and sadness)

stating Mother had been admitted into hospital with pneumonia – she died – unvisited ...

> STELLA
> (expression is grave but reliable)

I can't pretend to imagine how you felt, Spencer, other than to say, if it had been my mother – I'd hate to see the back of someone I love.

> SPENCER

The day after my mother's funeral, I

met my father for the first time in John Hinchcliffe's office and it was by instinct that I knew immediately who he was.

## SCENE 65
**INT. HINCHCLIFFE'S OFFICE - DAY (SPENCER'S MEMORY)**

We see HINCHCLIFFE sat boldly behind his large desk. A cigar posed in his hand.

We see SAM, attired in well-cut jacket and waistcoat, riding breeches, polished boots and leggings - seated eloquently - watching SPENCER regardantly.

               HINCHCLIFFE
        *(brusquely to SPENCER)*
When do you leave for Canada?
        *(without pause)*
Before you go will you endeavour to drop into my office - a question of the Compulsory Purchase Order documents served on the property - Woodclose Cottages, Holbridge.
        *(draws heavily on cigar, then*
        *forcefully exhales smoke)*
Furniture.
        *(lifts a prudent hand)*
No problem. Abe, a cousin of Sam's will more likely than not, take the concomitants off your hands.

               SPENCER
        *(sharply)*
You sound to me as though you are telling me to stand outside because

> it's not raining. I'm use to settling
> my own business affairs, Mr
> Hinchcliffe, and if that's all, I'd
> like to call it a day.

> HINCHCLIFFE
> *(raises a vestigial eyebrow)*
> Should there be more? I think so!

*We see SPENCER being handed the legal order to quit from his mother's home. We see SPENCER scanning the paperwork – he looks disturbed.*

> SPENCER
> You're asking me to vacate my mother's
> home immediately – when my mother's
> hardly gone cold in her grave!

*When SPENCER looks up at HINCHCLIFFE he is surprised to see HINCHCLIFFE'S selected – prepared – lit and puffing a new cigar – produced three glasses – bottle of whisky – measured three fixed rations, and in the process of pushing one glass toward SAM and the other into his direction.*

*We see SAM taking no vocal part in the given arrangements.*

*We see SAM setting SPENCER rather liken to an animal whose head is turned sagaciously – backwards – in an attitude of acute vigilance.*

*We see SPENCER thump the desk so hard that HINCHCLIFFE is so surprised that he knocks over the consolation drink.*

*We hear HINCHCLIFFE'S words spoken with just the right ring of the insinuation to introduce the suggestion he knows very well, what, and who, is here.*

HINCHCLIFFE
(pronounces)
What have we here?

SPENCER
(outraged)
Mr Hinchcliffe. I can not have you explaining me away. That would be just too much – I'm a man who cannot stand having assumptions inflicted upon me. I'd like to think I'm a man with a sense of morality – a fair man, therefore, I will not go out of my way – unless you go out of yours, to espouse causes or perform agrarian outrages.

SAM
(rasps)
No need to take it that far – I'll see to the Compulsory Purchase Order being waylaid or lifted.

HINCHCLIFFE
(rebuking)
You must let me be the judge of that, Sam.
(tops up his own drink generously)
After all, let's not lose sight of the fact Evelyn Ridgeholm and son were, but have not been local residents here in Holbridge for the last thirty or forty years ...
(takes a drink)
Taking into account Mother and son

>                       pleased everyone by staying in
>                       Australia then Canada.
>
>                               SPENCER
>                           *(coldly)*
>                       That last remark, Mr Hinchcliffe, was
>                       spoken with studied cruelty. If you
>                       were a younger man, I would knock the
>                       living daylights out of you ...

*We see SAM rise from his seating. He comes to within a stride between SPENCER and himself. We see the abdicator of fatherhood stare perspicaciously into SPENCER'S face. We see SPENCER'S face gradually superimpose onto SAM'S.*

>                               SAM
>                           *(without parting his jaw)*
>                       I'll see you get your dues.
>                           *(turns abruptly to HINCHCLIFFE)*
>                       I'll be back here in the hour.
>                           *(without taking breath)*
>                       The apple doesn't fall far from the
>                       tree.

### SCENE 66
### I/E. ROVER CAR - STOCKDALE FARMS - HAYFIELDS - 9:10 AM

*We see STELLA hauling the Rover's steering wheel – tyres spinning on the stingy heather – she comes to a fluctuating halt. Stiff legged she climbs out of the car – just in time to open the field gate for approaching car.*

*We see the veterinary, MR DAVIS accelerate through gateway, one hand on the wheel, other arm crooked over the drawn down window.*

*We see MR DAVIS shake hands within easy reach of STELLA without undue stretching - all done in a curious endurance - he moves his car slowly forward as he speaks.*

                  MR DAVIS
      Spencer tells me Nelson has made a
      vast change for the better and that
      Blanche is carrying on -

                  STELLA
Names!
        *(nose rises slightly)*
      Names strike more than they stroke, Mr
      Davis.

*We see exhaust fumes discharge as MR DAVIS revs engine, to quickly speed off.*

*We see STELLA surge back to the Rover to remove the food basket and ginger beer bottles - slams door down, before clanging the sneck on the five barred gate close behind her.*

*We see GRACE and SOPHIE spotting STELLA. They down the wooden hay-rakes and come to meet her, looking wonderfully suntanned and healthy in the June sunshine. We see STELLA hand out food boxes and bottles of ginger beer to them - they settle down for a break behind the shade of the wall-back to consume mid-morning snacks and cheese scones and apple pie.*

*We see STELLA heading for JAKE.*

                  JAKE
        *(shouting as he backs HORSE and*
        *machine before taking next cut*
        *of row)*
     <u>Back! Back!</u>

We see the cutting bar containing the long razor sharp zigzag blade moving rapidly as it cuts through the variegated grasses, clover and wild flowers, to fall down onto the long swath board at the end of the cutting bar - to roll over and form thick rain-logged cutaway swaths - which fall with exact formality just out of reach of the mowing machine when it comes back round the field.

                    JAKE
                  (bawling)
        <u>Woooaaahhh! Wooaahh!</u>

We see JAKE pulling on reins to bring the HORSE to an uneasy, sweating halt - we hear leather harness creaking, and connecting chains clanging.

We see the relentless plague of flies taking rise to make buzzing sounds around HORSE, JAKE and STELLA before resettling unmercifully around the HORSE'S moist nostrils and pestered eyes and along its sweating body.

We see JAKE, wrapping the reins loosely over and between an iron wheel spoke before he climbs down stiffly from the machine seat.

We see SPENCER - on another machine - mowing the other half of meadow.

We see STELLA pouring out a quota of ginger beer for JAKE, then reaching into the wicker basket for his snack box. JAKE covers her every movement with suspicious attention.

                    JAKE
              (drolly to STELLA)
    By hell ...
             (throws a mournful glance up

>           *the field)*
> Sam Asquith couplin' wi' that gurt
> mother o' his ...
>           *(grimacing)*
> It must have been like givin' ah
> French-kiss t' ah cow!

*STELLA rapidly blinks the image away. She doesn't reply - instead straightens the cloths in the basket.*

*JAKE guzzles on the cheese scones.*

>                JAKE
> Ta think it only took ah half-pissed
> copula t' produce that!
>           *(swallows noisily)*
> An' t' think - me an' missus -

>                STELLA
>           *(gallantly)*
> Intimacy can put a spin on our lives,
> but I'm afraid my memory might be too
> inadvertently selective.
>           *(changing subject in the same*
>           *breath)*
> It's as Sam use to say ...
>           *(smiles peculiarly)*
> "The best time for cutting grass is
> during the first days of June when the
> meadow grasses are in full bloom".

*JAKE drinks noisily across top of tin mug as he scrutinises her body language.*

*STELLA looks markedly resentful at his affront.*

                    JAKE
            (strives to put warmth and
            conviction into his voice)
        Ah see tha's been havin' ah
        conversation with thesen, like. Easy
        ta imitate, hard t' describe.

                    STELLA
            (adamant)
        I want you and Spencer to put your
        differences on hold until after
        autumn, at least -

*STELLA takes the empty mug and box from JAKE and places them in a linen bag before returning them back into the basket.*

                    JAKE
            (rancorously)
        An' what about thine?

*We see JAKE take a stride nearer to STELLA.*

                    STELLA
            (snarls)
        Yes! Me as well, Jake! Right now I
        care more about my hay and harvest
        crops being gathered in for winter
        than I do about personal or family
        vendettas! I could not stomach another
        winter like the last one!

                    JAKE
        Weel! Ah hope it'll not be too dull a
        time for thee.

*We see JAKE climb back on the machine and lower himself*

woodenly onto the iron seat. He gathers reins – then half-turns his face away, narrowing his eyes, and peers out of their corners at her. We see suspicion and morbid curiosity with a suggestion of disrelish spread across his rugged features.

                JAKE
            (slow and distinct)
    Tha'll be adoptin' him first! Then
    tha'll be weddin' him next!

**SCENE 67**

**EXT. STOCKDALE FARMS – FARMYARD - ONE WEEK LATER – 10 AM**

We see arrival of KIT SULLIVAN, aged 45, rough and ready Irishman, leads an unconventional lifestyle.

                SPENCER
    You must be Kit Sullivan. I've heard a
    lot about you, and I'm aware you've
    not heard of me – my father was Sam
    Asquith.

                KIT
    I've worked seasonal for Sam Asquith
    as regular as clockwork, the second
    week in June until September ... for
    the last twenty years without
    complaints.

We see SPENCER and KIT shake hands.

**SCENE 68**

**I/E. HARRY'S PARENTS' CAR - STOCKDALE FARMS – 11 AM**

We see HARRY'S PARENTS driving along cart-road next to

*hayfields - on their way to Stockdale - HARRY'S on backseat with crutches, left leg in plaster.*

*We see JAKE, SPENCER and KIT taking a snack-break behind a stone wall. HARRY'S FATHER winds down window and addresses them.*

>                     HARRY'S FATHER
>                 (speaking to countryfolk as
>                 though they are bumpkins)
>             Are we to believe that a search is
>             still mounted for the absconder and
>             the vehicle?
>                 (judicially)
>             After all, by leaving the scene of the
>             accident, this - this stealthy
>             personage has committed a criminal
>             offence -
>
>                     JAKE
>                 (rancorously)
>             Aye - an' we're all up against bloody
>             weather, so don't come hinderin' us by
>             spoutin' thee hoi polloi jargon in our
>             faces - fuck off!

*HARRY'S PARENTS are not offered any hospitality - the relief is proportionate as they drop HARRY off and drive away.*

>                     HARRY
>                 (sighting STELLA approaching)
>             So! So good to be back in the
>             countryside.
>                 (smiles happily)
>             You've no idea how good it feels to be
>             amongst you all again -

                        STELLA
            I hope, young man, you don't expect us
            all to wait hand and foot upon you.
            Let's get one thing clear. If you're
            staying on at Stockdale this summer,
            we will expect you to addle your keep.
            We're not running a charity shop here.

**SCENE 69**
**EXT. STOCKDALE FARMS - HAYFIELDS - 12:15 AM**

We see HARRY hoisted onto an iron seat attached to the horse-drawn hay-rake machine to rake the strewed dry grasses into windrows.

We see SPENCER spurring him on competitively, while using the pronged paddy sweep to samm-up lengths of each gathered windrow.

We see SPENCER back harnessed HORSE, then taking the strain from the side-chains, before dragging the hay-sweep teeth back from beneath the abundantly gathered hay, SPENCER manually lifts the sweep by its handles so that the wooden teeth-tips dig into the ground, and as the HORSE moves forward - off-side - allowing the implement to somersault over the sammed-up hay - to then right itself on the other side of the gathered mass - it is ready to be forked into hay-pikes.

                        STELLA
                     (to GRACE)
            I'm sure Harry's hugging himself in a
            perverse way - manoeuvring the levers
            with his one good foot and his right
            hand strategy of reining.

                    GRACE
          He's still in a preliminary stage, but
          I can see he's cottoning on ...

                    JAKE
               (shouting at HARRY)
          Tha's makin' as much impression as ah
          fart on ah drum, Sonny!

*No notice is taken of JAKE'S taunt.*

*We see STELLA bend to draw a couple of handfuls of hay out of the near bottom off the hay-pike. She begins to twist it methodically.*

*JAKE'S eyes are fixed on STELLA – watching her make a hay-loop then nimbly putting the loop over a tooth of GRACE'S hand-rake.*

*We see GRACE spiralling the rake handle – moving backwards as the twisted hay lengthens, as STELLA feeds the hay-rope with more strands of collated hay.*

*JAKE bides his time, forking hay onto his pike from the sammed-up heaps of dried grasses, now turned golden brown by the summer sun.*

*We see GRACE raise with the hay-rope still attached high enough to clear the top of the hay-pike and reach down to the other side.*

*We see STELLA then take another handful of hay from the pike's other side, and twist it to secure to the other, before tucking it into the side of the pike.*

STELLA

That should anchor the pike against any severe summer winds and small whirlwinds that could cause havoc ...

JAKE

*(unable to control his impatience)*

It's these friggin' new arrangements!

STELLA

New arrangements?

*(turns to face JAKE)*

What new arrangements?

JAKE

Ah'm tellin' thee. It's bloody unnatural to bunch all o' these menfolk into my home. Ah can't do a sodin' hand stir, nivver mind shit in peace for them – an' after ah hard day's work, ah want ah quiet life as much as an' maybe more than they ruddy well do!

GRACE

*(shouting)*

<u>A quiet life! You think you're entitled to a quiet life here at Stockdale. Well – that's damn rich coming from someone who helped string up my man – then half-kill my brother and maim Harry!</u>

JAKE

Tha what!

>             *(showing his teeth clamped*
>             *together in hostility)*
> What did ta say?
>
>                  KIT
>             *(strolls into earshot)*
> Pub talk has it, Sam Asquith, my boss
> here for over twenty summer seasons,
> left the place you call home, Jake, to
> his cryptic son, and it won't be over
> long before you're turned out to
> grass.

*We see JAKE like the snake of the hood – studying KIT, and KIT looking blatantly back at him. We see STELLA regarding them with sharp attention.*

>                  STELLA
> This is neither the time nor the place
> for such loose talk, quite scandalous
> and entirely injurious to the Asquith
> reputation!
>             *(her eyes flash with anger)*
> People should learn to place their
> hands over their mouths more.

*We see STELLA march off to start a new hay-pike.*

>                  JAKE
>             *(shouting)*
> <u>Ah'm not on ah blind, if that's what
> you're all damn well thinkin'</u>.

*We see JAKE lunging himself untidily down the field to work on his own hay-pike.*

                    JAKE
               (rancidly talking to himself)
          Fuckers - stealin' my home from me.
          Weel, ah'll button up that Asquith
          bastard for a start - as sharp as onny
          lady's maid could fasten the master's
          fly-buttons.

## SCENE 70
**EXT. STOCKDALE FARMS - FARMYARD - ONE WEEK LATER - 2 PM**

We see MR DAVIS examining NELSON. We see KIT riding NELSON in yard for final oversee.

We see JAKE, observing - unlit cigarette in mouth, walking-stick in hand.

                    MR DAVIS
          I can certify now that Nelson is
          sound.
               (pats NELSON'S rump)
          Yes, he's, again in full fettle.
               (turns to JAKE)
          I'll check the heifer to confirm she's
          cleansed thoroughly after calving.

We see JAKE light his cigarette as KIT, still astride NELSON, circles the yard. MR DAVIS heads for bottom cow-house.

We see through MR DAVIS' Point-Of-View: via cow-house window reflection - KIT and NELSON approaching open yard gate, JAKE stepping behind them - raising walking-stick and wriggling the tip into NELSON'S anal ring.

We see NELSON rear up and bolt through open gateway, leaping across the beck - with KIT clinging wildly to its halter -

*neither making contact with the first stone wall.*

*We see MR DAVIS grasping medicinal case and chasing after KIT and NELSON - just in time to see another wall looming.*

*We see KIT trying in vain to get NELSON level with wall.*

*We get a glimpse of NELSON skimming the top-stones as they pass over.*

*We see MR DAVIS climbing over second wall.*

*We see KIT sprawled behind the wall - between and through wild brier bushes, looking wetly blooded and showing convulsive motions.*

*We see NELSON grazing nearby.*

*JAKE disappears into a pig-house.*

## SCENE 71
**EXT. STOCKDALE FARMS - FARMYARD - TWO DAYS LATER - 6:30 PM**

*The sun has left the front of the homestead.*

*We see STELLA and SOPHIE turning out the last of the DAIRY COWS from the bottom cow-house after their evening milking time.*

*We hear SOPHIE whistling for BRIDIE to heel DAIRY COWS across beck to pasture land - repeatedly she whistles - no BRIDIE.*

*We see STELLA and SOPHIE searching - whistling - searching.*

**SCENE 72**

**EXT. STOCKDALE FARMS - GARTH - 6:40 PM**

*We see STELLA and SOPHIE finding BRIDIE in the garth, collapsed - vomiting.*

*We see BRIDIE'S spine arched and her head strained backwards grotesquely over her backbone, legs peddling the air frantically.*

>            STELLA
>         *(concerned)*
>    Bridie's in a bad way.

*We see BRIDIE suddenly go still.*

*We see SOPHIE throw herself down beside her dog, with shaking hands she tries to comfort BRIDIE, who again shows signs of spasms.*

>            SOPHIE
>    Is Bridie having a fit or ...
>       *(finds speaking difficult)*
>    Whaaat's happening to her, Mam?

*We see STELLA dropping to her knees beside them.*

>            STELLA
>         *(sorrowfully)*
>    By the look of her - Bridie's taken
>    poison -

>            SOPHIE
>    Poisoned!

*We see SOPHIE'S face crumble - tears glitter on her downcast lashes.*

*We see STELLA forcing her gaze over SOPHIE'S head and in the direction of the pastures.*

          STELLA
Strychnine poisoning is something that crops up now and then in the countryside after farmers have used it to control wild vermin.

          SOPHIE
But Bridie ...
    *(voice breaks)*
Not Bridie.

*We see SOPHIE stroking BRIDIE'S head, lovingly.*

          SOPHIE
    *(cries out with astonishing hostility)*
<u>Not Jake! Surely not Jake!</u>

          STELLA
I wouldn't put anything passed Jake these days, but let's not jump to conclusions – yet – it could be the hand of a gamekeeper, perhaps Hensley, over at the Smethers ...

          SOPHIE
But their estate is several farms from here, and Bridie has only been missing for the last half hour ...

*SOPHIE breaks off talking as BRIDIE suddenly jerks still –*

*then again – another tormenting spasm – her fine limbs straining wildly in the warm summer breezes – then – all her muscles reduce in a full suffering contraction.*

*We see STELLA placing her arm along SOPHIE'S shoulders.*

>            STELLA
> Bridie's dying, lass ... and there's
> no antidote to this poison.

*SOPHIE'S too overcome with misery to answer.*

*We hear BRIDIE'S breathing – death agony breathing – rattling in the depth of her throat ...*

*FADE OUT.*

*END CREDITS ROLLS TO SONG BY IDA BARKER, "I FORGOT TO FORGET".*

*END OF EPISODE 3.*

Episode 4

# Autumn

:

# EPISODE 4
# AUTUMN

:

## SCENE 1
**INT. STOCKDALE FARMS – BARN CAUSEWAY – 10 PM**

*Indian summer. We see three sets of eyes; SPENCER, STELLA and BLANCHE watching JAKE.*

*We see JAKE side-stepping, left hand gripping GELDING'S mouth-bit, his other hand pushing hard against its girth as he manoeuvers the HORSE, in the shafts of the empty hay-cart, from the inner barn causeway – to lead it outside.*

*We see the fading early September eventide lightness, projecting a broad warm dusky shaft of light through the open barn doors, while high above, through the glassless narrow slit-windows, strands of mellow light project down onto the hay mew and inner causeway – depicting SPENCER, STELLA and BLANCHE working within the stone building.*

*We see SPENCER leaning forward at the edge of the mew with his hands cupped round his knees.*

> SPENCER
> (shouting)
> That will be the last load of hay for the day, Jake. We'll see you back at the stables before long!

*We see JAKE turn and look up at him in such a way as to mean anything.*

                    JAKE
               *(bawling back)*
          Reight! Ah'll be takin' horse out from
          between shafts, an' ah'll leave cart
          tipped an' stabilised here before
          headin' back home wi' horse!

**SCENE 2**
**INT. STOCKDALE FARMS – BARN – 10:20 PM**

*We see SPENCER and BLANCHE spreading the last forkfuls of sweet, dried hay, evenly, before treading every square inch of it down.*

*We see STELLA raking down the loose crisp hay from the side of the mew.*

*We see BLANCHE stretching out her right hand for the long-sided barn ladder propped against the wall, and swinging her leg over the side of the hay mew.*

*We see BLANCHE blindly feeling with her foot for the right level rung under her shoe sole – finding it – she swings the other foot below it, putting her whole weight upon the ladder rungs.*

*We see BLANCHE warily descend – suddenly, without warning, the cross-pieces forming the steps give way beneath her feet – startled – BLANCHE opens her mouth wide and lets out a long drawn out penetrating scream!*

*We see SPENCER turn from treading – just in time to see BLANCHE'S head disappear below the perimeter of stacked hay.*

*We hear the scrapping of the long ladder against the stone wall.*

*We hear SPENCER shout to STELLA as he throws himself to the edge of the mew, to leap athletically onto the interlocking top arm of the barn door and scale down.*

*We see in the diminishing daylight STELLA swinging herself round towards BLANCHE.*

      STELLA
     (yelling)
  <u>No! Noooohhhaaahhh!</u>

*We see STELLA fling herself headlong at BLANCHE'S downfall - and somehow manage to grab and wrap her arms around BLANCHE'S posterior and the shunting ladder.*

*We see SPENCER ducking passed the tilted ladder. He places his hands under BLANCHE'S armpits.*

      SPENCER
  Blanche is in a state of shock, 'Ella
  - I've never seen such a blank
  expression on anyone's face ... and
  her perspiration is chilled on her
  body ...

*Neither STELLA or BLANCHE hear him.*

*We see SPENCER raising his eyes to squint up the ladder - seeing at least six rungs broken - splintered or missing.*

*There's an amplified silence.*

      STELLA
  Is this one more of Jake's monkey
  tricks, Spence?

*We see SPENCER considering the slight abbreviation.*

>              SPENCER
>           *(arbitrarily)*
> Hard to tell without inspecting the
> ladder, but there are several cross-
> pieces cracked and some missing.

>              BLANCHE
>           *(faint voice)*
> Miz ... ing ...

*We see BLANCHE moving her head slowly from side to side, she looks white and dishevelled and appears to have no idea where she is, or what time of day it is.*

*We see STELLA jostling herself half-round the leaning ladder to search BLANCHE'S face.*

>              STELLA
> Is Mother showing any interest,
> Spencer? Any interest at all? Mother's
> not usually this quiet.
>       *(noisy intake of breath)*
> She's – she's not ...

>              SPENCER
>           *(gravely)*
> Shock – I guess we'll have to carry
> Blanche home ...

>              BLANCHE
>           *(vaguely)*
> Kkkri ... keeeee ...

STELLA

(gasping)

Ruddy wars – I don't know whether to laugh or cry ...

(hangs onto BLANCHE'S posterior)

because Mother's still with us, despite having wet and soiled her clothes.

SPENCER

Dear Blanche. It's nature's calling card to an unexpected fall ...

(peers into BLANCHE'S face)

if this is another of Jake's dirty tricks, 'Ella ...

(rasps)

then someone will have to settle his ash before he kills one of us. You know as well as I do, that old man will never leave Stockdale, even though I've already offered him a cottage free of rent, next year at Woodclose.

STELLA

(discordant voice)

I know! We all know, and he knows we all know. But are we tamely going to let these things happen? Are we going to let this pernicious old man enjoy the dramatic aspects and plain curiosity of it all, before he goes in for the kill?

*We see STELLA pushing her perspiring face so close to*

SPENCER'S face, which almost blends into STELLA'S in the filtering shafts through slit windows.

                      SPENCER
                  (huskily)
         You are far too easy to follow these
         days, 'Ella. Your presence is far more
         disturbing than an overactive
         conscience.

We see, just, the dust particles rising and falling gently, as their hot breath creates currents of air to fan temperaments.

We hear BLANCHE let out a bellow of thanksgiving - it brings STELLA and SPENCER'S charged attention strictly back to her predicament.

                      STELLA
         Mother! Oh Mother!

We see BLANCHE extracting herself from them and the ladder.

We see BLANCHE hooking up her dress - dragging down her saturated and ordure bloomers, panting and crying from the sheer physical strain of it all.

                      BLANCHE
                  (miserable)
         I need a cigarette - and a good ...
         stiff drink.

We see BLANCHE covering her face with bleeding fingers, blood trickling down her arms.

                    STELLA
                  (disturbed)
            Dear God. My mother looks like the
            parent turning into the child.

*We see STELLA and SPENCER wrapping the resisting BLANCHE in several hessian meal sacks, to carry her home, lying in mercy, on the loft ladder.*

## SCENE 3
**INT. STOCKDALE FARMS - STELLA'S KITCHEN - 11:30 PM**

*We see JAKE butting his head around kitchen door. The room is empty and the linen curtains drawn. On the windowsill the hissing tilly lamp casts prismatic colours and darken shadows, modifying the corners of the large room.*

*We see JAKE step inside and close the door quietly, then strutting towards the table.*

*We see six table settings. Two have been used. JAKE picks up the white cup with blue border from matching saucer. He sniffs it, then places it back down.*

                    JAKE
                  (mutters)
            Cream an' sugar, the bastard! So he's
            been an' gone - or has he?

*We see JAKE taking his time to daintily place his forefinger and thumb tip on either side of the china cup handle to gingerly raise it from its flowery edged saucer - mockingly - taking off STELLA'S mannerism of slightly curling his little finger, half-closing his eyes, pursing his lips, to gradually bring the fluted edge of the cup to his mouth.*

                    JAKE
                (mutters)
        Her second cup of tea. She never
        finishes the second - says it never
        tastes as good as the first one - so -
        they are both standin' - or are they?

We see JAKE'S eyes move - to rest on a cluster of short
stemmed glasses turned upside down and left to drain on the
side of the sink running board.

                    JAKE
                (mumbles)
        So three have admitted t' need o' a
        drink.

We see JAKE turn back to the kitchen table and drop STELLA'S
cup onto its saucer.

We see BLANCHE'S place setting has not been touched.

                    JAKE
                (softly)
        So - it's her who's come a cropper.
        Her - not him.
                (grimaces)
        Weel, what t' hell - that bastard's
        turn will come - later.

We see JAKE plonk himself down at his own seating. He lifts
the tea-cosy off the teapot and places his hands around the
earthenware pot - speaks as though he's talking to an
invisible person.

                    JAKE
        Still fairly hot - been brewed I'd

                    say, about half-an-hour ago, at a
                    guess.

We see JAKE shoot a glance at the free-standing clock, near
the burning lamp.

                         JAKE
                       (softly)
                    Twenty-five t' twelve. Weel, Grace an'
                    Sophie won't be back for an hour or
                    two – aye, taken young townie t'
                    hospital t' have plaster removed then
                    visitin' gurt Winny an' Abe t' collect
                    a young dog.
                       (imitating SPENCER'S voice)
                    One of Cousin Mike's ... one trained
                    collie that hasn't come up to scratch
                    – one that does not follow commands
                    good enough for Mike's sheepdog trials
                    ...
                       (grinds his teeth)
                    Ah've half a mind t' do it all over
                    again – but where t' hell have they
                    hidden rat poison? Fuck them! All!
                    They've no idea what it's like t' be
                    without in the middle o' plenty.
                       (rives about on chair)
                    I'd nivver once thought twice about
                    brass until that son o' ah bitch came
                    here t' Stockdale.
                       (snarls)
                    But bloody soon ah'll show them, by
                    Gawd, ah'll show them!

We see JAKE suddenly lurch across the table to lift the
cheese dish lid and hack off a piece, then stab it onto his

*plate. He helps himself to a teacake under a glass cover - he tears it apart. Removes butter dish lid - scoops a knife blade full.*

      JAKE
     *(guttural)*
  Ah don't need a fuckin' Christian t'
  tell me ah've ended up sharin' me home
  like at workhouse wi' three friggin'
  drop-outs ...
     *(gormandising bread)*
  Aye. One who's dropped reight onto his
  feet - one who knows a good thing when
  he sees it - and one who makes his
  home wherever he lays his head.
     *(swills his mouths with*
     *lukewarm tea)*
  A cottage, ah God-damned cottage!

*We see JAKE wipe the back of his hand over his contorted mouth. He pushes plate away and stiffly rises from the chair.*

      JAKE
  Where's the bastard? What's he up ta?
  Not next door - ah searched there
  afore comin' here, an' Sullivan, after
  cartin' hay buggered off across fields
  t' Crown - late drinkin' there - aye.
  Busy knockin' landlady off, so he
  comes rollickin' back at dawn.

*We see JAKE pincer-toe his way to adjoining door - the living room - and place an ear to the hinges.*

*We hear mild snoring sounds - slowly he pushes door half-open to reveal the back of draped curtain - places a cocked ear to fabric.*

*We hear faint fire cracklings – there again – faint snorts.*

                   JAKE
                *(mutters)*
        Not the bastard – he nivver makes as much as a muffle, an' by Gawd ah've stood outside his bedroom door often enough t' wonder if the dingo sleeps wi' his eyes wide open – lamp-like.

## SCENE 4
**INT. STOCKDALE FARMS – STELLA'S LIVING ROOM – 11:34 PM**

*We see JAKE groping among curtain folds – twitch it aside.*

*We see BLANCHE laid asleep on the large sofa - spotlighted in the mellow glow of paraffin lamps.*

*We see SAM'S box of cigars and his pipe holder with various pipes jutting out of their holes – alongside a pile of farming weekly journals.*

*We see JAKE squinting in the temperate light – bends to select a pipe.*

                   JAKE
                *(softly)*
        Ahh – so they kept you. Aye – the one ah prised out o' bosses frozen teeth – an' from then on – all this friggin' change started.

*We see JAKE snap the pipe into pieces and savagely throw them into the fire – he watches them slowly spit and burn.*

                    JAKE
          Aye – burn – burn t' ashes.
                (watches ashes gently
                fluttering)
          Now, then yah little beggars – don't
          be givin' me any rascally ideas – cos
          ...

Suddenly BLANCHE lets out a loud snort.

We see JAKE judder upright.

                    JAKE
                (mutters)
          The fat sow ...

We see JAKE in a dance-like way – move to the head of the sofa and lean over the sleeping BLANCHE.

                    JAKE
          By hell – I'd ah given my eye-tooth t'
          have seen thee face drop.

We see JAKE place his middle finger nail into the pad of his thumb and flick his nail edge against BLANCHE'S nose-tip – he waits for reaction.

We see BLANCHE – in a spread-out way – seeing white cotton gloved hands crossed corpse-like over her ample breasts.

We see bandages poking out from her dressing gown cuffs.

We see her not moving an inch.

We see JAKE'S disappointment and distaste.

JAKE
Yah lazy old bitch. Ah expected ah better show from thee.

**SCENE 5**

**INT. STOCKDALE FARMS – STELLA'S LIVING ROOM – 11 PM (FLASHBACK)**

*We see BLANCHE washed, attired in flannelette nightdress and dressing gown.*

*We see STELLA and SPENCER insisting she should rest on the sofa.*

STELLA
Here, Mam.
*(hands BLANCHE a drink)*
Just sip this gently, it's your favourite tipple – Grace's homemade turnip wine – it will take your mind off things while Spencer attends to your injuries.

*We see SPENCER removing vicious splinters from beneath BLANCHE'S finger nails, wrists and others embedded into her upper arms.*

BLANCHE
*(weakly)*
I feel as though I've had all the stuffing knocked out of me – and my body feels numb ...

STELLA
You've had a shock, Mam. In fact – all three of us have had a shock.

>                    (strokes BLANCHE'S damp hair)
> I thought that you were having a heart attack, or ...
>                    (voice wavers)
> Even worse ...

                    BLANCHE
The flash-point came when I felt the rungs give way as soon as I placed both feet together – my weight ...

                    SPENCER
                    (tight-lipped)
I'll check each ladder rung tomorrow morning – I'm beginning to now feel for certain, the most innocent incidents happening here, are beginning to point to Jake.

*We see SPENCER placing lint, before bandages around BLANCHE'S discharging wounds.*

                    STELLA
I've seen the stone's throw in Jake's eyes when he looks at Mother.

                    SPENCER
And I've been at the blunt end of Jake's actions, you're right, 'Ella. He's stone to us, and we will all bruise ourselves against him – he needs no excuses, only opportunities.

                    BLANCHE
                    (with sedation)
I'm beginning ... to realise ... that

it's quite difficult ... to die.

          STELLA

Poor old you, Mam.
> *(eyes water)*

You always have taken the most hopeful view of life ...

          BLANCHE

Promise me, that both of you won't stray far away from me, tonight.
> *(rests her hands across her breasts)*

I need to try and sleep the worst off.

          STELLA

I'll just sip into the dining room to wind the gramophone up and pop one of your favourite Roaring Twenties records on the turn table ... Just to tide you over.

*We see STELLA disappear into adjoining room – the dining room.*

          SPENCER
> *(putting first aid box into sideboard cupboard)*

You can rest assure, Blanche, we'll not be too far away.

*We see SPENCER place a couple of logs on fire.*

*We hear music playing as STELLA re-enters living room.*

*We see SPENCER pouring out two generous measures of brandy.*

*He hands one to STELLA. They clink glasses.*

                    SPENCER
          Just to get the edge off things.

*We see BLANCHE closing her eyes on them – as she thankfully gives into her lassitude of body and mind.*

*We see STELLA and SPENCER induced to hum and dance to the music hall medley of songs.*

## SCENE 6
**INT. STOCKDALE FARMS – STELLA'S LIVING ROOM – 11:38 PM**

*We see JAKE staring down at BLANCHE – he turns aside to help himself to a glass of wine – gulps it down – pours another. We see him listening – intently.*

                    JAKE
                (mutters)
          Where the hell is she? Can't be far
          off – not wi' old lady laid flat on
          her back ...

*We see him alerted – as though hearing another sound – pauses – again we hear a faint swirling.*

*We see JAKE cross the room to stand behind the kitchen curtained door - we can hear the mellow hissing of the kitchen lamp.*

*We see JAKE juddering back to the dining room door – he brushes his ear to the keyhole.*

*We hear again, the faint swirling ... JAKE bars his teeth, slowly turns the door knob – pauses – butts head round door edge.*

## SCENE 7
## INT. STOCKDALE FARMS - STELLA'S DINING ROOM - 11:39 PM

*We see the dining room dimly lit by candle light - JAKE'S eyes dart around the room - he steps into room - careful not to let the door click behind him.*

*We hear, mulled whirling sound.*

> JAKE
> (mutters)
> Fuck me ...

*We catch the pale reflective surface of the gramophone horn.*

*We see JAKE bumping his way against furniture, to stand before the barely moving turntable of the gramophone. His hand closing over the handle.*

*We see JAKE slowly stoop to pick up STELLA'S crumbled dress from the carpet - he brings it up to his face - then lets it drop as though it's scalded him.*

*We see his eyes glitter in the dim light - as his sight pinpoints SPENCER'S pair of calf-leather boots slewed to the side of the middle door.*

> JAKE
> (through clenched teeth)
> Upstairs - bedrooms.

*We see JAKE incensed.*

*He returns back into the living room.*

## SCENE 8
**INT. STOCKDALE FARMS - STELLA'S LIVING ROOM - 11:40 PM**

JAKE towers over BLANCHE laid sleeping on the sofa.

> JAKE
> (mouths)
> Weel! Thou'll have t' go for ah fuckin' start.

JAKE pokes her. BLANCHE doesn't move one muscle.

> JAKE
> Ah case o' throttle or ...

BLANCHE suddenly snorts loudly and her mouth slackens sideways.

We see JAKE grab the nearest cushion – and as he lifts the cushion above her head – we hear SAM'S voice as though in JAKE'S ear.

> SAM (V/O)
> Murder shouldn't be rushed. It should be enjoyed by various degrees.

We see JAKE drop the cushion onto an easy chair, still straining to hear footsteps – nothing to be heard only the crackling of logs.

We see JAKE sidle back into the kitchen.

## SCENE 9
**INT. STOCKDALE FARMS - STELLA'S KITCHEN - 11:41 PM**

JAKE washes and dries his used crockery and cutlery – buffs

up container lids with his cuff – blows loose crumbs off table cloth and pushes his chair nearer to table.

**SCENE 10**
**INT. STOCKDALE FARMS – STELLA'S LIVING ROOM – 11:42 PM**

Giving ear, JAKE enters the living room.

We see JAKE standing over sleeping BLANCHE.

We see BLANCHE sprawled out oblivious to his presence.

**SCENE 11**
**INT. STOCKDALE FARMS – STELLA'S DINING ROOM – 11:43 PM**

JAKE enters.

We hear a board creak above – then creak some more ... JAKE shifts his burning eyes to the ceiling.

We hear vague voices and snatches of muffled laughter ...

>                     JAKE
>                  (mouths)
>          Brazen bitch an' bullin' bastard!
>                  (face twists into a storm of
>                  rage)
>          Fuckin' betrayer! An' gavelkind
>          bastard!

We hear BLANCHE snort from the living room.

**SCENE 12**
**INT. STOCKDALE FARMS – STELLA'S LIVING ROOM – 11:44 PM**

JAKE juts into living room – stares down at sleeping BLANCHE.

JAKE

Aye. Ah expected ah better show from thee. Ah see tha's eaten theesen out o' shape – ah real bloody luxury item bein' kept in clover.

   *(pause)*

Folk like thee expect something different an' then they're pleased ...

*We hear BLANCHE snort. JAKE'S all rage again.*

*We see JAKE straddling his knees on either side of BLANCHE'S ample thighs – he bends to reach for cushion – jams it down on her slackened face.*

*We see no retaliation ...*

*We see disappointment on his face.*

JAKE

   *(mumbles)*

Hasta already had enough?

   *(pants)*

Trust a bloody woman t' incite discontentment ...

   *(places extra pressure onto the cushion)*

Tha reminds me o' Carol Wray. Ah courted her for nigh on eight years – eight bloody long discontented years – wherein – all she'd wanted was kisses an' cuddles – while ah wanted more ...

   *(splutters)*

Ah can still hear dozy Carol parrotin' off what her bigoted mother had dinned into her fathead ...

>                    (mimics)
>          "Anything, our Carole that moves to
>          grow in your hand is better left
>          alone. And, our Carole, don't put
>          anything into your mouth unless it's
>          been boiled first."
>                    (pants)
>          Fuckin' women!

*We see JAKE so intense with rage, that he's caught off guard as BLANCHE'S muscular legs shoot open from beneath him – she brings up her knees with force, knocking him headlong into the fire-range structure.*

*We see JAKE stupefied – struggling violently to sit up.*

*We see a glimpse through partly open dining room door of car headlights reflecting through the windows.*

*We see JAKE floundering to his knees – crab-crawling to the dining room doorway.*

## SCENE 13
**INT. STOCKDALE FARMS – STELLA'S DINING ROOM – 11:46 PM**

*We see JAKE straining his head towards the stairway door.*

*We hear distant on-foot sounds – indicating arrivals and descendants.*

*We see JAKE bungling himself to his feet, banging and tripping into and over furniture.*

*We hear vaguely BLANCHE'S crouping from the living room.*

*We see JAKE grabbing for the window-ledge – swirl the lock-*

*arm round – shove the bottom half up – he screws his eyes shut and head dives into darkened space.*

## SCENE 14
**INT. STOCKDALE FARMS – STELLA'S LIVING ROOM – 8 AM**

*We see BLANCHE looking in poor shape, propped up on the sofa. STELLA is fussing around her.*

                STELLA

Would you like a fresh cup of tea, Mother, with a drop of brandy in it – before I redress your injuries?

                BLANCHE
            *(smiles wearily)*

Later – love – later. I feel full of aches and pains, and I'm not too sure if I've received more damage than I first imagined ...

                STELLA

Would you like me to go and phone Doctor Liddle ...? You don't look in apple-pie order ...

                BLANCHE

No! At close quarters, he's not easy company.
      *(stubs out a comforting*
      *cigarette)*
The worst of all this – is ...
      *(speaks through a coughing fit)*
We'll never know – when we're safe from one hour to the next – never mind a day – the most ordinary happenings,

>                   to my mind – will be sinister –
>                   menacing – and distraction offers no
>                   middle road ...

*We hear BLANCHE involuntary croup away the rest of her words.*

*We see GRACE enter living room from kitchen, carrying pot of tea, milk jug and mugs. She places the tray on side-table.*

>                         GRACE
>                   You'll be pleased to hear, Grandma,
>                   Spencer has agreed to move into our
>                   guest room – he no longer trusts Jake.

*We see a look of shrewdness – self-indulgence and defensible innocence cross STELLA'S handsome, rosy face.*

>                         STELLA
>                   Yes. I've decided – and I've been
>                   thinking of nothing else since
>                   Grandma's downfall.
>                        *(pours tea)*
>                   As an elementary precaution, I've told
>                   Spencer, that I have every intention
>                   to adopt then marry him!

**SCENE 15**

**INT. STOCKDALE FARMS – STELLA'S KITCHEN - 9 AM**

*Two weeks later.*

*We see BLANCHE joining STELLA, GRACE, SOPHIE and SPENCER at the table for breakfast, she only has plasters on thumbs and first two fingers on each hand – she's wearing a long sleeved cardigan over her blouse.*

SPENCER
Good to see that you're joining the family for breakfast again, Blanche.

BLANCHE
Resourcefulness doesn't desert a woman who assisted in the Women's Home Defence during the war years.

SOPHIE
Harry said he's not looking forward to returning to office work, on Monday ...

STELLA
But he knows he's welcome here each weekend – so he shouldn't be too down hearted.

BLANCHE
And what's this I hear – Kit, at the end of each working day, now legs it across the fields to The Crown ...

GRACE
*(helping herself to fried bacon and scrambled eggs)*
And he's back here by six o' clock for the morning milking ... then straight into the hayfields ...

SOPHIE
*(loving gossip)*
Kit told Harry that he's unfavourable towards Jake after the horse caper and he knows Jake holds it against him for

lodging at the pub – and ...

*We hear JAKE'S boots on the flagstone – before he butts his way into the kitchen, and plonks himself down to help himself to breakfast. Their conversation falls flat.*

                  SPENCER
                *(casually)*
If the weather holds up we should have finished haytime by this time – next week.

                  STELLA
The gardens need to be tided up.
            *(turns to SOPHIE)*
Now there's a job for Harry at the weekend.

                  GRACE
                *(abruptly)*
And one person's choice can be another's pain.

*The meal is finished in silence.*

## SCENE 16
**I/E. STOCKDALE FARMS – TOP COW-HOUSE – 3:30 PM**

*One week later. The last day of haytime.*

*We see a cart-load of hay being forked through the window (frame removed) of the first floor above top cow-house, then forked up to the above baulks.*

*We see JAKE standing on the load outside – pulling off one forkful of hay after another and tossing them with expertise through the window gap to KIT, who stabs his fork into each forkful, to heave it high above his head to SPENCER who's stacking it onto the baulks.*

*We see SOPHIE treading the hay down, barefoot.*

>SOPHIE
>*(to SPENCER)*
>Do you think Jake will ever leave here to live in the cottage?

>SPENCER
>No!

>SOPHIE
>*(quietly)*
>Why? Why not. Retirement should be embraced. He's been working here at Stockdale, day in day out, since he was fourteen years old ...

>SPENCER
>That's the whole point — he feels he belongs here.

*We see SPENCER jab his fork into another forkful of hay from KIT, to shake it evenly out.*

>SPENCER
>Grandfather and my father gave him their word — for his loyalty to them he'd earned the right to live here until he dies ...

>SOPHIE
>But that was their promise, not ours!

SPENCER

Yes, you're right, Sophie, and he probably knows that, trouble with Jake is he's so entrenched in the old ways of farming that he can't see modern farming has great advantages.

*(takes another forkful of hay to spread evenly about)*

Which means, intensive farming – petrol machines – implements modified and we need electricity, gas – hot water laid on – cattle tested for TB.

*(sounds excited)*

So many advantageous changes, all if only Jake could open up his mind to their changes, there would still be a place for him here – but he can't see that – he'd rather play a deadly game of roulette with all our lives ...

SOPHIE

*(voice breaks)*

And are we going to pretend nothing is happening ... I mean, Bridie for a start ...

SPENCER

*(patiently)*

But we have no real proof of certainty to Bridie's demise.

*(pause)*

As we know, Sophie, poison is often laid down at random in the countryside, and –

SOPHIE

And Grandma's downfall! She did say, in her sleeping mind, she somehow felt stifled through some sort of presence. So Grace had the insight of re-checking all the closed windows, and found the bottom-half of the dining room window open, and she also noticed that the hollyhocks were lolling against the wall with their flowers crushed.

*(lips quiver)*

We've not told Grandma yet ...

SPENCER

*(nods his head repeatedly)*

Grace told me in no uncertain manner before I inspected the barn ladder carefully ... bearing in mind the ladder is as old as the barn – and yes, several rungs were broken, and two others dislodged, so, we're left with these findings against, dear Blanche's fourteen stone body weight against the age of the ladder ...

SOPHIE

*(angrily)*

You sound as though you're on Jake's side ...

SPENCER

*(stabbing his hay-fork into KIT'S high-rising forkful of hay)*

I'm a fair man, Sophie. I don't

believe in surmising – in my experience, it causes more trouble than what it's worth, besides – Jake was on the hay-carts, loading and unloading them all day – and Blanche and myself had used the ladder, twice earlier – but that doesn't mean I don't suspect him, so don't get me wrong, Sophie ...

          SOPHIE
          *(uneasily)*

Suspect! How can you say that, when yourself and Harry witnessed and received injuries from him after the milk machine celebration. That was grotesque behaviour, yet Harry and you, act as though it never even happened?

*We see SOPHIE stomping down with extra vigour on the loose hay.*

          SPENCER
          *(rasps)*

We are well aware, Sophie, that Jake's getting sadistic pleasure from inflicting these preliminary warnings as a procedure of controlling changes – modern farming changes, which he is profoundly against, all deeds instigated to impel self-preservation so, believe me when I say, we're watching him like rapacious hawks.
          *(joins SOPHIE to trample down the hay)*

> Jake Swales is a very cunning man, on the other hand, he can be very blatant ... we all have to be vigilant! Because he'll already be planning his next synchronous! We just have to catch him in action.

                    SOPHIE

> Harry says he's a psycho. And Grandma says, when Jake sits at our meal table, it's as though he's taking a ringside seat at a Greek orgy!

## SCENE 17
**EXT. STOCKDALE FARMS - BARLEY AND OAT FIELDS - 11:30 AM**

*Two weeks later.*

*We see STELLA and JAKE with the young COLLIE dog walking the borders of the blond fields of barley and oats. They are inspecting the oncoming harvest.*

*We see JAKE has taken to wearing extra old clothes, including an old khaki overcoat.*

                    STELLA

> Don't you think you're carrying things a bit too far, Jake? All those clothes - you must be boiling hot, the weather is still warm enough for shirt sleeves.

                    JAKE

> Nah, boss! Just a bit off colour.

*We see both eyeing each other severely for several seconds.*

> STELLA
>
> We could still work out our real and imaginary problems, Jake, if we all pull together, before it's too late, Sam would have ...

*Protuberant of eye, JAKE'S mouth slips sideways – he mutters something uncatchable.*

> STELLA
> *(tries again)*
> Can't we get things out and into the open instead of merely inferring their presence?
> *(looks him over, hesitates, stretches her point of view)*
> After all ...
> *(smiles appealingly)*
> Put yourself into my shoes ...

> JAKE
> *(snarls)*
> An' have me touchin' me forelock while he pokes up me arse?!

*We see STELLA'S better nature dissolve immediately. She clenches her teeth and looks nauseated.*

*We hear vehicle approaching. They lurch away from each other and head for the field gateway to stand on the cart-road.*

*We see SPENCER driving Rover car. See him primped, matched and laundered to the hilt.*

> JAKE
> Tha wants t' be on thee guard against

lone bastards dressed like a toff an'
drivin' thee car.
>(lips twist)

Tha'll start findin' out about why
they're lone bastards when it's too
late! Thee mark me words, lady!

    STELLA
>(stumpy)

I've learned not to run down corridors
with a pair of scissors, and Sam
always had his entourage of rodents.

We see SPENCER approaching - draws up alongside them. We see
JAKE incensed. He abruptly takes off back into cornfield,
whistling young COLLIE to heel.

We see no guilt on STELLA'S face as SPENCER winds down window
to thrust his head over the rim.

    SPENCER
>(looking worried)

Be careful, 'Ella. Remember the old
horseman's bitterly disturbed, and I
do believe his problems are so deep
seated because he can't let go of the
past handrails, therefore he can't let
go of his shame or blame of being
brought up in the paupers' workhouse -
>(arches an eyebrow)

He should be kinder to himself and
remember that childhood memories are a
prism, not always understood, if not
sufficiently explained.

We see SPENCER reach out his hand from the open car window,

to grasp hers – to press the back of her palm against his moving lips.

We see JAKE moving sprightly into sight through the gateway and onto the cart-road.

> JAKE
> When tha's finished slatherin' over boss's hand, ah suppose tha's headin' for that committee meetin' on electric job, then tha'll be back t' Stockdale like ah blue-arsed flee t' tell us we'll be lit up like a bloody Christmas tree in middle o' next June!

> SPENCER
> *(firm resolution)*
> All things considered.
> *(shoots laconic glance at JAKE)*
> It's high time Stockdale is modernised and brought right into the twentieth century. Electricity laid on would enable us and our neighbouring farmers, to farm more effectively – more intensively. It will enable us to do ...

> JAKE
> Cuttin' down! But better than idleness – eh, lad!

We see STELLA, tousled and weather rosy, looking on with an unsettled smile.

We see SPENCER without expression.

*We see JAKE looking like a field scarecrow.*

*STELLA is the first to come round.*

>                    STELLA
>              *(breathing heavily)*
>         For heavens sake, let's not get
>         mangled in the machinery of change.
>         We've been through all this several
>         times already. We must guard against
>         going round in circles.

*We see STELLA placing a hand to her throat. We hear her sucking in and out her breath, noisily, then as though something urgent has swept across her being – she sets off back along the cart-road.*

>                    JAKE
>              *(rasping voice penetrating the
>              air)*
>         Tha's not gone an' put ah bun in owld
>         Sam Asquith's missus's oven - has t'
>         lad?

*We see STELLA spluttering inarticulately – hand across her mouth – as she strenuously distances herself from JAKE and SPENCER – only to see SOPHIE running swiftly to meet her.*

*We see STELLA begin to break into a run.*

>                    STELLA
>              *(shouting)*
>         <u>Sophie - Sophie - What's the matter?</u>
>         <u>What's wrong - Sophieeee - Sophieee?</u>

*We see SOPHIE coming to a staggering halt – then drop down onto the grass verge – gasping – pushing her hair behind her ears.*

*We see STELLA'S arms and legs flailing. She throws herself down on her knees beside SOPHIE – with shaking hands – shakes SOPHIE by her shoulders.*

>STELLA
>
>What's the matter, lass? Is it our Grace? Grandma?

>SOPHIE
>
>No!
>>*(unbridled distortion)*
>
>It's Kit Sullivan! He's dead!

>STELLA
>
>Kit Sullivan! Dead!

>SOPHIE
>
>Yes. He was found battered ...

>STELLA
>
>Battered!

>SOPHIE
>
>Yesterday! The postman told Grandma – less than ten minutes ago ... said ... Kit had been found stone cold behind the chapel ...

>STELLA
>>*(disbelief)*
>
>Chapel! Kit was a Catholic – not a Methodist. He never showed the slightest signs of going near a chapel

                    - not in all the twenty odd years he
                    worked for us.
                              *(raises her harassed eyes to*
                              *the blue sky)*
                    The Crown - yes - not the chapel.

*We see SOPHIE plucking STELLA'S sleeve.*

*We see STELLA moving her eyes to SOPHIE'S face.*

                              STELLA
                    Oh, God, Sophie - I caught a glimpse
                    of the child in your eyes ...
                              *(blinks eyes)*
                    You're scared stiff ...

                              SOPHIE
                              *(whispers)*
                    Mummy ... do you think Jake had
                    anything to do with Kit's death?

## SCENE 18

**EXT. STOCKDALE FARMS - CORNFIELDS - HARVEST TIME - 10 AM**

*Two weeks later.*

*We see Holbridge Constabulary's vehicle driving through Stockdale's main gateway - along the cart-road - halt - turn off engine. TWO CONSTABLES step out and head for the cornfields.*

*We see SPENCER climb down from horse-drawn binder machine to check the mechanics of it. STELLA, GRACE, BLANCHE and JAKE are stooking sheaves - they look cool and seemingly prepared for any eventuality.*

We see the TWO CONSTABLES approaching them as they continue to work perpetually, stooking the long golden corn sheaves – tucking a twined sheaf under each arm – walking a few steps while casting a few words this way and that way. As they drop the sheaves – blunt end down into the stubble ground at such an angle so that they lean against the other – eight sheaves a stook, all aligned in neat rows so the autumn sun and crisp breezes will dry and ripen the grain dead-ripe.

SPENCER makes his way across the field towards them.

>             CONSTABLE 1
>           *(judicial manner)*
>     It seems to me, that countryfolk
>     prefer a good funeral to a good
>     wedding any day of the week.
>               *(pause)*
>     We're seeking further information ...

We see the TWO CONSTABLES surveying them with unfavourable regard. Noting their bending – lifting – placing – all done with natural dexterity without breaking sweat or time.

>             CONSTABLE 1
>      *(producing note book and pen)*
>     Christopher – Sullivan – a few more
>     personal questions required ...

We see STELLA with a sheaf of corn under each arm – striding purposely to start a new eight sheave stook.

>               STELLA
>       *(speaks over her shoulder)*
>     Kit Sullivan – as we said in our
>     statement, Constable, we knew very
>     little about him – he was so private.

We didn't ask, and he didn't offer.

          BLANCHE
     *(tilting two sheaves left then*
     *right against each other)*
He always turned up here, at Stockdale, as regular as clock-work ...

          GRACE
     *(bending to pick up two sheaves*
     *by their tied twine)*
Always the second week in June ...

          STELLA
For the last twenty years and always leaving September time –

          CONSTABLE 2
Family? Did he talk about his family – we'll need to contact them ...

*We see SOPHIE taking out a small jar of homemade ointment from her dungaree pocket, unscrew the lid to finger out a helping portion to rub along her scratched arms in a sensual way – not lost upon the TWO CONSTABLES of peace.*

          SOPHIE
Kit always kept himself to himself ...

          STELLA
     *(parental tone)*
Now that ungtous ointment, Sophie, will attract the flies and blue-bottles ...

GRACE
*(adding two more sheaves to make up her stook)*
As far as we know, Kit was a traveller - a sort of bohemian.

BLANCHE
But he didn't deserve what the postman described as foul play.

STELLA
*(brings the heads of two sheaves together to lock the grains)*
We finished haytime two weeks ago, Constable, so we paid Kit off - we believe he usually heads for Bradford - or was it Sheffield?

SPENCER
*(joins them)*
Barnsley, he said ...

CONSTABLE 1
*(consults his note book)*
Huddersfield!

STELLA
Huddersfield, you say! Well, I never knew that ... fancy Sam not mentioning that after all these years ...

We see the TWO CONSTABLES throw knowing glances at SPENCER.

CONSTABLE 2
Seems by all accounts, Sam Asquith

didn't tell you everything, Mrs. Asquith.

          STELLA

And what do you mean, by that underhanded remark, Constable?

We see the women exchanging fiery glances between the TWO CONSTABLES and SPENCER.

We see JAKE suddenly loom amongst them all.

          JAKE
      *(talking at the top of his voice)*

<u>Ah don't know what all this questionin' an' bloody wonderin' is all about! Ah'm not use t' workin' wi' folk that's always pesterin' an' fuckin' wonderin' all ovver t' place!</u>

The women's residing cold eyes dwell upon JAKE unblinkingly.

          CONSTABLE 1
      *(to JAKE)*

Any further contempt from you, old son, and we'll throw the book at you!

          JAKE
      *(looks back at CONSTABLES with disregard)*

Nah! Perhaps, The Crown landlady cun't git off Sullivan's shirt-flap quick enough afore owld Alf - landlord - brayed livin' daylights out o' him. Owld Alf always were ah religious

>           zealot!

*We see the TWO CONSTABLES depart abruptly and accelerate their vehicle off the cart-road – to speed up the road towards The Crown Inn.*

**SCENE 19**
**EXT. STOCKDALE FARMS – FORECOURT – 6:28 PM**

*One week later.*

*We see ABE driving over water-splash. Parks car on forecourt. We get a flash of the local newspaper: THE HOLBRIDGE HERALD under ABE'S arm as he steps out of his car.*

**SCENE 20**
**EXT. STOCKDALE FARMS – STACK-YARD – 6:29 PM**

*We see JAKE, SPENCER and HARRY stacking the corn sheaves onto a corn-stack.*

**SCENE 21**
**EXT. STOCKDALE FARMS – FORECOURT – 6:30 PM**

*We see BLANCHE meeting ABE half-way.*

>                    BLANCHE
>                 *(pleasantly)*
>       I would have thought you would be far
>       too busy with your own harvesting to
>       be able to take time out visiting us,
>       Abe.
>            *(spots newspaper under ABE'S
>            arm)*
>       Must be bad news, paper doesn't come
>       out until tomorrow ...

                    ABE
Aye, that's as may be, but ah know the
advertisin' manager, an' he slipped
this early copy my way - so here ah
am!
          (looks about him)
And where's Stella, I want a word or
two with that lady.

We see BLANCHE inviting ABE into the kitchen.

## SCENE 22

**INT. STOCKDALE FARMS - STELLA'S KITCHEN - 6:31 PM**

BLANCHE pours ABE a glass of John Smith's ale. He settles on a chair, and begins to thumb through newspaper.

                    BLANCHE
We're running behind time today, Abe.
The weather forecaster predicted heavy
rain coming our way, so the menfolk
are striving to cart as much as they
can onto the yard corn-stacks ...

                    ABE
Ah'll not be keepin' your lot from
workin' t' long, but ah thought you
might be interested in what's being
said in farmin' community an' Wheat
Sheaf pub concernin' Kit Sullivan's
unexpected an' unexplained damnation,
like ...

                    BLANCHE
          (nods head violently)
We're all concerned - there's no

> getting away from it - I mean -
> everyone who met Kit were perversely
> delighted by his ability to rub folk
> up the wrong way and not always a good
> thing ...

*We see STELLA enter kitchen. She looks sun bleached, her ginger hair has golden highlights giving her illuminative beauty.*

*We see ABE - after a prodigious intake of breath, dredge up a thin smile of welcome.*

>           STELLA
>         *(congenial)*
> Sophie told me that she'd seen your
> car pull up on the forecourt - so it
> would be churlish not to break off -

>           BLANCHE
> Abe's taking time out to be here to
> fill a gap or two in relation to Kit's
> demise and -

>           STELLA
> I hope you're not going to be too long
> winded in detail, Abe, because we're
> all behind time with the second
> milking of the day and against the
> weather forecast ...

>           ABE
>     *(hands over the newspaper to*
>     *STELLA)*
> Never mind weather. Just turn t' page
> four and read it aloud. I've marked it

out wi' red crayon.

*We see STELLA accepting newspaper – then turning pages, she scans page four quickly, then reads it out slowly.*

    STELLA
Alfred Keld, landlord of The Crown Inn, Norhard Moor, Kayshaw, near Holbridge, has been held in custody on suspicion of the murder of Christopher Sullivan, forty-five, Irishman of no fixed address ...
  *(pulls out a chair and sits
  down slowly, to BLANCHE)*
Have you read this?

    BLANCHE
  *(looks at ABE)*
No. Abe's been holding onto it as though it's family silver.

    ABE
  *(dead-pan expression)*
I've just dropped Clarence off at The Crown, so ah thought I'd best call here – wouldn't like you t' think we'd not spared yah a thought over this local tragedy – ah mean ...
  *(looks from one to the other)*
Weel, you're ah man short – an' our Mike said, he'd come an' give yah a helpin' hand if bein' in need.
  *(plonks glass down onto table)*
An' while ah'm about it, ah thought I'd bring you up t' date wi' what farmers are sayin' in Wheat Sheaf,

about ...

                    STELLA
                *(sharply)*
We don't pay much attention to rumours
or gossip, Abe.


                    ABE
But yah must pay some attention surely
- as ah primary precaution.


                    STELLA
                *(folds up newspaper)*
Precaution?


                    ABE
Aye, precaution. Rumour has it, that
old Alf, landlord, weel - he's too
frail a man t' tackle ah man like
Sullivan -


                    BLANCHE
                *(sits at table)*
There's usually a thread of truth
within rumours - I remember Kit saying
years ago, when Jake challenged him
about his seasonal dalliance with the
landlady, and Kit saying - "If you
don't stand up to your principal when
the going's hard, then it's just a
hobby, and -"


                    ABE
                *(forcible)*
Jake! Jake Swales! Now ask yourselves
- could he have had ah hand in this

matter – Clarence said, landlady told him – on the side –
*(winks at STELLA)*
that Kit had a fractious relationship with Jake due to Jake prodding a walking stick up thee stallion's arse ...

STELLA

*(glassy eyed)*
Horseplay – mere horseplay!

BLANCHE

*(rising from chair)*
I need a good strong cup of tea and a cigarette – it's times like these ...
*(points at newspaper)*
when you run into human nature in a raw kind of way ...

STELLA

Which offers scope for Clarence, now that the coast is clear ...

ABE

*(bulbous of eye)*
Aye, you're not wide off t' mark theer, Stell'. Clarence always had an eye for owt for knowt!

## SCENE 23
**INT. STOCKDALE FARMS – STELLA'S LIVING ROOM – 10 PM**

*Following week.*

*We see STELLA, SPENCER and BLANCHE seated in easy chairs*

*before a fire burning.*

*STELLA sipping a cup of tea, SPENCER reading THE HOLBRIDGE HERALD, BLANCHE smoking cigarette.*

                SPENCER
Doctor Liddle stated, and here I quote, "Due to head injuries and excess drink, Christopher Sullivan, of no fixed abode, had inhaled copious amounts of vomit which had started a chain of reactions which had led to his death – asphyxiation." Unquote.
    *(jabs finger at report)*
I feel the evidence does not fully disclose the means by which Kit's death was caused.

                BLANCHE
No one in their right mind will ever convince me that Jake Swales had nothing to do with Kit's death.
    *(with rancour)*
There's been too many queer happenings here at Stockdale since Sam went ...

                SPENCER
We've had a heavy basting – but try telling that to the jury – lies can only exist where there is truth telling, and truth is more deadly than fiction.

                BLANCHE
    *(aggressed and cigaretted)*
I'm afraid it's no good expecting a

lunatic to have reason for what he does.
> *(turns to STELLA for approved continuity)*

Later, you said yourself, Stell', after my ladder incident, that you distinctly remembered bolting all the windows. Yet Grace found the dining room window unlatched and the flower bed beneath was crushed ...

*We see STELLA nod and her mouth tighten.*

*We see BLANCHE face SPENCER attentively.*

> BLANCHE
> And it's no good Jake trying to blame the new sheepdog for lifting its leg and urinating over the plants to mark out its new territory – because it wasn't let loose from the Humber until the dairy cows were brought in from the fields for their morning milking.

*We hear murmuration of: "Wouldn't put anything passed Jake Swales."*

> SPENCER
> The trouble is, Jake's solely convinced, quite wrongly – we are planning to place him back into the workhouse.

> STELLA
> Honest to God, tell me, what will it take to drive him to further carnage

amongst my family?

                    BLANCHE
                 *(expounded)*
I'll tell you what - cruelty doesn't
need excuses, only given opportunities
in very dangerous portions, and Jake's
a master at them!

*We see STELLA, SPENCER and BLANCHE sat stiffly erect on their chairs - taking refuge in their own afraid thoughts.*

                    SPENCER
                 *(voice low)*
It's with the sad ache of pain, how
can I - an Asquith man say aloud, I am
afraid?
                 *(pause)*
These words are as difficult to
pronounce as saying out aloud, I love
you.

*BLANCHE is the first to move - she goes into the kitchen - we hear her siding away the meal things - toing and froing.*

*Eventually SPENCER rises, as does STELLA, they face each other.*

                    STELLA
                 *(quietly)*
I can see you have that blinkered look
of Sam Asquith, which means - you're
not of mind to talk about it. And
given time, I rather think you'll turn
out just like your father - but if it
means living with this knowing - then

I can live with that - inbred -
peculiar pettifoggery.
    *(disarming smile)*
An understatement I know.

## SCENE 24
**INT. STOCKDALE FARMS - STELLA'S KITCHEN - 2 PM**

*We see STELLA and BLANCHE seated at kitchen table, BLANCHE is pouring out tea, STELLA'S ticking off whereabouts listings.*

    STELLA

Yes, I'll call round at your home, Mother, and leave message, stating you'll be staying here - until further notice ... And yes, I'll call in at Shadman's, to book the threshing days ...

    BLANCHE

Have you wrote an order for more draining pipes to be delivered?

    STELLA
    *(looking up from list)*

Kit voluntarily stayed on to finish digging the trenches - never prolonged his seasonal labouring before - if only he'd left, perhaps he'd still be alive.

    BLANCHE
    *(pats STELLA'S arm)*

You're looking a little under the weather my dear, call into Doctor Liddle's surgery and get a tonic to

>                     tone you up -
>
>                           STELLA
>                 You will keep an eye on the girls
>                 while I'm away - shouldn't be too long
>                 - and make sure you stay vigilant,
>                 Mother.

**SCENE 25**
**EXT. STOCKDALE FARMS - FORECOURT - 2:10 PM**

*We see BLANCHE walking STELLA to the Rover parked on the forecourt.*

>                           BLANCHE
>                       *(grinds her teeth)*
>                 Spencer told me where he keeps his
>                 hand gun, so if needs be, I'll help
>                 myself, and by hell, I'll shoot Jake
>                 with pleasurable disgust - you mark my
>                 words!

**SCENE 26**
**EXT. STOCKDALE FARMS - WATER-SPLASH - 2:12 PM**

*We see STELLA drive over the water-splash to disappear from sight up the cart-road.*

**SCENE 27**
**INT. DR LIDDLE'S SURGERY - 2:55 PM**

*We see DR LIDDLE usher STELLA into his surgery.*

>                           DR LIDDLE
>                 And what brings you here, Stella,
>                 lass? Harvest time's not over yet ...

                    STELLA
          Just feel a trifle fatigued.

                    DR LIDDLE
               (patting her shoulder kindly)
          Pop yourself on the couch and I'll
          examine you thoroughly.

**SCENE 28**

**INT. DR LIDDLE'S SURGERY - 3:05 PM**

*DR LIDDLE looks a twinge or two distracted as he seats himself behind his desk. STELLA takes a seat opposite.*

                    DR LIDDLE
          Nothing wrong that I can detect, lass
          - nothing out of the way ...

                    STELLA
          I have missed a period, but then, I've
          been a little patchy, since Sam died.

                    DR LIDDLE
               *(with approval)*
          Stress! Forty-six Stella. Could well
          be the change of life.

                    STELLA
               *(swallows her disappointment)*
          You must have said that a thousand
          times and more over the years - to
          women - such things as belong to only
          women.

                    DR LIDDLE
          I always recommend to my special

                    patients a glass of port wine, each
                    day, just for the iron – prevents
                    anaemia.
                         *(smiles)*
                    Bolsters your energy.

*We see DR LIDDLE disappear into his well-stocked wine and spirit cellar – reappearing with crate of various bottles – money and bottles exchange hand.*

                         DR LIDDLE
                         *(gravely)*
                    No one, Stella, has claimed the body
                    of Kit Sullivan ... but he's entitled
                    to a pauper's funeral – unmarked
                    grave.

                         STELLA
                    No! We'll give Kit a decent burial and
                    marked stone. He was a decent man, and
                    always a willing worker.

                         DR LIDDLE
                         *(places paper notes into his
                         wallet)*
                    I expected to hear you say that, lass.
                         *(with clarity)*
                    It was another peculiar case – John
                    Hinchcliffe passed it my way –
                    confidentially – Stella – the Irishman
                    of yours – he had been crudely
                    castrated!

*We see STELLA utterly stunned.*

                    STELLA
               (inarticulate)
          Mother Mary - rest his soul.

We see STELLA stagger - place her hands to her temples - she
swerves.

We see DR LIDDLE guide her back to the examination couch,
where she lands heavily on her back.

                    STELLA
          Ooh - poor - Kit. He didn't deserve
          that, and found behind the Methodist
          chapel. A Catholic - not a Wesleyan.

                    DR LIDDLE
          Now, take it easy Stella.
               (props her up)
          I'd pour you a glass of port, but all
          I've got here are containers -
               (smiles convivially)
          Urinals.

We see STELLA blink herself back to near normality, as she
swings her legs over the edge of the couch, and sits with one
knee crossed over the other.

                    STELLA
          Just bear with me a little longer,
          Doctor Liddle.

                    DR LIDDLE
               (nods)
          And while you're bearing up, lass, I
          understand the police have still not
          traced the whereabouts of the hit-and-

                          476

absconding-driver, and I don't suppose they ever will. Jake, what's his surname ...
>(impatiently waves the name aside)

I think you should know, Stella, when he gets a drops too much drink, I'm told, he quarrels incessantly with those he ought not to.
>(helps her off couch)

He's awkward, and ritual! You should pension him off - for all your sakes.

>STELLA

What are you trying to tell me, Doctor Liddle?

>DR LIDDLE

I think you need a friend, lass.

## SCENE 29
**INT. STOCKDALE FARMS - STELLA'S KITCHEN - 9:30 AM**

*We see BLANCHE move across to the sink.*

*We hear the front door iron sneck lift then drop with force.*

*We see JAKE stood framed in the doorway.*

*We see STELLA, GRACE, and SOPHIE seated at the table having breakfast - they turn in cold silence to face JAKE.*

>BLANCHE
>
>(deceptive mildness)

We were expecting the veterinary - has he not arrived? He usually knocks to the seven beat before calling out his arrival ... always been perfectly pleasant to me ... Shallow, but amiable.

*We see JAKE not moving a muscle – his stance: I can wait!*

          STELLA

The words, always and awful, Mother, are good. It makes a compliment go further, so much further.

*We see STELLA smothering goose grease onto her hands, and circulating it along her palms and between her fingers.*

          STELLA
        (to JAKE)

About Macilla. Is she still straining?

          JAKE
        (drolly)

Yah say vet's comin' but then, nobody tells me owt these days. Any road – it's nobut a bloody calvin' when all's said an' done – it's a one man job.

          SOPHIE
      (rising from chair)

Spencer said, Macilla is a big cow with a long pelvis, and the calf's head is too far back, and –

          JAKE

Me old arms are t' short t' reach inta that gurt cow's inside.

*We see JAKE take a step back, then pull out his battered tobacco tin, and delicately select a half-smoked cigarette – strike a match against protruding boot nail, shield flame with cupped hands, draw deeply on stubbed cigarette and close his eyes against them, to slowly dispel little whimsical wisps of smoke down through flared nostrils.*

*We see their wary eyes following his every imponderable movement.*

              JAKE
           *(eyes opened)*
Aye.
           *(brightens up under their*
           *attention)*
Aye. A wire job. Sam Asquith an' mesen tackled a calvin' like this back in 1938. Just before wartime. Aye – war years ...

*We see a look of obscurity cross JAKE'S face.*

*We see a flash of self-preservation – even a flash of sadism in BLANCHE'S face.*

              BLANCHE
Remember the war time ... how can anyone forget? Some people shy away from the memories – all that make do and mend business.
           *(turns to GRACE and SOPHIE)*
We use to put newspaper between the blankets for extra warmth.
           *(laughs)*
And what a terrible noise it made when one turned over your bed-companion to

punish him with the back of a
hairbrush laid on his bare bottom with
a heavy hand - then when he confessed
to not bringing four pairs of silk
stockings ...

    *(captivating laugh)*

Plainly determined to hang on for the
bristle side-up to descend on his
quivering buttocks - and I made double
sure that I permeated the punishment
area ...

*We see an open brazen expression illuminating BLANCHE'S face.*

        BLANCHE

And I didn't want to laugh, it would
have been unprofessional - when he
pleaded - "this is so distasteful for
you".

    *(smiles)*

I often wondered if one really started
to hate or get too excited - a lady
might not be able to stop.

*We see BLANCHE etched by fatigue, suddenly collapse onto a chair.*

        BLANCHE

I'll be back to my old self soon ...

        JAKE

    *(dismal dolorance)*

Er - er, thee watch thee tongue,
m'lady, rakin' over old ground. No
wonder yah fall for incognito games
an' black bottom remedies.

JAKE grinds his teeth in perverse pleasure.

>                    JAKE
>           (speaks over his shoulder as he
>           heads for outside door)
>      Hasta ivver wondered, boss, ah know I
>      have - when readin' local obituary
>      columns ...
>           (tone of mock puzzlement)
>      it's bloody marvellous how folk die in
>      alphabetic order?

We hear the door slam into place behind him.

## SCENE 30
**EXT. STOCKDALE FARMS - COW-HOUSE ADJOINING A BARN - 9:40 AM**

The autumn blanket of mist is lifting.

We see STELLA and GRACE heading for the cow-house.

We see JAKE meeting them half-way.

>                    JAKE
>      Ah reckon there's putrefyin' dead calf
>      inside yon cow an' ...

We see STELLA and GRACE exchange hollow glances, heartfelt glances.

We see JAKE taking morbid enjoyment in their interaction.

>                    JAKE
>      Ah son, did ta say, lass? Another
>      bastard son -

STELLA
(eyes flashing)
Now, that's taking things a step too far, Jake. Our mourning can't take that kind of buffeting, so shall we stick to countenance, at least, for today?

GRACE
(finds her voice)
I find those remarks rather macabre, Jake, and if nothing else, at least I had six months of sheer joy carrying my baby son – and that's more than your wife ever had in her lean life with you.

*We see JAKE'S mouth fall open and his eyes become bulbous – he's distracted when we hear a vehicle approaching the beck waterway – it's SPENCER returning.*

JAKE
(nods head violently)
Trust him t' arrive back afore bloody vet – an' I'll bet yah owt for nowt, that he's come back wi' a wire.
(spits to the side of himself)
If onnybody had t' ask me I'd say he's as smooth as a cat's back – but then what do ah know!

*We see the Humber speeding – wheels spinning jagged impressions along cart-road edges as SPENCER slews to a sudden stop on forecourt.*

JAKE
*(turns and heads for the cow-
house, snarls over shoulder)*
He's headin' for a real dressin' down!

*FLASH – STELLA witnessing HERTZ, the young German Prisoner Of War, naked – hanging by the neck – mutilated – blood – so much blood. Pig cratch – (whereupon they dressed slaughtered pigs) – HERTZ'S toes curled through and round the cross-bars. We see STELLA looking nauseous – but she holds on.*

STELLA
*(to GRACE)*
We cannot live by keeping ourselves half-dead – Jake's toying with us ...

GRACE
*(speaks under her breath)*
Somehow, Mam, we have to settle the horseman's ashes, before he kills one of us.

JAKE
*(turning)*
Ah can hear yah both mutterin' an' see yah both carryin' conversations in yah heads, aye, easy t' imitate harder t' follow.

*We see SPENCER approaching them.*

JAKE
Nah, we'll see what yon bastard's made o', wire or no wire t' tip scales. That Macilla's – she's ah wick bugger.

*We see SPENCER is carrying a bucket of hot water in one hand and a carpet bag in the other.*

> SPENCER
> *(calling out)*
> <u>Mr Davis is overrun with farm calls this morning, but his receptionist said she would endeavour to chase him by the telephone, so I called at the cottages to collect a few things ...</u>

*We see concern tighten STELLA'S face and hear it squeeze her voice to sharpness.*

> STELLA
> These kinds of dilemmas only belong to the female species.

*We see STELLA turn to GRACE.*

*We see GRACE stood, immobile and white faced, seemingly unable to lift her eyes to STELLA or SPENCER, but plainly determined to hang on.*

> STELLA
> *(voice softens)*
> Go ask Grandma to make, and bring a jug of Doctor Liddle's cocoa. He recommends it highly as nutritious –

> JAKE
> Promises cost nowt. Any road, it gripes me stomach an' it meks me want t' shit!

*We see SPENCER'S eyes scald JAKE.*

*We see JAKE screen his eyes beneath his cap neb.*

                JAKE
           *(voice holds mockery)*
Ah mean, who wants reunions studded wi' tears an' hugs an' lipstick kisses all given as if ah was a damp baby.

                STELLA
           *(ludicrous sternness)*
There will be no altercation on my cow-house door-step – remember, we have a calving to attend to. A problematic calving and a solution is urgently required.
        *(glares at JAKE and SPENCER)*
And I'm saying what we're all thinking, Macilla could die from septicaemia.
        *(pause)*
As Sam said –

                JAKE
Aye! As we said back in 1938 the medicines were bloody useless, but thee father were a dab hand at concoctin' ...

*We see JAKE pause inside the cow-house doorway, then turn to stare at the baggage grasped in SPENCER'S hand.*

                JAKE
Er – er, what's tha carryin' in that handbag?

*We see SPENCER shoulder him aside and enter cow-house.*

**SCENE 31**

INT. STOCKDALE FARMS - COW-HOUSE ADJOINING A BARN - 9:45 AM

*SPENCER places carpet bag on inner windowsill - goes over to calving cow, MACILLA, standing uneasy in her stall - there's no protruding signs of a calf.*

*STELLA and JAKE enter.*

> SPENCER
> Stillborn. More than we bargained for
> - she's loosing fettle as I speak.
> This is a case one could not see
> coming - a dead calf - it's a tragedy.

*We hear footsteps from outside - see BLANCHE come into sight.*

> BLANCHE
> There's still no sign of the vet.

*We see BLANCHE holding a jug of hot cocoa in one hand, and in the other hand are mugs hanging from each one of her fingers. BLANCHE smiles a welcome.*

> BLANCHE
> Resourcefulness doesn't leave women
> when their marriages are over and done
> with. It's reticence that breeds that
> sort of dreariness which calls for
> sleep and then prevents it.

*We see BLANCHE pouring out equal measures of cocoa, JAKE turns away. We see JAKE hanging up his coat on a nail, and settling himself on a milking stool, placed in far corner. He lights a cigarette.*

We see STELLA, SPENCER and BLANCHE blowing – sipping – blowing over their drinks while observing MACILLA lifting her roan head and tail simultaneously, then hunching her back – straining – bellowing.

We hear the chain around MACILLA'S neck clattering and clinking as the slack of the steel links come in contact under her neck with the stone feeding trough – and once more, the metallic clanging resounds as she jerks her head upwards – carrying the linked-chain rapidly up the chain pole with another bellowing of distress – to abate.

We hear murmurings of empathy between STELLA and BLANCHE.

                SPENCER
We'll give the veterinary another five minutes ...
      *(opens his bag to extract a*
      *wire instrument)*
before I make another internal examination –

                JAKE
Wi' thee long arm.
      *(sarcastically)*
An' as for that contraption in thee hand, lad. We call it cheese wire, but then – ah don't know what yah call it in bloody Canada!

                SPENCER
An embryotome instrument.

                BLANCHE
      *(ogling SPENCER then JAKE, to*
      *STELLA)*

It's not as if they were still on
speaking terms – their silences have
been very lowering.
>(pours herself another cocoa)
You know, Stella, loneliness isn't
just a case of being short of people,
it's –

          JAKE
>(ominous)
Likelihood same as puttin' shutters
down!

*We see STELLA, SPENCER and BLANCHE back on their guard.*

*We hear MACILLA'S bellows – see her astride tremulous hind-quarters, instinctively trying to bear forth her young calf.*

         SPENCER
>(impatiently)
We've waited long enough.

*We see SPENCER stripping off his shirt – revealing his washboard stomach, before lathering his hands and arms with carbolic soap – to then rinse them off in the bucket of hot water, followed by a dousing of iodine.*

        BLANCHE
I always liked a good solid backside
on a man, myself.

          JAKE
Nah! An' the bloody cow mee-oooowed!

*We see SPENCER thrust his disinfected arm inside MACILLA – then begin to talk the women through the procedure.*

SPENCER

Yes ... long pelvis ... almost up to my armpit ... calf's feet ... Oh, yes ... as suspected the calf's head is turned back ... damn ... tucked away ... somewhere ... A second ... guess ... somewhere behind the ribs ... can just about, yes -

JAKE

Bloody cleft.

SPENCER

Fissure, and it's beginning -

JAKE

T' putrefy!

SPENCER

I would estimate that this calf has been dead for -

JAKE

Ah day an' a half!

SPENCER

No room for straightening the -

JAKE

Bend in t' neck!

SPENCER

Flexion of the neck ... and judging by the sweet saccharin smell, the emphysema -

                    JAKE
       Cracklin' under t' skin like teeth
       chewin' on fuckin' crispy bacon rind
       ... Ah can hear it from ovver hear,
       lad!

*We see SPENCER struggling with his hatred of JAKE as he
withdraws his arm, now covered with decaying discharge – he
flexes his arm and fingers.*

                    JAKE
       Squeezed sensation out o' thee arm –
       lad. Weel, she's a strong beast –
       strong uterus contractions.

*We see STELLA and BLANCHE looking upon SPENCER'S sweating –
bespattered face to the discharging vulva of MACILLA with
compassion.*

                STELLA and BLANCHE
       Cush – cush. Cush – cush.
              *(as oneness)*
       Cush – cush.

                    SPENCER
       Will you be good enough to fetch me
       another bucket of hot water and a
       towel, Blanche, so I can finish the
       job properly?

                    BLANCHE
              *(nods head ruefully)*
       A stillborn must be something like a
       terrible absence following you around
       for the rest of your life ...
              *(lowering voice)*

> As for praying, how shameful to use prayer as a diversionary tactic.
> *(gathers jug and mugs)*
> Poor Grace – dear Grace. Her sadness is so private ...

*We see BLANCHE leave the cow-house.*

> SPENCER
> It's pointless waiting for the vet. Any further delay will prove to be very serious. The calf's dead, and beginning to decompose, and if putrid matter is absorbed into Macilla's bloodstream, she will have to be slaughtered.
> *(pause)*
> As for the calf –

> JAKE
> Thee father an' mesen used a wire t' saw a two headed calf's head reight through ...
> *(throws tab-end into manure channel)*
> Aye, in spring o' 1938. Joined at forehead but cloven-faced ... Aye.
> *(ponders)*
> Aye, we had t' slice its deformed head reight down middle ...

*We hear JAKE cough, and cough loudly to give his words effect, then to spit out saliva.*

*We see STELLA suppressing a scream – a harrowing sound escapes her lips.*

SPENCER
(matter-of-fact)

I'll have to cut the calf's head off with the embryotome wire. It's the only way to remove her calf and save her life or -

JAKE

Maa-cill-ah, will end up sold as dog meat t' knackerman an' go same road as old Bonny went - remember? Boss!

STELLA

Trust you, Jake, to get to the point a bit too obviously.
(pause)
But never mind ...

*We see the wire instrument resting on brown paper - see a heavy metal weight with a small hole at one end of the cord, and a bigger one at the other end for a finger-hold.*

*We see SPENCER demonstrate as he speaks.*

SPENCER

If I can force the metal weight forward and feel it fall down on the calf's fissure - and - then - get hold of the lead weight on the -

JAKE

Underside o' its bent neck!

SPENCER

And pull it through the cord attached - then the rest will be easy -

                        JAKE

          An' if tha can't catch it wi' thee
          long arm then job's all ovver an' done
          wi', lad -


                        STELLA

          Just stop it! Jake. You're rubbing my
          soul raw with your despotic manner.

We see SPENCER turn his back on JAKE - and look at STELLA.

                        SPENCER

          The knack is to join the cord to the
          wire and pull it round the neck, then
          thread the wire through the steel
          tubes of the -


                        JAKE

          Cheese wire -


                        SPENCER

          Embryotome! Which protects the cow's
          vaginal wall from the cutting edge,
          then -


                        JAKE

          Saw its putrid head reight off!

We see BLANCHE re-enter cow-house with second bucket of hot
water and a towel.

                        BLANCHE
                    (bustles in)
          I've come as fast as I could, and
          there's still no sign or sound of the
          vet, but then -

> STELLA
>
> *(to BLANCHE)*
>
> The receptionist told Spencer that the vet was out numbered with farm calls this morning ...

*We see STELLA giving SPENCER an exquisite troubled, but brilliant glance.*

> STELLA
>
> Which offers Spencer scope to go ahead immediately.

> SPENCER
>
> *(to STELLA)*
>
> Thank you, for your assurance.
> > *(squeezes BLANCHE'S arm affectionately)*
>
> And you're a real gem to have around, believe me - Blanche.

> BLANCHE
>
> *(acquiescing)*
>
> I'm glad at least that cheek pinching seems to be on its way out. Men use to do that to little girls. It disarranged their hair and facial expressions - and it even bruised their skins.

*We see SPENCER rescrubbing and dousing his hands and arms in iodine, then re-enter MACILLA.*

> JAKE
>
> Thee grandmother use t' say ah was always theer, friendly an' diligent in

t' background as if ah were some
relation who had come t' stay an' from
sheer absence o' mind had nivver taken
mesen off ...
>   *(gives a violent controlled
>   cough)*

Aye, that's how ah came t' be part o'
Stockdale until carried out feet
first.
>   *(shouting)*

<u>Can yah hear me Grandmother? Can t'
hear meeeee?</u>

*We see BLANCHE looking at her wrist watch as though planning escape then she smiles like someone contented in dormancy – sometimes she pauses – looks up and down the cow-house as though asking herself a question or two.*

*We see STELLA trying to put BLANCHE back on her guard.*

### STELLA
>   *(sharply)*

Grandma! Grandma thinks of others'
unhappiness rather than her own as a
contrivance for getting to sleep. It's
to be seen in all her stops and
starts.
>   *(stares at BLANCHE)*

And old habits are hard to break.

### JAKE
>   *(raillery)*

An' kept incommunicado!
>   *(rolling a new cigarette)*

Old John's missus use t' think ah lot
about me, aye. Wallflowers! Ah even

did her flower arrangements an' –

                BLANCHE

Like trampling on hollyhocks and treading down our flower-beds.
     *(flash of malice)*
You nasty, perverted old man!

                JAKE

Er – eerr!

*We see JAKE'S eyes bulge as he rotates his head around cow-stall partitions to stare at BLANCHE.*

                JAKE

Tha's lettin' thee tongue run away wi' itsen just like that spittin' image daughter o' Sam Asquith's.

                STELLA

Stop right there! Both of you!

                SPENCER

Please be quiet, everyone. I need concern here, not conflict ...
     *(pause)*
Just need a few more steady sawings ... yes ... I can feel the resistance ... it's –

                JAKE

Slackened off.

                SPENCER

It's yielding ... Oh, yes – the head's truly cut off!

                    BLANCHE
              *(eager to mourn)*
        Oh! Mother Mary of God! Only a man
        could say that without emotion.

We see BLANCHE catch SPENCER'S penetrating eyes.

                    BLANCHE
        It's not what you said, Spencer, it's
        more the way you men say it that makes
        it sound wrong.
                *(pause)*
        Perhaps we lose something in the
        translation.

We see BLANCHE cross herself.

We see SPENCER withdraw his blooded arm and blood-covered wire instrument from MACILLA'S distressed body – he drops cutting tool into bucket of water and re-swills his limb under stand-by cold water tap.

We see STELLA and BLANCHE taking the protruding CALF'S back hooves in a separate share – to deliver the headless CALF without complication.

We see STELLA spread a forkful of hay over the pitiful sight of the CALF.

We see SPENCER bring forth the severed head.

                    STELLA
        Poor – little – bugger. The little
        calf didn't ask for that.

> BLANCHE
> (laments)
> I'm afraid I view life unadorned. Do you know, our Stell', what I was thinking of when I was holding onto the calf's foot?

> JAKE
> It's like takin' hold o' family silver!

*We see STELLA, SPENCER and BLANCHE feign deafness.*

> BLANCHE
> (perseveres)
> I was reminded of a neighbour who suffered from consumption in the war years. She told me, while she was in the sanatorium, under observation, they fed her on calves foot jelly, blood and dirty jokes ...

*We hear a soft cough coming from the doorway.*

*We see STELLA, SPENCER and BLANCHE turn retentive faces towards the sound.*

*We see the veterinary, MR DAVIS stood perfectly still framed in door-opening.*

*We see JAKE not moving a muscle.*

> MR DAVIS
> I called at the farmhouse, but I felt – a knock or a shout would hardly be sufficient to open it.

STELLA
The girls have gone through to
Holbridge to collect provisions and at
the same time pick up Harry - and it's
no exaggeration to say, he's now
practically one of the family.

JAKE
(to STELLA)
Which is more than thou could say
about me!

*Fleetingly STELLA and JAKE'S eyes meet.*

*We see JAKE reach for his jacket hung from rusty nail, and without looking left or right - he leaves the building.*

*We see MR DAVIS walk towards MACILLA and briefly examine her and the CALF. We see him administer cautionary injection.*

MR DAVIS
Well, all looks as honest as the day.
(turns full circle on SPENCER)
This sort of operation is not taught
in kindergarden, so where?

STELLA
(spur of moment)
Canada?

BLANCHE
(re-offers)
Australia?

*We hear STELLA and BLANCHE laugh affectionately.*

*We see MR DAVIS doing his best to conceal the single irritation of resentment.*

*We see a ghost of a smile hovering on SPENCER'S face.*

                    SPENCER
        As a matter of fact ...

*We see SPENCER putting his shirt back on, as they wait on him for an answer. He shrugs.*

                    SPENCER
        It's a mistake to go back into the
        past.

                    STELLA
        But the importance of constructive
        leakage, Spencer, is to condition
        minds. I mean, it's common-sense
        philosophy.
            *(looks at MR DAVIS)*
        The matter of the fact should be
        introduced into every conversation.

*We see MR DAVIS, not quite comfortable in STELLA'S presence, refuse to be button-holed, we hear his explanation while avoiding STELLA'S hostile eyes.*

                    MR DAVIS
        My apology to you all, for not
        arriving sooner rather than later.
            *(spreads his fingers)*
        You see, I hate telephone calls, as
        you must appreciate, I arrange my
        daily diary to suit my morning in-
        coming calls - I've found this saves

people, particularly farmers, re-phoning me which allows them to call me at moments chosen by them.

              BLANCHE
Like a saxophonist coming in like a clumsy husband.
     *(face clouds then brightens)*
I shall always remember this morning, as another lesson on how not to catch a man.

*We see MR DAVIS pick up his pharmaceutical case and move mechanically towards the doorway.*

              MR DAVIS
     *(turns to them)*
Will you be burying the calf, or ...?

              SPENCER
In the next hour.
     *(comes forward and holds out*
       *his hand)*
I do hope you don't feel that I've usurped your position, Barry, but –

              MR DAVIS
Needs must.
     *(smile comes and goes)*
There's a limit to what anyone can ever do. I can only be in one place at a time.

              SPENCER
     *(back to his jaunty self)*
Did I ever tell you, Barry, my mother

was a cattle drover back in Canada? She journeyed on horseback - crossing and re-crossing wild and open country tract for years. She called it ...
    *(smiles roguishly)*
"The seat of Misery" so you see, Barry - I've been around cattle and horses for most of my life.

*We see them shaking hands.*

          MR DAVIS
I can't cure old habits, but I'll still charge you for my visit. Good day.

## SCENE 32
**EXT. STOCKDALE FARMS - STACK-YARD - TWO WEEKS LATER - 3 PM**

*We see the threshing machine and tractor engine pulling out of Stockdale Farms stack-yard.*

*We hear FARM MEN'S loud voices traversing across the revving and reversing of the heavy machinery - as they direct the CONTRACTOR manoeuvring out of the narrow stack-yard and onto the hardened cart-road.*

          FARM MAN 1
    *(shouting)*
<u>Turn front wheels ah bit more t' under carriage!</u>

          FARM MAN 2
    *(loudly)*
<u>Full lock!</u>

                    FARM MAN 1
                  *(shouting)*
Whooo-whaa ... mind bloody wall!

                    FARM MAN 2
                  *(loudly)*
Steady on ... Wheels t' right!

                    FARM MAN 1
                  *(shouting)*
Nah - then - straighten up - back!
Back!

                    JAKE
                  *(bawling)*
Put fuckin' brake on - yah bloody
pillock!

**SCENE 33**

**INT. STOCKDALE FARMS - STELLA'S KITCHEN - 3:01 PM**

We see STELLA and BLANCHE seated at kitchen table, drinking a cup of tea.

                    STELLA and BLANCHE
                  *(speak as one)*
Jake!

                    BLANCHE
This constant, never taking your eyes
off Jake, is beginning to take it's
toll on the family.
          *(lights cigarette)*
I'm plagued by worry as regards to our
safety - and he's been far too quiet
these last two days ... he's like a

                    ticking bomb, just waiting to go off
                    ...

*We see SOPHIE enter kitchen, she leaves door ajar, we hear the heavy machinery.*

                    SOPHIE
We've not been eaten out of the house, have we? I'm ravishingly hungry – so hungry that I could eat a bought-out cake!

                    BLANCHE
We must have peeled and cooked a hundred weight of potatoes and vegetables, not to mention all that basting onto joints.
          *(rises to fill teapot)*
I'm beginning to feel Cinderella-like, you know what I mean, our Stell'? These last two days catering for ten hungry men.
          *(sits down)*
Rather reminds me of when I use to work in the soup kitchens in the war years.

                    STELLA
The consensus of agreement between the farm men was that you are a brave little woman –

                    BLANCHE
Yes, I heard that.
          *(passes a hand over damp*
          *forehead)*

> And the one wearing his Glengarry hat throughout the meals – repeatedly called me a, "brave wee woman who appears unwilling to remain in the state" cheeky sod.

> SOPHIE
> A good job you're almost completely without self-pity, Grandma.

*We see SOPHIE turn to STELLA, who knows SOPHIE'S hungry look.*

*We see STELLA rising – opens cupboard door to reach for prepared sandwiches, then several bottles of brown ale and glasses.*

*We see the women raise their full glasses to a toast of longevous.*

> BLANCHE
> *(manages to eat as well as talk)*
> I'm too old to hunt or want another husband or companion – too antiquated to start again – behaving like a madwoman screaming and whining like a horse.
> *(takes large gulps of ale)*
> In my experience, unless a discontented wife has made a husband utterly wretched, they do not want a divorce. They simply refuse to leave the house.

> STELLA
> And a wife who divorces too

impetuously is left alone and uninvited to rich, elegant country houses.

*We see STELLA help herself to another brown ale.*

          SOPHIE
I can't say that I've heard anything about stray husbands or divorced wives ...
      *(carries on eating)*
when I've heard nothing whatsoever about either.

          BLANCHE
The last time I was invited to the Mullard's Grange ...
      *(closes eyes in memory)*
Oh – yes – it afforded a good view, and the proprietor, was a property agent, come – auctioneer at the corn-exchange in the city ...
      *(makes her face inviting)*
He was very gentle and careful to rest his weight on his elbows.
      *(voice drops)*
If only men – more men did that ...
      *(takes leisurely drink)*
He use to call me his little corn-marigold ...

          STELLA
Just flash talk, Mother ...

*We see STELLA gather a handful of pronged forks and cutting edged knives from the sink draining board and begin to dry them vigorously - then one by one, drop them into their allotted compartments in the dresser drawer.*

                STELLA

Everyone knows those kind of flowers are very common in the cornfields.

                SOPHIE
           *(suppressing a giggle)*

Flowers of fine thoughts, eh, Grandma, but you do sound as though you use to be quite a naughty lady.

*We see STELLA and BLANCHE acknowledge SOPHIE'S summary with only their eyelids.*

                BLANCHE

I should have married him, but we were both in-between marriages.
           *(looks apologetically at*
           *STELLA)*
Your father was one of the boys at the front, so men were very scarce to come by, but yes, I'm sure I still have the telegram ...
           *(looks optimistic)*
I never saw either of them again after the autumn fall, did not want to, although I'm sure we would be friendly if we met again.

                STELLA

           *(kindly)*

I'm sure you would, Mother. Sam use to say, and quite often, your special skill of affability was seeing that no

one felt slighted or was over-looked
...

We hear the sound of grating reverse gear of the traction engine which causes SOPHIE and BLANCHE to rise from their seating and with STELLA, move towards the open door.

**SCENE 34**
**EXT. STOCKDALE FARMS - FORECOURT - 3:04 PM**

We see STELLA, SOPHIE and BLANCHE as by-standers on the flagged forecourt.

We see the heavy machinery moving slowly on the cart-road, heading for the water-course; seeing SPENCER and GRACE striding from one stepping stone to another - to pay attention to the crossing over the stream without the CONTRACTOR driving the iron wheels over the edge stones of the waterfall.

          STELLA
        (thoughtfully)
If the stream was flooding, they'd never make it to the other side of the water-course, and it wouldn't be the first machinery to go down the deep descent, as Sam once said ...

We see SOPHIE lock her arms tightly through STELLA and BLANCHE'S.

          SOPHIE
        (whispers hoarsely)
Was it an accident, or ... was it deliberate murder?

**SCENE 35**

**EXT. STOCKDALE FARMS - FORECOURT - 12:20 PM**

*We see JAKE crossing the forecourt - in the driving rain - he has a hessian meal sack draped over his shabby overcoat. He's heading for the kitchen.*

**SCENE 36**

**INT. STOCKDALE FARMS - STELLA'S KITCHEN - 12:20 PM**

*We see JAKE stood right there on the newly scoured kitchen doorstep - his hob-nailed boots caked and slathered with mud. The sediment now beginning to drip and form a sludgy pool round his worn boot soles.*

*STELLA is wearing a smart rustic coloured costume.*

> JAKE
> *(to STELLA)*
> Ah thought ah'd better tell thee afore
> tha buggers off t' Christening ...
> *(accusing tone)*
> Ah called round here earlier in
> mornin', but tha weren't here!

*We see STELLA swallowing her anguish with difficulty, but she controls her movements, as though to please herself and no one else.*

> STELLA
> I don't owe you any whereabouts
> explanations, Jake Swales, so kindly
> get to the point and have done with it
> or I'll be late as usual ...

                    JAKE
              (no sign of moving, his eyes
              fixed on STELLA)
         Weel – I've come t' say ah'm off t'
         put mesen inta bed, ah don't feel over
         clever – liverish, full o' bile ...

                    STELLA
         Bed! Good farmers are never found in
         bed! They only come indoors at
         mealtimes and at bedtime, besides,
         it's scarcely half past twelve in the
         afternoon.

We see STELLA take a step closer to JAKE.

We see JAKE'S dark face under his saturated cap neb is indeed bloated.

                    STELLA
              (uneasily)
         I don't see how it can be your liver –
         you don't look yellowish – more – more
         – animated – you've always had a good
         bill of health.

We see JAKE press his hand to his chest and set-up a loud, controlled fit of coughing.

We see STELLA turn her head towards the window, she sees SPENCER, cutting across garden lawn, leaning forward against the rain.

We see SPENCER in the doorway, waiting courteously for JAKE to move aside.

*We see JAKE bristling with wrath. He shuffles inside doorway and into the kitchen.*

*We see STELLA'S anger rise as JAKE drags the puddle of mud from beneath his boots and wipes them on the cocoanut interwoven matting.*

*We see SPENCER step over the residue, and head straight for STELLA.*

> SPENCER
> You look magnificent, 'Ella in these rustic colours.
>     *(smiles)*
> They set off your fiery hair and wonderful complexion ...
>     *(laughs)*
> And ...

*We see STELLA with her head proudly held high and her beautiful eyes smiling into his.*

> SPENCER
> Everyone in the world should see you, as you look to me now.

*We see SPENCER take her outstretched hand and raise it to his lips, as though they are alone together.*

> SPENCER
> 'Ella, I never knew what happiness was until I came home and met you and my sisters.

*We see SPENCER press his cheek against STELLA'S.*

*We see STELLA smiling into his ear – and over his shoulder STELLA sees JAKE, watching them – staring – and in that stare – hatred.*

*We see STELLA press her hand warningly against SPENCER'S chest.*

*We see SPENCER turn round – JAKE has gone.*

## SCENE 37
**EXT. HOLBRIDGE CHURCH – 2:55 PM**

*Through the rain we see ABE, WINNY and MIKE leading the way towards The Wheat Sheaf on foot, only a stone's throw from the church.*

*We see EDNA'S father, RALF and his wife, ROSE following them.*

*We see STELLA and SOPHIE with EDNA, wheeling pram with baby, ALICE-ROSE within, at the tail-end.*

*We see the procession led by ABE, entering The Wheat Sheaf.*

## SCENE 38
**INT. THE WHEAT SHEAF INN – 3 PM**

*We see ABE, WINNY, MIKE, EDNA with sleeping ALICE-ROSE in pram, RALF, ROSE, STELLA, SOPHIE and a few LOCALS are sat looking wetly dispirited around ornate cast iron tables – seated on settles in the bar-room.*

      ABE
     (with acritude)
  It's time tha took thee turn, Ralf,
  an' took thy Edna and bairn off our
  hands an' under thee roof, at least

until spring time, an' while yah at it
...
    *(glares)*
give our Mike some extra work now he's demandin' ah married man's wage.

*We hear ABE smack his empty beer glass onto table top.*

    RALF
    *(with severity)*
They made their bed so they can lay on it!

    WINNY
    *(usual rationale self)*
Now the nights are drawing in, Ralf ... we've all become conscious of how best to accommodate the extended family ... We're restrained ... cramped ... and the child won't stop crying -

    RALF
Edna's not goin' to land herself an' that bairn back on our doorstep to make us the local laughin' stock.

    ROSE
    *(sits stiff backed on settle)*
And your Mike had no business in taking advantage of our Edna. If he'd kept his appendages inside his trousers, our Edna wouldn't have ended up caught in this poverty trap!

*We see ABE and WINNY open their mouths to speak - ROSE hold's* up her hand like a marshal.

                    ROSE
          And if Ralf and I had had our way, she
          would have wed young Gerald Beck. He
          was always sweet on our Edna - and
          everybody knows the Becks have never
          been short of brass. It's no wonder
          the baby can't and won't stop crying!

                    STELLA
                  (gallantly)
          Putting ethical considerations to one
          side, what about Edna and Mike? How do
          they feel about these crowded
          circumstances, and what about the
          marriage? Do they love each other?

*We see faces - hardboiled faces turn swiftly upon STELLA, while blinking back at her in astonishment - replaced quickly by argumentative expressions.*

*We hear a nasty, amplified silence.*

*We see MIKE looking sullen.*

*We see EDNA'S beautiful, large eyes circled with dark shadows, unblinkable.*

                    RALF
          An' what's fuckin' love got t' do with
          it?

                    STELLA
                  (grandly)
          Adversity does set things back a bit,

Ralf. But in the end it's the clearing up that matters.

     RALF
    (inflamed)
Don't thee come sittin' on thee high horse wi' me. It's got nowt t' do wi' you!

     WINNY
    (coolly)
Control. It's a common trait with selfish women who marry rich men, then seduce their sons.

     STELLA
And jealousy, Winny, is the hallmark of a killjoy. So, to avoid deep tiredness through baby crying, may I propose as Alice-Rose's Godmother and as a goodwill gesture, that Edna, Mike and baby, live as tenants in the first renovated cottage on Woodclose Terrace.

     ABE
Tha's already thinkin' o' linin' thee own pocket!

*We see MIKE looking uneasy, but silent.*

*We see EDNA sat sipping a lemonade in thoughtful reverie.*

*We see ALICE-ROSE beginning to wake-up.*

*We see SOPHIE gently rocking the pram.*

STELLA

No! Money has never been my first consideration ...

ABE

Pull t' other leg, Stell', John Hinchcliffe said tha turned up at his office in thick o' winter like a pan o' milk unexpectedly boilin' over when tha discovered old Sam had left half o' his wealth t' ah kept-in-the-dark bastard son!

STELLA

*(roguish)*

John Hinchcliffe wouldn't know the difference between a woman having a false orgasm or a real orgasm.
    *(looks point-blank at WINNY)*
I'm sure Winny could vouch to that.

WINNY

*(clicks her tongue)*

According to impeccable sources, Stella, dear, you certainly know the difference between Father and son.

SOPHIE stops rocking the pram - comes to sit next to STELLA.

SOPHIE

*(sportively)*

Mummy's a sophisticated lady who knows the value of simplicity when it comes down to family matters ...

We see STELLA throw a warm glance to SOPHIE.

STELLA

Yes. I'm in partnership with Spencer, and this cottage will be fully modernised to a high standard by the new year. There will be no rent to pay for the first year - to get you both on your feet.

*We see STELLA look to EDNA then MIKE for a reaction.*

*We see MIKE looking unsettled.*

*We see the shyness of the strong in EDNA'S face.*

STELLA
(encouragingly)

And as for an extra earning wage - Mike could cycle to and from Abe's farm, and still have time left over to lend a hand on the building site ...

MIKE

Eight miles each way ... each day -

STELLA

A mere nothing to such a strapping young man, and -

RALF

Tha'll not be short changing, lad, or our Edna?

STELLA
(firmly)

Mike would be paid the hourly going wage, if he cares to take up our offer

for the sake of his own family, after
all, there are eleven more cottages to
be renovated.

*We see WINNY rise and move across to the bar counter.*

                  STELLA
Take your time.
     *(genuinely)*
If you're interested in taking things
further, then, call into John
Hinchcliffe's office and ask for
Harry. He'll show you both around the
premises. He's our overseer.

                  EDNA
     *(convivial tones)*
We'll take your offer, Aunt Stella
with both hands, and thank you.

                  STELLA
     *(warmly)*
What are Godmothers appointed for if
they can't give a helping hand ...

                  MIKE
     *(leans forward)*
Thanks. Aunt.

*We see WINNY advancing towards them from the bar counter - carrying a plate of sandwiches in each hand. ABE rises to meet her.*

*We hear ABE'S discontentment in his loud voice as he answers WINNY above the juke-box playing - IVOR NOVELLO, "WE'LL GATHER LILACS".*

ABE

Did ta hear me say they deserved cottage given?

We see WINNY'S lips moving, her voice is inaudible.

ABE

How could yah? Ah swallowed me words – fuckin' nearly choked mesen.

WINNY is still inaudible.

ABE

Aye, ah know yah can understand anything ah can – but ah was too taken aback t' not go along wi' convention!

WINNY still incoherent.

We hear juke-box stop playing!

We see ABE and WINNY not realising it's finished playing the record.

ABE
(takes plates of sandwiches from WINNY, still bawling)
Ah know yah was fond o' Edna for five minutes an' by accident. We all were until ...

RALF
(rasping)
Until?

                    ROSE
                (sarcastic)
            We could all hear you shouting unequal
            criticism, making us feel like
            children who hear their parents
            squabbling when they think they're
            asleep. Well it won't wash with us!

                    ABE
                (blusters)
            Oh, for Christ's sake. Let's all wash
            it down wi' one last round.
                    (plonks down plates, waves to
                    BAR-TENDER)
            Same again, lad. An' shake thee
            feathers!

*We see SOPHIE reaching out for a beef sandwich. She takes a large bite then tongues it sideways.*

                    SOPHIE
                (companionably)
            Let's not deplete goodwill by sounding
            tribally different.
                    (smiles at baby)
            It's Alice-Rose's special day, so we
            young ones don't want her baptism day
            ending up less so.

*All turn to face the winsome, wholesome SOPHIE, reflecting harmony.*

*ABE, from the other side of the table reaches out to tap SOPHIE'S arm.*

                    ABE
          For an instant - theer - ah'm not sure
          if ah resent such insight from you,
          young lady.

                    RALF
          Ah can't see why tha should be
          resentful - she's an Asquith.
                    (bites into sandwich)
          Peopled by increasingly difficult
          womenfolk ...

We see ALICE-ROSE open her eyes - then her mouth, to rally attention.

                    ABE and MIKE
                    (as one)
          Amen t' that!

## SCENE 39
**I/E. ROVER CAR - HIGH ST - HOLBRIDGE - 4:55 PM**

We see HARRY waiting in the rain outside J. W. HINCHCLIFFE AND CO SOLICITORS with his weekend case.

We see STELLA pulling Rover up onto pavement. SOPHIE is sat on the back car seat.

                    HARRY
          I really thought you had forgotten me,
          what with the invitation to Abe's
          family Christening.

We see HARRY'S feet hardly tucked behind the driver's seat before STELLA presses her foot down on the accelerator.

STELLA

I'm afraid Abe and Winny will never change. We'll always be fighting off their constant sense of having been deliberately denied their dues by circumstance ... vague, yet conspiratorial, and it's eating away at them like a virus ... which brings my mind strictly back to Jake -

SOPHIE

*(urgently)*

Yes! Jake! - Hurry Mam ... it's getting dark. And the rain's not letting up.

*(leans forward)*

We heard Grandma saying last night she'd had a previous premonition, something she couldn't quite place her finger on - but never-the-less ...

*(voice wavers)*

something shocking and debasing.

HARRY

The more I think about Jake Swales, the more troubled I am ...

*(grips SOPHIE'S hand)*

Yes. Please hurry, Mrs Asquith.

STELLA

You're both right ...

*(changes into top gear)*

It struck me as odd earlier today when Jake said he'd take time out - because he felt effected by jaundice ...

                SOPHIE
              *(sharply)*
        And did he look yellow?

                STELLA
        I couldn't really see the whites of
        his eyes ...

*We see and hear STELLA skidding round a corner on locked brakes.*

*We see SOPHIE and HARRY bounding up and down to the rhythm of the car's coiled spring seating.*

                STELLA
        His eyes were shaded by the neb of his
        cap.

*We see and hear STELLA reversing back on skid marks before turning the bend. We hear the window wipers scraping on the front screen.*

                HARRY
              *(imperfect tone)*
        Stop talking ... please ... Mrs
        Asquith, just concentrate on the road.

**SCENE 40**
**I/E. ROVER CAR - STOCKDALE FARMS - 5:20 PM**

*We see STELLA driving the Rover through the flooding water-splash to swing the car steering wheel towards the forecourt.*

*We see in the car headlights GRACE staggering - to lurch sideways, her arms held upwards as though shielding herself against attack.*

*We see by the beams of headlights – dark red splotches of blood stains down the front of GRACE'S white jumper.*

          STELLA, SOPHIE and HARRY
            (shouting in oneness)
  <u>Grace!</u>

*We see and hear STELLA brake so suddenly that the engine cuts out and the car jerks to a sudden stop!*

*We see STELLA, SOPHIE and HARRY piling out of the Rover. Hear car doors slam – young COLLIE dog barking.*

          STELLA
            (wild-eyed)
  Grace!

*We see dimly – their anxious ridden eyes looking towards their home and the adjoining farmhouse and outer-buildings. Nothing stirs. No front doors open – no others appear.*

*We see only faint glimmers of lamplight tinged through drawn curtains.*

*We see STELLA, SOPHIE and HARRY running headlong in the driving rain towards spasmodically moving GRACE.*

*We see GRACE bent over, right hand groping for kitchen door sneck – left hand clutching her ribs.*

          GRACE
            (mutters through clenched
            teeth)
  Jake. He's really not fit to be let
  loose – he's completely haywire ...
  We've got to stop him ... before ...

We see HARRY fling open the door, while STELLA and SOPHIE assist GRACE into the kitchen.

## SCENE 41
**INT. STOCKDALE FARMS - STELLA'S KITCHEN - 5:22 PM**

STELLA and SOPHIE help to gently lower GRACE onto a chair. SOPHIE leaves kitchen to enter living room.

> **HARRY**
> *(disquiet)*
> I'll search your farmhouse rooms then the gardens ...

HARRY follows SOPHIE.

> **GRACE**
> *(crying)*
> Harry did say Jake was a psychopath, and he's right.
> *(tears slide down her damp face to settle under her chin)*
> Jake, he's simply not – plumb-rule ...

We see GRACE beginning to rock herself.

> **STELLA**
> *(coldly)*
> Jake Swales will pay for this! He's exercised far too much malice to be safe around.

We see SOPHIE re-enter the kitchen. She's carrying a bowl, kettle and first aid box. She hands them over to STELLA.

We see HARRY stepping back into the kitchen.

                    HARRY
              *(anxiously)*
I've not seen head nor tail of Jake –
and I can't help but feel a chill
running down my spine when I think
about him.
              *(leans against Aga rail)*
It's hard to find someone who doesn't
want to be found.

                    SOPHIE
              *(whispers)*
Jake just doesn't care anymore – he's
a dangerous old man – and –

                    STELLA
Not anymore! We're finished with Jake
Swales!

We see BLANCHE bustle into kitchen from outside. She's carrying a torch and SAM'S double barrelled gun clamped under her arm. She looks risky.

                    BLANCHE
I've just been in the top barn and
cow-houses to investigate why the
young collie dog was barking so
profoundly – and at the same time
looking for our Grace –
              *(pin-points GRACE and is
              outraged)*
It's that blasted Jake Swales, isn't
it! I knew something like this was
going to happen – I could feel it in
my bones ... all this bloody
mindedness and lunacy that gets into

old men. It's the disease of
persecution mania - he's crackers!

*We hear sounds of agreement.*

*We see STELLA cleaning and dressing the swelling wounds. We see GRACE sat awkwardly - sipping a brandy - eyes red rimmed - face showing signs of bloating and bruising - nose blooded and when bathed it looks decidedly off centre.*

          STELLA
        *(aghast)*
A broken nose! My God, he's given our Grace a boxer's nose ...

          SOPHIE
       *(close to tears)*
I think we should fetch Doctor Liddle.

          GRACE
     *(taking deep breaths)*
No! When the dizziness spins itself - out of my head - I will attend to it myself -

*We see GRACE vacate her seat with galvanised jerky movements. She enters the living room.*

## SCENE 42
**INT. STOCKDALE FARMS - STELLA'S LIVING ROOM - 5:26 PM**

*We see GRACE swaying before the sideboard back-mirror.*

*We see and hear STELLA, SOPHIE, BLANCHE and HARRY begging to differ as they crowd into the room behind GRACE.*

*We see all their reflections ogling back at GRACE – each one having individual expressions superimposed over another, as we see GRACE bravely, take her nose between her fingers and thumbs, mercilessly crunch it back into its rightful place.*

                STELLA
              *(mutters)*
    Just what her father would have done.

## SCENE 43

**INT. STOCKDALE FARMS – STELLA'S LIVING ROOM – 6:15 PM**

*We see STELLA, GRACE, SOPHIE and HARRY seated round the room. BLANCHE is standing by GRACE'S side.*

                BLANCHE
              *(to GRACE)*
    Now, flower – in your own time. How did this assault happen?

                GRACE
              *(nasal)*
    I was working with Spencer – taking drainpipes up to the six acre field –
              *(takes shuddering breaths)*
    rained off –

                BLANCHE
              *(gently)*
    Don't keep stifling your screams, love – just bloody well scream –

                STELLA
              *(pressing cold flannel on GRACE'S forehead)*
    We'll understand. In fact, we could

all scream for you, lass.

                GRACE

Came home on our new tractor ... checked young stirks chained up for first time ... discovered one had its foreleg caught up in its neck chain ... swollen knee-joint ... I'd gone for the animal medication box ...
    *(sips brandy with difficultly)*
Couldn't find it in the grainary ... then remembered it had been cleaned out of the store place ... last week ... ready for threshing time ... saw Jake carry the box across the yard before he disappeared with it into his kitchen –

                STELLA
    *(astonished)*
You went into his home after all we've said! When we all know he's here, but not altogether there! You know as well as we do, our Grace, he's a stranger to reason these days!

                GRACE
    *(fidgets her forehead)*
The door was open –

                BLANCHE
    *(cries out)*
<u>Oh, my God!</u>

*We see BLANCHE dropping down onto the nearest chair, the gun straddled across her wide spread-out knees.*

BLANCHE

Our Grace – she's going to tell us next – she saw old Jake playing in a four piece band!

GRACE
(jerks upright)

I spotted the medication box on the windowsill, and just as I reached for it ... the door slammed shut ... and there stood Jake ... behind the door ... smiling.

*We see GRACE break off from speaking to take a gulp of brandy. We see her numbed mouth buckle sideways automatically.*

*We see STELLA mopping up the spillage as though GRACE is a child.*

SOPHIE
(tears brimming over)

Oh, Grace. Grace ... you're not going to be a damp baby ... for the rest of your days.

HARRY

There's many a slip between the lip and the cup, Sophie, love, but it doesn't mean that it's permanent. Grace will heal.

GRACE

For the first time in my life ... I felt fear ... real fear ... and I really thought about Hertz's fear ...

>           and I thought ... I should have shot
>           Jake down, and left Father to clear up
>           the matter. He was so good at that.
>                   *(begins to whimper)*
>           "Money talks" he use to say with the
>           authority of a payroll master.

*Silence falls.*

*We see GRACE turn from them as though listening and automatically their heads turn in the same direction.*

>                           GRACE
>                   *(muffled tones)*
>           I remember Jake's voice now ... sort
>           of sing-song tones ... as he said,
>           "Come here, lass. You could do with ah
>           bit of proper shame instead of that
>           nose in the air stuff." Then he
>           strutted closer ... sort of chanting
>           ... "Ah've come to take thee away,
>           away, away. To join thee father away,
>           away, away."

*We see them nodding – willing GRACE not to clam up on them.*

*Eventually GRACE speaks again.*

>                           GRACE
>                   *(voice quakes)*
>           Then he moved in closer. In a dance-
>           like way as though he had a tune going
>           on in his head ...

*We see GRACE hesitate, she begins to tremble.*

> BLANCHE
> (distressed)
> Our Grace, she's trying not to lose heart.

> GRACE
> (reliving her fears)
> For the first time I really and truly began to realise the enormity of fear and dread Hertz must have experienced in that fatal day.

We see SOPHIE begin to cry again.

> BLANCHE
> (shouting)
> <u>I'll swing for that wicked old man myself!</u>

We see and hear BLANCHE cranking away at the lever on the gun.

> STELLA
> I've just thought – where's Spencer? Oh, God – there's no safeguards against falling into love – Grace – there's no manuals ... no –

> GRACE
> I heard myself shouting for Jake to go back to bed ... he was suppose to be ill – but he kept side-stepping towards me ... then I saw what he had in his hand ...

We see – all – shaking their heads mournfully from side to

*side, trying to catch each other's eyes, not catching each other's eyes, not knowing or having the courage to ask.*

*They all stay silent, waiting.*

                    GRACE
        *(distressed)*
Bridie's collar ...

          STELLA, SOPHIE, BLANCHE and HARRY
        *(all at once)*
Bridie! Dog collar!

                   STELLA
        *(repellency)*
Bridie was buried with her collar round her neck. I know that for a fact. I was with Spencer when we buried her.

                    GRACE
Jake was motioning with Bridie's collar, and smiling ... "Let's get on with it!" he said. Then he started whistling as though calling me to heel ... I dived for the doorway – but he rammed the kitchen table in front of me.
        *(pause)*
So I darted under the table but he managed to kick me on the head, and my ribs ...
        *(shudders)*
I tried not to moan as he circled the table, and I could hear him snapping his fingers and singing to a slow

>           three beat ... "Come closer, come
>           closer, my dear come closer. You're
>           safe in killer hands." Then suddenly
>           he stopped singing.

*Silence.*

*STELLA hands GRACE a handkerchief. SOPHIE, HARRY and BLANCHE can't take their eyes off GRACE.*

>                    GRACE
>           "I'm not going to hurt you," he said.
>           "Why should I ... I've come to take
>           you home."

*We see GRACE rocking herself – trying to breathe regularly, but she is choking, swallowing, coughing.*

>                    GRACE
>           I couldn't believe he meant ... what I
>           knew he meant ... until then ...
>                 (gasps)
>           Feeling desperately alone. I saw him
>           crouch and saw him place his elbows on
>           his knees, leaving himself splayed
>           wide open, so I lashed out with my
>           feet and kicked him right between his
>           crutch. He bawled out and I rolled out
>           from under the table and bolted
>           through the doorway.

*We see GRACE hold her head in her hands.*

>                    BLANCHE
>               (wiping her eyes on her
>               pinafore)

                    Poor lass. Her head must be pumping
                    mad with all this talking, never mind
                    her injuries.

                              GRACE
                    I'm sorry, everyone ... but I feel
                    overly sad about myself and another
                    self ... Hertz ... and my lost baby
                    son.

We see GRACE'S body go into violent shudders and she starts
to weep as if what is being wept about is growing faster than
it can be wept about.

                              GRACE
                    So-rry ... so-rry ... so-rry ...

## SCENE 44
**EXT. STOCKDALE FARMS - FORECOURT - 7 PM**

We see STELLA and HARRY leaving the farmhouse and into the
heavy rain. STELLA is carrying a storm lamp.

We see BLANCHE standing on the kitchen doorstep - SAM'S gun
clasped in her hands.

                              STELLA
                    Don't move an inch from our Grace or
                    Sophie, Mother, while Harry and myself
                    re-check the young stirks - and God
                    only knows where Spencer is? And as
                    for Jake ...?

We see STELLA take out SPENCER'S hand-gun from her inner coat
pocket and check its contents - she replaces it into her
pocket.

                    BLANCHE
              *(flushed with anger)*
          If that Jake Swales comes within one
          inch of Grace and Sophie, I swear I'll
          shoot him dead on the spot!

*We hear BLANCHE drop the iron sneck as she closes the kitchen door.*

## SCENE 45
**I/E. STOCKDALE FARMS - TOP COW-HOUSE - 7:05 PM**

*We see STELLA and HARRY entering cow-house where STIRKS are chained within separate stalls. There is a lit storm lamp hanging on a nail.*

*We see STELLA handing HARRY her lamp, he holds it aloft – light reflecting on his spectacles.*

*We see STELLA elbowing and pushing her way between restless young SKIRKS - while running her hands over their hot, sweating backs, chains clanking as they jerk their heads up and down their chain poles.*

                    STELLA
              *(talking to STIRKS)*
          You'll get use to the chains - given
          time - after a day or two - cush, cush
          ... cush, cush ...
              *(to HARRY)*
          Spencer's been and gone.
              *(points to empty stall)*
          He must have removed the injured stirk
          and taken it into one of the loose-
          boxes ...
              *(turns down the lighted lamp*

> *hanging on wall)*
> They'll settle down better in the darkness. Come on, Harry, let's try and catch up with Spencer before Jake does.

*We see STELLA and HARRY leave cow-house and enter the rainfall of the night.*

## SCENE 46

**EXT. STOCKDALE FARMS - HEADING FOR OUT-BUILDINGS - 7:07 PM**

*We hear the rainwater gushing over the stepping stones - to rushing over the stone edge of the flagged causeway to pound down into the deep waterfall - to merge with the other stream - swelling their banks to overflow.*

> HARRY
> Don't you think ...
> *(shivers)*
> Mrs Asquith, it would be advisable to call Doctor Liddle and at the same time - the police?

> STELLA
> *(snarls)*
> Poppycock! It's too late for that now! Anyway, we, nor they, would be able to drive safely over the swollen becks - so - Harry Bletchford don't you even try!

> HARRY
> Mrs Asquith, I wouldn't do anything to jeopardise ... not like Jake.

*We see HARRY beginning to lag behind – his feet clumsy – caught in the cart-tracks. He stumbles – lamp swings from limp hand. We hear him curse – pant for breath.*

> STELLA
>
> Autonomy! That's what we call it here in the countryside! Harry!

*We see STELLA turn to HARRY, and collar his arm tightly – to bear him upright.*

> STELLA
>
> We hold our own counsel here at Stockdale, Harry Bletchford. And if you don't have the gall or the balls for it, then bugger off, lad! Back to the town-life!

> HARRY
>
> I can't argue with you, Mrs Asquith, because I'm too much in love with your Sophie – and I'm already far too much enmeshed into your family's lives. And I've already decided to avoid any mention of Spencer's loaded gun that you're carrying on your personage ...
> *(rashly)*
> In fact, my instincts tell me – to say nothing, for as long as it takes.
> *(squares shoulders)*
> A lifetime if need be!
> *(stumbles alongside STELLA)*
> I can't be – or do without Sophie in my life!

## SCENE 47
**I/E. STOCKDALE FARMS - OUT-BUILDINGS - 7:09 PM**

*We see STELLA and HARRY - heads down against siling rain, moving from and into one outer building to the next.*

*We hear rain smacking down onto the slate roofs.*

*We hear the mellow cushing - grunting and stirring of the animals as they settle down for the night with their prismatic shadows.*

> STELLA
> There's no sign of Spencer - or ...

*We hear something - other - then a bang! A resonant bang!*

> STELLA
> *(grabs HARRY'S arm urgently)*
> Did you hear that noise?

> HARRY
> *(croaks)*
> It's Blanche - she's pulled the trigger!
> *(clutches STELLA)*
> Surely not Sophie caught in the cross-fire - Sophieee!

*We see HARRY stumble into a run, with STELLA chasing after him.*

## SCENE 48
**EXT. STOCKDALE FARMS - FARMYARD - 7:10 PM**

*We see HARRY fling the yard gate open - he and STELLA blunder* through.

We see HARRY fumbling and riving at the bottom garden gate – he can't encounter the sneck.

We see HARRY moving faster than he has for weeks – streak along cart-road to disappear round the stone wall corner, lamp flickering precariously.

>STELLA
>(shouting after him)
>Take care! Take care, Harry!

We see STELLA staring wildly up at the rain-darkened stone adjoining farmhouses.

JAKE'S house: STELLA catches a brief glimpse of JAKE with wavering light behind him drawing bedroom curtains together with one hand – and in the other hand, the silhouette of a hammer – or is it?

>STELLA
>(to the darkness of the night)
>Oh! No! God! No!

We see STELLA squinting – blinking – and peering from different angles before the edges of the curtains meet.

>STELLA
>(shouting)
>Spencer! Spenceeeerrr ...

We see dimly, STELLA'S legs – convulsively jerking her back through the yard gateway. It clanks shut. She runs across the flagged yard – passing the pig-houses, cow-houses – barn and grainary, and onto JAKE'S frontage.

We see STELLA stagger onwards – wet grass squelching under her rubber soled boots.

We see STELLA steadying herself, before entering JAKE'S home.

**SCENE 49**
**INT. STOCKDALE FARMS - JAKE'S KITCHEN - 7:12 PM**

We see STELLA quietly entering the kitchen.

We see on the windowsill, a single white candle waxed onto a cracked saucer. Its slender wick glows dimly showing empty bottles, old jam jars; shaving brush - bristles worn down, next to shaving mug and cake of soap.

There's no sign of the farm medication box.

We see STELLA gripping SPENCER'S gun, finger on its trigger, she moves to stand in the open living room doorway.

**SCENE 50**
**INT. STOCKDALE FARMS - JAKE'S LIVING ROOM - 7:13 PM**

We see the fire has fallen – embers taken the place of flames.

We see a table lamp with its wick burning unevenly – sending a curl of smoke spiralling lazily up one side of the blackened glass globe to trail gently towards the darkened ceiling.

We see a tin egg cup stood on a dinner plate. Its surrounded by egg shells and stale egg yolk covered teaspoons - one half-eaten loaf of bread - gone mouldy, leaned isolated on wooden bread board.

We see used drinking mugs with tea dregs and cigarette butts afloat.

We see STELLA brushing against furniture – shabby furniture as she enters the room.

> STELLA
> *(talking to herself)*
> Poor Lizzy – you had a very lean life with Jake – never spent a penny on his home – he must have just secured his wage somewhere – else – like his attitudes and feelings – Jake never observed – so they bloody well ceased to exist ...

We see STELLA reaching an adjoining door – she pauses – we see her carefully turning the door knob – clenching her teeth as dry hinges creak – and creak some more.

We hear movements – dampened down movements. We catch a sound – a dronish, humming sound – coming from above.

> STELLA
> *(to herself)*
> Jake – that sounds like Jake – what was Mother's warning words ...?
> *(pause)*
> "I'm afraid it's no good expecting a lunatic to have reasons for what he does".

We see STELLA shiver.

We see STELLA ease door more open – to stand in the gap – looking across at the hallway.

We hear an inner upstairs door open, and the melodic droning becomes louder.

> STELLA
> *(to herself)*
> Grace – that's what Grace heard ...

We hear a bang from above!

## SCENE 51
**INT. STOCKDALE FARMS - JAKE'S STAIRWAY - 7:15 PM**

We see STELLA crossing the hallway – and as she places her foot on the bottom step of the uncarpeted stairway we hear muffled shuffling noises, followed by a dull thud from above.

> STELLA
> *(as clean as cold to herself)*
> I'll protect my own ... family ...

## SCENE 52
**INT. STOCKDALE FARMS - JAKE'S LANDING - 7:16 PM**

We see STELLA reaching the landing. We see several bedroom doors. We hear hobnailed boots striking nail heads in the bare wooden floorboards of the far bedroom, then the sudden crash of pottery and glass colliding – breaking!

> STELLA
> *(whispers to herself)*
> Jake ...

We see halted footsteps cross the band of light beneath the far bedroom door. We see the door suddenly jerk open, and strands of mellow light shafts across the landing to reflect upon the whitewashed staircase wall opposite.

We see STELLA dart into the nearest bedroom – leaving a pencil width of view: she waits, holding the gun ready.

We hear dulcet sounds, as though JAKE'S marching to a three beat ... one step striking down hard, lighter touch on other two beats.

We see JAKE come out of the far bedroom onto the darkened landing.

We hear JAKE strutting closer to where STELLA is.

              JAKE
          (singing with dulcet tones)
  Come closer, come closer, my dear,
  come closer ...

We see, as he passes STELLA'S snippet of view – the glowing end of his cigarette. We see STELLA'S nostrils flare.

             STELLA
          (to herself)
  Fresh cigarette smoke, and chloroform.

STELLA places her hand over her mouth to smother a scream.

We hear JAKE'S boot steps clomp to a halt at the top of the stairs.

We see STELLA move instinctively two steps backwards and point the gun to centre of the doorway.

She waits.

We hear JAKE'S rasping voice reverberate along the length and breath of the silent landing.

> JAKE
> Tha should be bloody grateful ah'm
> makin' it possible so tha can have
> some peace!

*We hear his tone alter – as though his sense of humour is so strong it enables him to think with humour.*

> JAKE
> There was nobody t' teach me what I
> had t' know t' be peaceful! Thee
> grandmother once said t' me ... an'
> ah'll nivver forget it, she said,
> "Jake, lad, you are your own
> experience".
> *(laughs)*
> Aye, we are our own experience. By
> Gawd. She was a real Christian. Ah
> real bloody Christian thee grandmother
> was!

*We hear JAKE laugh again as he descends the stairs – to stop abruptly.*

> JAKE
> By hell, lad. Tha should see theesen.
> Tha looks ah real bobby-dazzler!
> *(shouting)*
> <u>Can't t' hear me, Francis bloody
> Spencer-Asquith?</u>

*We hear JAKE stomping his way further down stairway in transport of peculiar laughter, then in a change of mind, he bawls up from last few steps with approval.*

                    JAKE
                (shouting)
    Tha was much better about it, lad,
    than onnybody had ah reight t' expect.
    But ah'll not keep thee waitin', lad,
    ovver long or tha might get t' enjoy
    it t' much!

We see JAKE rounding the balustrade and disappear through living room doorway.

                    JAKE
              (singing loudly)
    Um-ta-rye, um-ta-rye-ay. Come closer,
    come closer, my dear, come closer.
    You're safe in killer hands. Let the
    moonlight serenade yah, no don't be ah
    stranger. Um-ta-rye, um-ta-rye-ay ...

We see STELLA throw herself down the landing and swing round into the far open bedroom doorway - closing it behind herself.

**SCENE 53**
**INT. STOCKDALE FARMS - JAKE'S FAR BEDROOM - 7:19 PM**

We see STELLA looked stunned!

                    STELLA
        Ss-ammm ... Penceeer ... Spenn-ceer
        ... Ashclifff ...

We see a chloroformed, gagged SPENCER collapsed onto a soiled, flock mattress, stark naked, positioned on his back as though he was a colt.

We see the old fashioned method of casting by side-lines has been used on SPENCER – trussed up by placing a rope around his neck – then between and round his legs and forearms, and back through the neck loop – tightened – leaving the operation area exposed.

We see STELLA'S eyes jerking from one knot to another.

              STELLA
   Oh! No! Noooooo!

We see a fire burning brightly in fire grate; a branding iron already thrust among the glowing coals; instruments on the hob boiling away in battered saucepan.

We see the dressing table surface crudely covered with a stained bed sheet and cattle instruments laid out methodically.

We hear JAKE singing from bottom of the stairs

              JAKE (O/S)
   Um-ta-rye, um-ta-rye-ay ...

We see STELLA propel into action – with rage and hatred.

We see STELLA shoving the loaded gun back into her pocket and pulling away SPENCER'S mouth gag.

We see SPENCER shaking his head violently from a dread beyond explanation.

We see SPENCER'S eyes swell in desperation – to meet STELLA'S.

                    SPENCER
                  (garbles)
            Ah'mmm ... affaa ... aahfr ... dda ...
            Ah'mm heelp-less ...

*We see STELLA lunge to the fireplace – nose-dive to the red-hot fire-iron and yank it out of the embers, then swing back round to SPENCER.*

                    STELLA
                  (wildly)
            Trust me!

*We see STELLA tugging at the rope for leverage, then plunge the fire-iron – white with heat – upon the rope, barely a hair-breath away from SPENCER'S sweating, cringing body.*

*We see smoke smouldering and rising from the scorching, to a burning.*

*We hear JAKE strutting slowly up the uncarpeted stairs.*

                    JAKE (O/S)
                  (singing)
            Take me to heart when I say, come
            closer, come closer, my dear, come
            closer, yah safe in killer hands ...

*We see SPENCER frantically straining his trussed body against the taunt rope in desperation to quicken the burning progress.*

*We see sweat pour down from beneath SPENCER'S thick hair – to slide down his forehead, off his eyebrows, over contorted face, to run under his chin, down his chest and beyond.*

*We see the rope catch fire, and the cords spring apart making SPENCER'S head jerk back and his bare body twist and contort towards wild-eyed STELLA, still dexterously manoeuvring the fire-brand.*

                    JAKE (O/S)
                (sing-songing)
            Let the moonlight serenade yah, no
            don't be a stranger. Um-ta-rye, um-ta-
            rye-ay ...

*We hear SPENCER let out a bellow of excruciating pain.*

*We see SPENCER drop onto his knees.*

*We catch a glimpse of three burnt – raw initials – SJA grooved on SPENCER'S masculine thigh.*

*We see STELLA staring momentarily mesmerised at the initials of Samuel John Asquith's brand mark – then – with female ferocity, she attends to SPENCER'S roped, right forearm and leg – untying to release the dividing rope.*

*We hear a clatter just beyond the closed door – then halted boot steps.*

*We see STELLA undoing knots, focusing on precious moments.*

                    JAKE (O/S)
                (shouting from other side of
                the bedroom door)
            <u>Tha can bawl all tha likes, lad! Ah
            can't come any faster, damn yah!</u>

*We see SPENCER, still with cauterised rope halter round his weltered neck – now with an arm and cramped leg free. We see him going into a series of uncontrolled sporadic movements.*

      JAKE (O/S)
    (shouting)
  <u>Ah've always been over worked an'
under paid – ten bob ah fuckin' week –
owld John used t' pay me – an' he
considered that almost over generous!</u>

*We see door handle move, then slowly turn.*

*We see STELLA'S fingers instantly fly off unfinished knots.*

*Without further warning, we see and hear the door kicked open with such violent force, that it bangs back against the wall to rebound shut – leaving JAKE on the inside of the room.*

*We see JAKE'S face – full of grime: a scythe with its almost straight shaft held high with bent nib resting on his shoulder.*

*We see JAKE'S thickened fingers gripping round the lower straight nib.*

*We see the five foot long by six inch wide steel blade glinting sharp as a razor as it curves down JAKE'S back – the tapered blade visible as it catches the light between the straddle of his legged stance.*

*SILENCE!*

*We see STELLA and SPENCER staring into the vacuum of JAKE'S unfathomable stare.*

*We see STELLA, icy calm, move forward protecting SPENCER'S naked contorted body, with her body, while SPENCER fumbles* with rope knots.

We see the gun held in her right hand – arm bent, pressed hard to herself in a decision making position.

We see JAKE'S sudden reaction when noticing the gun. He grips the bent handle – and swipes out with force to strike a forward sweep with the scythe blade to cut STELLA down. Too late!

STELLA PULLS THE TRIGGER!

We see JAKE'S blood splatter STELLA'S face, JAKE takes an involuntary step sideways, the scythe judders round from the snug of his shoulder ...

STELLA pulls the trigger again. The force spins JAKE a full step backwards hard against the closed door, forcing his lips to hang open – his eyes to startle wide as the bullet and the silent razor blade slice like butter through his worn clothes and flesh.

We hear a bellow of enraged painfulness and burning hatred, JAKE remains on his feet – clothes seeping blood. He drops the scythe. He slews round to fling the door open – to slam it shut behind himself, as the third bullet strikes, embedding in the woodwork.

We see SPENCER forcing his cramped limbs into breeches – thrusting bare feet into his boots. He blunders to STELLA to hug her.

We see STELLA with preservation worthy of a saint, detach herself and run out of the room after JAKE.

We see SPENCER grabbing for jacket and with pronounced limbs *chase after her.*

**SCENE 54**
**INT. STOCKDALE FARMS - JAKE'S LIVING ROOM - 7:25 PM**

*We see STELLA and SPENCER lurching into the living room.*

*We see the table lamp has been knocked onto scattered newspapers - hungry flames travel to make a trail of destruction.*

*We hear the front door slam.*

> SPENCER
> *(face set hard)*
> Don't take any chances, 'Ella ... I did - and you've seen the results ...

*We see SPENCER gather up the hearth rug and smother the flames.*

**SCENE 55**
**INT. STOCKDALE FARMS - JAKE'S KITCHEN - 7:26 PM**

*We see STELLA and SPENCER enter the kitchen.*

*We see a weak, leaning candlewick about to be submerged into the cooling pool of wax.*

*We see SPENCER reloading his gun.*

*We see STELLA looking attentively out of kitchen window.*

*We hear rain pattering against panes of glass - seeing barely nothing.*

                    STELLA
                (desperately)
            He's out there, somewhere, and ...

                    SPENCER
                (pants)
            Jake will go for the girls - my
            sisters!

**SCENE 56**
**EXT. STOCKDALE FARMS - JAKE'S FRONT DOOR - 7:27 PM**

*We see SPENCER fling the outside door open.*

*We hear the uproar of a reversing vehicle - then the sweep of headlights as the Fordson tractor swings round to gather speed.*

*We see the corner stones of the pig-houses impact the tractor. We see the silhouette of JAKE as he recklessly drives towards yard gate.*

*We see JAKE crash through, leaving it dashed to pieces.*

*We see STELLA and SPENCER, side by side, lunging with aggression, chasing after JAKE.*

                    STELLA
                (shouting to JAKE)
            You'll never make it over the flooding
            water-splash!

                    SPENCER
                (shouting to STELLA)
            He's going to take the tractor with
            him ...

                    STELLA
            (shouting to JAKE)
    Stop! Damn you! Tractors are too
    scarce to come by these days ...

We see STELLA firing a fourth bullet.

**SCENE 57**
**I/E. FORDSON TRACTOR - STOCKDALE FARMS - CART-ROAD - 7:28 PM**

We hear JAKE grinding through the tractor's gears along the
cart-road, just as SOPHIE - unexpectedly, rounds the walled
gardens with the young COLLIE dog lopping behind her.

                    SOPHIE
                  (shouting)
            Spencer! Oh, Spencer!

We see SOPHIE depicted in the headlights - suddenly she
stops, as the tractor swerves, hemming her against the stone
wall.

                    STELLA
                   (screams)
        Go back! Go back! Sophieeeee!

We see STELLA surpassing SPENCER, too late even to touch
SOPHIE before JAKE lurches sideways to seize SOPHIE by her
head of hair and drag her kicking and screaming onto the
tractor and beneath his knees.

We see in the distorted light JAKE'S arm lift, the fist drop,
and blurred sighting of SOPHIE before she flops from sight.

We see STELLA stumbling, almost fainting with shock. She
fires the gun.

We see SPENCER grasping a mudguard with one hand while taking a toe hold on the draw-bar of the tractor.

We see the tractor zig-zagging along the uneven cart-road.

We see SPENCER head butt JAKE.

We see JAKE malignantly drive into path of the barking, excited young COLLIE dog.

We see the tractor knocking the COLLIE backwards and off its feet, still alive, we hear it yelp in pain.

We hear the tractor accelerate – the tractor jolts. We hear the last yelp beneath the wide grooved wheels.

We see STELLA sobbing, staggering, legs wide apart as she steps over the crushed body, still chasing the moving vehicle towards the flooding becks.

We see BLANCHE clutching a storm lamp in one hand and SAM'S gun in the other, already ankle deep in saturated ground. Running towards the wooden footbridge.

We see GRACE and HARRY catching BLANCHE up and seizing her arms.

**SCENE 58**
**EXT. STOCKDALE FARMS – WATER-SPLASH – 7:30 PM**

We see images and hear echoes fainter.

We see JAKE unrepentant driving the tractor into the rumbling waters, the stepping stones no longer visible, and the infernal waterfall now forming a deep river basin of water.

We see STELLA, BLANCHE, GRACE and HARRY terrified – stood as bystanders, as the swells of the moving dark waters sweep the tractor into a wide semicircle – headlights rising and falling – the water force tilting, lifting the machine onto its side.

We see in the dipping light, SPENCER and JAKE lashing out at each other.

We catch a glimpse of SOPHIE bunched up in the foetal position with JAKE'S legs pinning her down.

We hear as one accord as STELLA, BLANCHE, GRACE and HARRY shout out SOPHIE'S name.

We see HARRY fling his soaking jacket away and throw himself towards the tipping, dipping tractor.

                  STELLA
             (shouting to GRACE)
      <u>Bring the Rover down here ... need
      more light. A rope ...</u>

We see HARRY being claimed by the water, and pounded unmercifully against the angles of the moving tractor.

We see JAKE still gripping steering wheel.

We see SOPHIE'S hair break the waters.

We see HARRY, choking – heaving for breath – to be submerged beneath the surface of the pounding waters.

We see SPENCER gripping the driving seat.

We see the blurred face of SOPHIE, still trapped beneath

JAKE'S knees.

We see SPENCER lunge to punch JAKE and seize and drag, shocked SOPHIE to the surface of torrid waters.

We see BLANCHE in the imperfect light swaying on the footbridge with SAM'S gun already cocked.

We see GRACE pull up with the Rover, headlights on. She and STELLA run to wet bridge and kneel down, desperately tying the rope ends around the bridge posts to form a rope-rail.

We see the water level less than two feet beneath the bridge.

We see SOPHIE flaying about in SPENCER'S grip - to see her thrashing loose from his hold.

We catch a glimpse from the Rover headlights of SOPHIE being dashed from the turning tractor and into the swell of the waters, to be tossed, floundering onto the overflow on the embankment.

We see STELLA run off the footbridge to struggle towards SOPHIE.

We see the tractor plunge, turning over and down into the inferno, taking JAKE and SPENCER with it.

We see HARRY suddenly surface, but before he can see or grasp onto the rope-rail, the force of the rapid flow sweeps him under the bridge and beyond.

      BLANCHE
     (shouting)
  <u>Did Harry have his glasses on?</u>

We see BLANCHE in despair, drop SAM'S gun on the bridge to stumble along the water edge, swinging the storm lamp.

> BLANCHE
> (shouting)
> <u>Harry! It's the best I can do - I'm coming ... I'm coming ...</u>

We see GRACE staring into the churning waters, trying to spot SPENCER and JAKE.

We see SPENCER being thrashed against the tractor. We see GRACE shouting to him, signalling, shaking the rope-rail. Somehow SPENCER manages to grab onto the hand-line, choking - coughing - choking - belching up the stenching water.

We see a blurred image of STELLA stumbling within a stone's throw of SOPHIE, who distressed, sways to her feet, arms outstretched towards STELLA.

We see SOPHIE'S legs buckle - she falls and slithers, flaying to be drawn back into the depths of the pounding waterfall.

We can just make out patchy reflections of the overturned tractor's paintwork, see the vehicle is wedged against the stone embankment and now slowly revolving away towards the bridge.

> GRACE
> (grabbing SPENCER'S arm)
> Sophie! Look! She's floundering!
> (waving and shouting)
> <u>Sophieeee!</u>
> (to SPENCER)
> I don't know who to go to first ...
> (sobs)

Run to Mother or jump to save Sophie!

>           SPENCER
>       *(shouting to GRACE)*
> Go to your Mother before she jumps
> into the waters after Sophie. She
> can't swim – I'll see to our Sophie!
>       *(shouting to SOPHIE)*
> Hold on! Hold on!

>           GRACE
>       *(wild-eyed to SPENCER)*
> You sounded – just like Father!

*We see SPENCER undoing one end of the rope-rail, making a running noose. He lasso's distressed SOPHIE.*

*We see STELLA treading heavily back onto the bridge, GRACE follows, sludge oozing from the tops of their wellington boots.*

>           STELLA
>       *(telling herself)*
> I'm so lucky to have stayed so sane
> ... a good job I have a spiritual
> sense ... of strength ... and ...

>           GRACE
>       *(crying)*
> Compared to my little sister's
> experience ... my ordeal was merely
> pinpricks.

*We see SPENCER lifting SOPHIE from the artificial respiration position on the footbridge.*

We see STELLA, GRACE and SOPHIE sobbing, wrapping their arms around each other.

GRACE is the first to recover her emotions.

> GRACE
> Jake! We have to find him! Find him for all our sakes – and for our peace of mind!

We see STELLA combing SOPHIE'S hair with her fingers.

> STELLA
> (yelling)
> Jake could be anywhere – any whereabouts – anyway –

> SPENCER
> (shouting)
> Jake's in poor shape. If we don't find him – the flood waters will harbour him – later than sooner.

We see JAKE suddenly surface – he somehow manages to grab onto the hanging rope – water pressure driving his body beneath the bridge.

We see JAKE jerking his head backwards – looking for help – his face twists in excruciating pain.

We see STELLA, GRACE, SOPHIE and SPENCER, eyes glittering – staring back at him from the footbridge.

We see GRACE beginning to untie the end of the rope from the bridge's iron frame.

We see BLANCHE suddenly reappear onto the bridge – re-gripping SAM'S gun – she ram's barrel into JAKE'S upturned face.

>             BLANCHE
>           (shouting)
>     I'll bloody well swing for you – Jake
>     Swales! – I will – I'll swing for you!
>
>              JAKE
>          (clenched teeth)
>     Bitch! Fat! Bitch!

We see HARRY limping onto bridge, still wearing spectacles – he's staunching an open gash on his head with shirt sleeves.

We see HARRY wrestling SAM'S gun from BLANCHE'S clutching fingers.

We see JAKE moving his eyes from one to the other – as they lean over bridge rail and stare down at him.

>              JAKE
>         (shouting haltedly)
>     No fuckin' Asquith – can break me –
>     done long afore – onny one o' yah knew
>     me ...
>           (voice breaks)
>     Long ago ...

We see HARRY point the gun at JAKE.

We see JAKE jerking his head to look at STELLA.

We see STELLA turn away – done with him!

                    JAKE
                (to STELLA)
        Aye - that's reight ... walk away ...
                (voice breaking)
        Don't go ... ah luve yah ... lub yah
        ...

We see JAKE screw up his eyes tight - so no saltwater can be
seen to glisten - or escape.

We see an image of a four year old JAKE - superimposed onto
JAKE'S face.

                    JAKE
                (screams)
        Mam-maaa ... Mammm-ahhhhh!

We hear the blast.

The blast knocks JAKE'S head sideways - blowing the right
side of his head clean off.

The battered tractor elevates from the embankment to turn
over and over towards the bridge ...

JAKE SWALES IS DEAD!

We see no triumph on their faces as they stagger off the
footbridge, onto the overflowing grass verge of the cart-
road, and when they all turn round - we see the heaving
tractor hit the span of the bridge with immeasurable impact -
smashing the wooden structure to ruin.

We see the flood churning away the smashed pieces - to leave
the banks unoccupied - deserted of the footbridge and its
supporting framework.

**SCENE 59**
**EXT. STOCKDALE FARMS - THE BECKS - 11 AM**

*We see the rain has cleared - the becks are slowly subsiding.*

*We see STELLA, SPENCER, GRACE and HARRY searching becks for JAKE'S body - not sighted.*

**SCENE 60**
**EXT. STOCKDALE FARMS - THE BECKS - 12:10 PM**

*We see SPENCER and HARRY with TWO CART-HORSES towing the smashed tractor out of the waters.*

**SCENE 61**
**EXT. STOCKDALE FARMS - THE BECKS - 12:15 PM**

*We see SPENCER and HARRY spotting JAKE'S dead body.*

**SCENE 62**
**EXT. STOCKDALE FARMS - FIELDS - 1 PM**

*We see STELLA, in haste, riding STRAWBERRY, her bay mare, across fields towards The Crown.*

**SCENE 63**
**EXT. THE CROWN PUBLIC HOUSE - 1:10 PM**

*We see STELLA within the Public Kiosk. She is speaking to someone on the telephone. Hangs up. Dials another number.*

**SCENE 64**
**EXT. STOCKDALE FARMS - THE BECKS - 2:30 PM**

*We see MR HOLMES surveying the smashed tractor with STELLA and SPENCER.*

                    MR HOLMES
It might be cheaper to buy a new
tractor than to have this one
repaired.

                    STELLA
Mr Holmes, tractor's are too hard to
come by, we bought this one via the
War Agg' sale -

                    SPENCER
Yes. Bought second-hand at the
agricultural auction in Lincolnshire -
one raffle ticket per farmer, at one
pound a ticket, and we held the lucky
draw ...

                    STELLA
Tractors, Mr Holmes, are scarcer than
poultry teeth.

**SCENE 65**
**EXT. STOCKDALE FARMS - THE BECKS - 2:40 PM**

*We see MR HOLMES assisted by SPENCER and HARRY hydraulically hauling the smashed tractor onto breakdown vehicle.*

**SCENE 66**
**EXT. STOCKDALE FARMS - THE BECKS - 3 PM**

*We see STELLA and GRACE removing bridge debris from waters onto flat cart.*

*We see departure of break-down vehicle transporting tractor away.*

We see SPENCER and HARRY recovering JAKE'S body from broken bridge planks. They lay his lifeless body onto back of cart.

**SCENE 67**
**EXT. STOCKDALE FARMS - THE BECKS - 3:30 PM**

We see DR LIDDLE swinging his car onto the grassy verge.

We see GRACE bring HORSE and cart to a stand still as STELLA accompanies DR LIDDLE as he examines JAKE'S body.

> DR LIDDLE
> Half a head! Both his legs amputated! Taken quite a bite out of him!

We see STELLA give DR LIDDLE a tired, resigned look, then she nods her head.

> STELLA
> Jake was such a grand worker ... and his demise, so soon after Sam, dear Sam. It's just been one disaster after another this year ... The landlady at The Crown told me, less than two hours ago, that Alf suffered a cardiac arrest the other day, and she doubts if he'll pull through ...

**SCENE 68**
**EXT. STOCKDALE FARMS - THE BECKS - 4:15 PM**

We see the ambulance arrive.

We see JAKE laid on stretcher and placed into the vehicle by TWO PARAMEDICS.

*We see DR LIDDLE checking HARRY'S head wound.*

                DR LIDDLE
            *(to HARRY)*
Looks like a nasty inflamed gash – needs a stitch or two – how did this happen?

                HARRY
            *(catching STELLA'S eye)*
Lost my footing on the stepping stones – sick headaches – but I'll be all right.

*We see DR LIDDLE'S insistence as HARRY is manoeuvred into ambulance alongside JAKE.*

                HARRY
            *(protesting)*
There's a world of difference between the two of us, Doctor!

*We see the ambulance depart.*

                DR LIDDLE
I insist, Stella, that I give you all a good check over before I leave ... polluted water is a dangerous commodity. A little jab will be in order.

                STELLA
            *(graciously)*
In that case, you'd better stay for tea, Doctor Liddle. Please leave your car at this side of the watercourse to

prevent water damaging the components.

*We see STELLA mount STRAWBERRY.*

*We see GRACE, SPENCER and DR LIDDLE follow on the backs of the CART-HORSES.*

**SCENE 69**
**INT. STOCKDALE FARMS - STELLA'S LIVING ROOM - 5:15 PM**

*We see STELLA, SPENCER, GRACE, SOPHIE seated at tea-table, DR LIDDLE is hovering over BLANCHE, who is fending him off.*

> BLANCHE
> We could go on talking about the accidents for as long as you like, Doctor Liddle ... We could select bits as far-fetched as you like, after all, there's very little from my marriage that has stayed clear in my mind.

*We see BLANCHE vacate the room to enter kitchen.*

*We see GRACE looking like a bluish-mauvish exquisite wild flower, she brushes DR LIDDLE aside - radiating a certain capriciousness that keeps him at bay.*

> GRACE
> I will work my aches and pains off ... Doctor Liddle. I've always worked things off ... work has been my salvation ... work is the only four letter word I know!

*We see SOPHIE has made a remarkable recovery - she's rested - and looks too wholesome - too innocent - too sexy for DR*

LIDDLE at this time of day.

We see SPENCER, sat a trifle uneasy - shirt buttoned up.

        DR LIDDLE
        *(to SPENCER)*
I see from here, that you have skin ruptures around your neck and wrists ...
        *(raises eyebrows)*
Horse-play!?

        STELLA
We suspected shingles, Doctor Liddle, so I applied salicylic antiseptic, which is ...

        DR LIDDLE
        *(knowingly)*
Usually reserved for livestock only, my dear Stella.

        SPENCER
        *(jauntily)*
But not as primitive as the Canadian cattle drovers' ancient culture of applying bovine faeces to inflamed areas ... and ...

        DR LIDDLE
        *(politely)*
There's no substitute for shared history - well, that just leaves you Stella.

                    STELLA
          (pats empty chair next to her)
     Just be off duty for once, Doctor
     Liddle.
          (smiles fetchingly)
     It's your occasional tenderness which
     I dread ...

We see BLANCHE re-enter the living room, manoeuvring the
overloaded hostess trolley up the two steps. DR LIDDLE goes
across to assist her.

                    BLANCHE
          (panting)
     Think of them as oil changes, Stella,
     dear.

                    DR LIDDLE
          (straight faced)
     Or hair-brush perforations ...?

We see four sets of eyes move from DR LIDDLE to BLANCHE with
various expressions of - the penny has dropped - dear
Grandma.

                    STELLA
          (gracefully breaks the silence)
     May the Lord make us truly thankful
     for our daily bread, Amen.
               (gives an exquisite troubled
               but brilliant smile)
     Scarcely a day goes by these days
     without myself feeling giddiness and
     deep tiredness.
          (pause)
     I've been taking infusions of orange

>               blossom to help this silly weakness
>               and nonsense ...

*We see tears gather in STELLA'S eyes. Their eyes all questioning her.*

>                    STELLA
>          No particular reason.

*We see STELLA looking different within this moment from the moment before - a leakage of expecting.*

**SCENE 70**
**INT. STOCKDALE FARMS - STELLA'S LIVING ROOM - 9 PM**

*We see DR LIDDLE placing his empty glass onto the side-table then squeak the stopper back into the half-empty brandy decanter. He slowly rises from the fireside easy chair.*

*We see STELLA, GRACE, SOPHIE, SPENCER and BLANCHE seated relaxed around the room, they lean forward.*

>                    DR LIDDLE
>               (pats STELLA'S shoulder)
>          I hope I've not over stayed my
>          welcome, but your hospitality has
>          overwhelmed me as usual, Stella.
>               (nods graciously to rest of the
>               family)
>          But I must love and leave you all.

**SCENE 71**
**INT. STOCKDALE FARMS - STELLA'S KITCHEN - 9:02 PM**

*We see DR LIDDLE reach for his coat, trilby and medical case.*

*We see STELLA and SPENCER see him to the outside kitchen doorway.*

      DR LIDDLE
    *(turns half-circle, speaks with*
    *overdone reasonableness of*
    *sobriety)*
  Now – tell me – my dears, and it will
  mean a lot to me to know.

*We see STELLA and SPENCER nod gravely.*

      DR LIDDLE
  Would you say ... that a situation in
  which half a dozen family members ...
  conspire together to murder one
  individual ... in such a way – that
  suspicion cannot fall on anyone of
  them ...
    *(pauses overlong)*
  is likely to be found in real life?

*We see DR LIDDLE step back from STELLA and SPENCER to firstly give SPENCER a searching look, then to cast his eyes upon STELLA'S vivacious face in a most conscientious manner – not seen before.*

*We see DR LIDDLE with deliberation, touch his trilby and take his leave.*

**SCENE 72**
**INT. STOCKDALE FARMS – STELLA'S LIVING ROOM – 9:04 PM**

*We see BLANCHE, GRACE and SOPHIE setting out glasses, bottles of brown ale and bottles of homemade wines as STELLA and SPENCER enter.*

BLANCHE
*(grandparental tones)*
We feel tonight calls for a homely, none triumphant drink. The dead need no earthly comfort, nor can they be any longer harmed or blamed.

*We see them all raise their full glasses and drink to that in oneness.*

SPENCER
*(re-raising his glass)*
To the Asquith women and Grandma Blanche for all their noble resilience by way of defending the home ground.
   *(pause, his eyes settle earnestly on each face in turn)*
And to think in the war years the Home Guards would not take women ...

STELLA
A toast to the innovative female doctor.
   *(raises her glass)*
That brave woman tipped the scales by founding the Women's Home Defence!

BLANCHE
*(flashes a distant spiritual smile)*
And to cap it all, anyone could join. I know that because I did, and I'm jolly glad I'm alive to tell the tale, but for now, all I want is peace and quiet, because I can't find words to match my feelings.

We hear general murmurings of: "We'll drink to that!"

We see BLANCHE sink thankfully down on the sofa. We hear silence fall between them, as they seek comfort before the log fire.

>                    BLANCHE
>               (breaking silence)
>      I know I shouldn't say it, but I will
>      anyway ...
>               (hesitates)
>      which up to now hasn't been pandered
>      to ...

We see heads turn – thoughts stilled – anticipating – while BLANCHE stubs out her cigarette.

We see BLANCHE look intense – modifying her personality.

>                    BLANCHE
>               (speaks as if she's alone)
>      The more I think about it ... the more
>      it bothers me ... not knowing with
>      certainty if Doctor Liddle remembered
>      that the footbridge is no longer
>      there?

FADE OUT.

END CREDITS ROLLS TO SONG BY IDA BARKER, "I FORGOT TO FORGET".

END OF EPISODE 4.

END OF SERIES.

## GLOSSARY

### Screenplay terms

**Ext.**: Exterior
**I/E.**: Interior and exterior
**Int.**: Interior
**(O/S)**: Off-screen; action or dialogue
**(V/O)**: Voice-over; dialogue by a character not on screen


### Yorkshire words and the meaning

**Afore**: Before
**Agenst**: Against
**Ah**: A (or) I (or) of (or) yes
**Ah'd**: I had (or) I would
**Ah'll**: I will
**Allus**: Always
**Ah'm**: I am
**Ah've**: I have
**Aye**: Yes
**Brokken**: Broken
**Cud**: Could
**Cudn't**: Could not
**Cun't**: Could not
**D'**: Do
**Didta**: Did you
**Doesta**: Do you
**Drempt**: Dreamed
**'Ellow**: Hello
**'Em**: Them
**Etiket**: Etiquette
**Evvery-one**: Everyone
**Friggin'**: Fucking

**Frozzen:** Frozen
**Gawd:** God
**Gurt:** Large
**Hasta:** Have you
**Hissen:** Himself
**Hoss:** Horse
**Inta:** Into
**Inter:** Into
**In't:** Is not
**Ista:** Are you
**Itsen:** Itself
**Ivver:** Ever
**Ivvery:** Every
**Knowt:** Nothing
**Lig:** Lay
**Lub:** Love
**Luve:** Love
**Mek:** Make
**Mesen:** Myself
**Nah:** No (or) Now
**Nivver:** Never
**Noan:** None (or) Now
**Nobut:** Nothing but
**Noha:** No
**No-ha:** No
**No-ha-body:** Nobody
**Nohow:** No way
**Nowt:** Nothing
**O':** Of
**Ollus:** Always
**Onny:** Any
**Onnybody:** Anybody
**Ont':** Onto
**Onta:** Onto
**Oppened:** Opened
**Ovver:** Over

**Ower:** Over
**Owld:** Old
**Owt:** Anything
**Pillock:** Idiot
**Raither:** Rather
**Reakon:** Reckon
**Reight:** Right
**Summat:** Something
**T':** The (or) to
**Ta:** To (or) you
**Tek:** Take
**Tekin':** Taking
**Tha:** The (or) you
**Tha'd:** You had (or) you would
**Tha'll:** You will
**Tha's:** You are (or) you have (or) you is
**Theer:** There
**Theer's:** There is
**Theesen:** Myself (or) yourself
**Thesen:** Myself (or) yourself
**Thou'll:** You will
**Thrang:** Vicious
**Upt':** Upped
**Un:** One
**Un's:** One's
**Vetnerie:** Veterinary
**Weel:** Well
**Wheer:** Where
**Wheer's:** Where is
**Wi':** With
**Wi'out:** Without
**Yah:** You
**Yan:** That
**Yer:** You
**Yon:** That (or) yonder

## LIST OF CHARACTERS

**Who's who – the main characters**

SAM ASQUITH – (72) landowner. A man cast in a mould of iron. Caught in snow blizzard on moorland. Found dead.

STELLA ASQUITH – (46) widow. Full of metal, yet eccentric. Her family and status are paramount to her well-being – with vengeance, come what may – she aims to keep it that way.

GRACE ASQUITH – (26) land-girl daughter. Strong willed. Speaks her mind. She was evacuated from the home farm, due to bringing disgrace to 'old moneyed' farming family – via becoming pregnant by a German Prisoner Of War. She returns home. Bitter, her soul raw.

SOPHIE ASQUITH – (22) land-girl daughter. Wholesome. Splendidly indiscreet yet winsome. She lives and loves by the light of nature.

JAKE SWALES – (65) farm-man. Stoic. Vigorous with psycho-leanings. Worked and lived at Stockdale Farms for 50 years. He was a 'workhouse' inmate – sees himself now, being ousted out of his home – the adjoining farmhouse.

FRANCIS SPENCER-ASQUITH – (42) son of Sam. A tall attractive, eloquent man, yet quietly ruthless. He has the combat skills of a survivor.

HARRY BLETCHFORD – (25) Sophie's latest love. A city guy with hidden grit. From being the outsider, he becomes a deadly insider.

BLANCHE – (74) Stella's mother. Promiscuous as a snowdrop. Family adviser – one-sided peacemaker.

ABE ASQUITH – (64) Sam's cousin. A stout man with dead-pan expression. His nature brusque, to point of being brutal. He's less fortunate – begrudging – as he's not mentioned in Sam's will.

WINNY ASQUITH – (50s) Abe's wife. A large woman with a calm frame of mind, to be almost chilling. Deeply resentful.

### Supporting characters

CLARENCE MOORHOUSE – (55) farmer and handyman
J. W. HINCHCLIFFE – (60s) solicitor
DOCTOR LIDDLE – (60s)
MR DAVIS – (30s) veterinary
MICHAEL/MIKE ASQUITH – (early 20s) Abe and Winny's son
EDNA ASQUITH nee BIGGERDYKE – (20) Mike's wife
VICAR SIMMS – (50s)
KIT SULLIVAN – (45) Irishman. Seasonal farm worker
MR HOLMES (50s) garage owner
BLACKSMITH – (60s)
HERTZ – (24) German Prisoner Of War (in flashbacks)
EVELYN RIDGEHOLM (70s) Spencer's mother (in flashbacks)
RALF & ROSE BIGGERDYKE – (40s) Edna's parents
MR & MRS BLETCHFORD – (40s) Harry's parents
BEST MAN – (early 20s)
CARETAKER – (old-timer)
ALICE-ROSE ASQUITH – (Mike & Edna's baby)
CHURCH WARDEN (60s)

## About the Author

It use to be said, you could recognise a Yorkshire person by the way they don't suck they crunch a boiled sweet! Gwen Hullah, (maiden name), was born and bred in the West Riding of Yorkshire. Educated at Braithwaite School, Dacre, and Pateley Bridge Secondary Modern, Nidderdale. By tradition in those days, farmers' daughters became home-land-girls wherein horse-power ruled – as the saying goes – 'Shake a bridle over a Yorkshire man's grave and he'll rise up and steal your horse'.

Married for twenty-eight years, Gwen resided in Grantham, Lincolnshire for most of those years. She became a free-lance writer, amidst other chance jobs – and the instigator of Radio Witham, Grantham Hospital Broadcasting Service in 1976.

Gwen has one brown-eyed daughter, Ida, who is a musician singer/songwriter/guitarist and author (pseudonym Zizzi Bonah); whom she is very proud of. They now live back home in Yorkshire.

'Wapentake' – revenge fiction – is a new writing genre created by Gwen to suit her style of writing. Her debut novel: Safe In Killer Hands – Money, Madness, Murder, was published in 2016 by She And The Cat's Mother.

**Become a Tattle Head by clicking follow at Gwen's blog site: SilverSplitter.com**

CLARENCE HOUSE

18th April, 2018

Dear Rosen and Ida

I am glad that you share my passion for reading and enjoyed the recent article about literacy.

Thank you for sending me a copy of 'Alice Returns Through the Looking Glass' by Zizzi Bonah. I look forward to discovering more about Alice's adventures…

With best wishes

Camilla

A letter-of-acknowledgement from *HRH the Duchess of Cornwall* to book publishers, She And The Cat's Mother

Paperbacks | ebooks | audiobooks
by this publisher include:

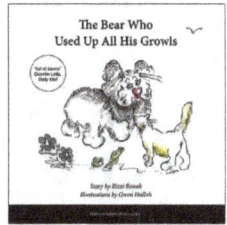

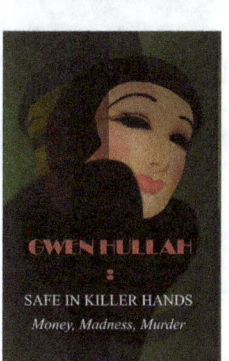
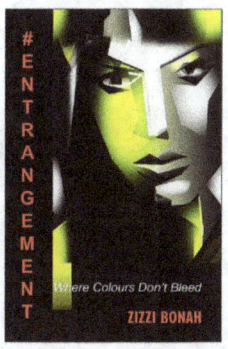

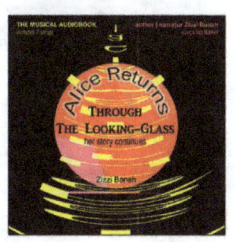

SheAndTheCatsMother.co.uk

# How to format your script, play, musical, novel or poetry & self-publish to eBook & paperback

'Self-publish in *one* week!
I've done the hard work
so you don't have to'
- Author Ida Barker

BUY

eBook | paperback at amazon
myBook.to/GirlLikeYou

Praise for **She And The Cat's Mother** book publisher's works
'beautifully published' - *Dame Julie Walters*

Ida
(also writes phantasy
under pseudonym Zizzi Bonah)

## #GirlLikeYou
written by Ida Barker
edited by Gwen Hullah

www.ingramcontent.com/pod-product-compliance
Lightning Source LLC
Chambersburg PA
CBHW071327080526
44587CB00017B/2754